W. Etherington

The Student´s Grammar of the Hindi Language

Salzwasser

W. Etherington

The Student´s Grammar of the Hindi Language

1. Auflage | ISBN: 978-3-84605-260-0

Erscheinungsort: Frankfurt, Deutschland

Erscheinungsjahr: 2020

Salzwasser Verlag GmbH

Reprint of the original, first published in 1870.

THE

STUDENT'S GRAMMAR.

OF THE

HINDÍ LANGUAGE,

BY THE

REV. W. ETHERINGTON,

MISSIONARY—BENARES.

1870.

PREFACE.

HINDÍ is the mother-tongue of, probably, not less than twenty-five millions of the people of India. It is spoken throughout the North Western Provinces, the Panjáb, the greater part of Rájputáná, Central India, and Behár; and, in the form in which it is used in Benares, it is readily understood by Sikhs, Guzaráttís, Mahrattas, Nepálís, and other tribes having distinct dialects of their own. Whether, then, we think of the extent of country over which it is spoken, or of the number and importance of the tribes that speak it, Hindí, if any, may be regarded as the language of Northern India.

A similar claim is often set up for Urdú, the vernacular of the Mahommedans, a comparatively small community. But though spoken in the cities and in many of the larger towns of Northern India by many educated Hindús also, as a second language, Urdú has predominance in no province of India, it never has been, and, in the nature of things, it never can become the language of any class of the people except the Mahommedans.

Hindí is a derivative from the Sanskrit to which it bears a greater affinity than any modern Indian tongue, except the Bengálí. Not less than nine-tenths of its vocabulary is traceable to Sanskrit roots, many of the words being pure Sanskrit and others varying only in the permutations of certain letters. The existence in Hindí of some words apparently not traceable to Sanskrit, together with the fact that many of its grammatical forms differ from that language has given rise to the theory that Hindí may have once existed apart from Sanskrit. The theory has but little to support it, for though it may now be impossible to account for all the changes that have taken place in words and grammatical forms during the centuries that have elapsed since Hindí was formed from Sanskrit, yet many words that at first seemed obscure have been satisfactorily traced to the Sanskrit through the Prákrit, and the most peculiar grammatical construction in Hindí, *viz.*, the use of the particle ने with the nominative in the past tenses of transitive verbs, has been clearly traced to Sanskrit. (See the note at p. 140.) Further study of the Prákrit, in which the Sanskrit began to be broken up and which formed an important part of the process by which Hindí and other living languages of Northern India were formed, will tend to throw light upon the origin of many words that are now not satisfactorily traceable to Sanskrit or to any other language; changes, for instance, so great as *láthí* from *yashtíh*, *nách* from *nrittya*, *mor* from *mayúrah*, *bís* from *vinśuti*, are accounted for by means of the Prákrit.

Hindí has been but little cultivated, its vocabulary is therefore poor as compared with other languages; it possesses, however, the elements of a fine language and has in its parent, the Sanskrit, ample resources both as to matter and form from which it is continually being enriched. It needs no foreign aid, and all attempts to force such aid upon it only tend to mutilate it and obstruct its natural growth. In the following pages I have rejected all words of Arabic, Persian, or Urdú origin, as well as all constructions that seem to me to belong more to Urdú than to Hindí. The jargon in which several educational books have lately been published, some may be pleased to term Hindí; but in reality it is a strange medley of Sanskrit, Arabic, Persian, Urdu, and Hindí. To understand some of it would imply considerable acquaintance not only with the words, but also with the syntax of three or four languages. It is much to be regretted that such books have found favor with any; they interfere with the spread of education, and are most offensive to a correct taste.

The want of a Hindí grammar has been long felt: no attempt that I am aware of has hitherto been made to supply it, except "The elements of Hindí and Braj Bhákhá grammar by the late Dr. Ballantyne," which, though good so far as it goes, contains but the bare outlines of the subject in thirty-seven large print pages. I have endeavoured to make the following work as comprehensive as the present state of the language will admit. As Hindí varies a good deal in different provinces, it was necessary to adopt some one form of it as a standard; and, as that of Benares is generally acknowledged to be the purest, I have followed it.

I have consulted the works of Shakespeare, Forbes, and Monier Williams, and have derived some aid from them. I am especially indebted to the last named writer, whose Sanskrit Dictionary, Sanskrit Grammar, and Urdú Grammar have been of great use to me. I have also read the *Bhásháchandroday* and the *Sandhí* in the *Vyákaran kí Upakramaniká* from which a few of my examples are taken. I am most of all indebted to the suggestions of the late Rev. John Parsons,

Missionary at Monghir, perhaps the most accomplished Hindí scholar that has yet appeared among Europeans. He most kindly undertook to revise my manuscripts before they were sent to the press; the latter part of the syntax was with him when he died. Paṇḍit Rám Jasan also, the head Sanskrit and Hindí teacher, Queen's College, Benares, read with me nearly all the examples in the syntax and approved of them. My thanks are also due to John Christian, Esq., of Monghir who at my request wrote the chapter on Prosody for this work. From his extensive acquaintance with Hindí poetic writings, he is more capable than any one that I know to perform such a task. The following remarks from his pen bearing upon the study of prosody are important and worthy of the reader's attention. "Students of language should not think that Prosody constitutes but an ornamental part of Grammar. In the study of Hindí Grammar, especially, prosody will be found to be no less useful than ornamental. The Hindús have a natural predilection for numbers, which is evident from the fact that few books of any note are written by them in prose. Their ideas whether relating to art, science, language, or philosophy, are embodied in measured language which is brought to bear upon even the concerns of their every-day life. Few Hindús will be found whose memory is not the repository of some scraps of their proverbial poetry which they readily and aptly quote.

The Hindú mind is exhibited in poetry, and it is in the poetry of the people that their manners and customs are portrayed; hence, if the student, whether of a literary or philosophical turn of mind, whether a minister of the Gospel or an official of Government, be desirous of studying the Hindús, a highly interesting nation, he must study their poetry.

The study of the prosody of the language is in itself delightful. The student will find in his progress towards the Indian Parnassus that his path lies through a rich and variegated field of orient flowers to be culled by every traveller who has a taste for what is pleasing and beautiful."

BENARES:
20th *March*, 1870.

WM. ETHERINGTON.

CONTENTS.

	Page.
CHAPTER I. The Alphabet, vowels, ...	1
consonants, ...	2
The vowel system, ...	″
Pronunciation of the vowels, ...	3
″ ″ consonants, ...	6
Classification of the letters, ...	11
Vowels classified, ...	12
Consonants ,, ...	13
Compound consonants, ...	″
1. Doubled letters, ...	16
2. Nasals in combination, ...	″
3. Sibilants in combination, ...	″
4. Semi-vowels म and य in combination, ...	17
5. Miscellaneous Compounds, ...	″
6. Combination of three letters, ...	″
CHAPTER II. Euphonic permutations of letters, ...	18
I. Permutations of vowels, ...	19
1. *Gun* changes, ...	″
2. *Vriddhi* changes, ...	20
3. *Dírgh* changes, ...	21
4. *Antargat* changes, ...	″
II. Permutations of Consonants and *Anuswár*, ...	24
III. Permutations of *Visarg*, ...	27
CHAPTER III. Parts of speech, ...	28
Nouns, ...	29
Gender, ...	30
Number, ...	35

CONTENTS.

Case, ... 36
Declension, ... 39
First Declension—all masculine nouns, ... "
   Class I. 40
   Class II. 41
Second Declension—all feminine nouns, ... 44
   Class I. ... ... "
   Class II. 45
Chapter IV. Of Adjectives, ... 47
Comparison of Adjectives, ... 50
Chapter V. Of Pronouns, ... 52
Personal Pronouns, ... "
Observations on the personal pronouns, ... 54
Demonstrative pronouns, ... 57
Possessive and reflexive pronoun, ... 59
Relative pronouns, ... 61
Interrogative pronouns, ... 62
Indefinite pronouns, ... 65
Chapter VI. Of the verb, ... 69
Conjugation of a transitive verb—Root ending in a consonant, ... 72
Conjugation of a transitive verb—Root ending in a vowel, ... 79
Conjugation of an intransitive verb—Root ending in a consonant, ... 83
Conjugation of an intransitive verb—Root ending in a vowel, ... 85
The Passive voice, ... 86
Anomalous forms tabulated, ... 92
Uncommon tenses, ... 95
Derivative verbs, ... 97

CONTENTS.

Compound verbs, ... ·102
Chapter VII. Of indeclinable words—Adverbs, ... 107
Prepositions, ... 111
Conjunctions, ... 112
Interjections, ... 113
Chapter VIII. Numerals—Cardinals, ... 114
Aggregate or Collective, ... 117
Ordinals, ... "
Fractional, ... 118
Chapter IX. Divisions of time, ... 120
Chapter X. On the derivation of words, ... 123
Prefixes, ... 124
Affixes, ... 127
Derivative nouns, ... "
adjectives, ... 132
verbs, ... 134
Chapter XI. Syntax, ... 135
Chapter XII. Prosody, ... 193
Hindí Selections. ... ... I to XLVIII.

ERRATA.

Page	Line	For	Read.
1	19	दखे	देख
21	4	टीर्घ	दीर्घ
35	28	words	most words
98	21	पढ़वाना	पढ़ाना
99	12	कमकाना	चमकाना
110	30	ruly	truly
120	7	ond	and
140	15	यमा	मया
142	23	कमवारी	फूलवारी

THE
STUDENT'S GRAMMAR
OF THE
HINDÍ LANGUAGE.

CHAPTER I.

1. Hindí is written in the Sanskrit or what is generally termed the *Deva Nágarí* character.*

The Alphabet consists of fourteen vowels and thirty-three simple consonants, and each letter has but one invariable sound.

THE ALPHABET. वर्णमाला *Varṇamálá.*

VOWELS, स्वर *swar.*

अ आ इ ई उ ऊ ऋ ॠ ऌ ॡ ए ऐ ओ औ

a, á, i, í, u, ú, ri, rí, lri, lrí, e, ai, o, au.

With the vowels are generally enumerated the nasal symbol (˙), a dot written above the letter which it affects, called *Anuswár* and the vowel aspirate (:), two dots written to the right of the letter and called *Visarg.*

---

* देवनागरी *devanágarí*, the alphabet of "the city of the gods;" from Sanskrit देव *deva*, a god, and नगर *nagara*, a city.

CONSONANTS, व्यञ्जन *vyańjan.*

क ka,	ख kha,	ग ga,	घ gha,	ङ ńa,
च cha,	छ chha,	ज ja,	झ jha,	ञ ńa,
ट ṭa,	ठ ṭha,	ड ḍa,	ढ ḍha,	ण ṇa,
त ta,	थ tha,	द da,	ध dha,	न na,
प pa,	फ pha,	ब ba,	भ bha,	म ma,
य ya,	र ra,	ल la,	व wa,	श śa,
ष sha,	स sa,	ह ha.		

THE VOWEL SYSTEM.

2. There are nine original or principal vowels, viz., अ a, इ i, उ u, ऋ ri, ऌ lri, ए e, ऐ ai, ओ o, औ au; of these the first five are simple and short, and each of the five has a corresponding long form; the remaining four are considered long, being in reality diphthongs.

Long (दीर्घ *dírgh*); आ á, ई í, ऊ ú, ॠ rí, ॡ lrí, ए e, ऐ ai, ओ o, औ au,

Short (ह्रस्व *hrasv*); अ a, इ i, उ u, ऋ ri, ऌ lri.

3. Observe that the preceding are the initial forms of the vowels and are never used except at the beginning of a word, or when two vowels occur, one immediately after the other. The second vowel then assumes the initial or full form; thus *ág* is written, आग, with the initial or full form of the vowel; but *gá* is written, गा, with ा, an abbreviated form of the vowel.

4. All the vowels, with the exception of the first, अ *a,* which is never written unless it begin a word, take other forms when they occur in the middle or at the end of a word; thus:—

Initial form :— अ आ इ ई उ ऊ ऋ ॠ ऌ ॡ ए ऐ ओ औ

Medial or final form :— ा ि ी ◌ु ◌ू ◌ृ ◌ॄ ◌ॢ ◌ॣ े ै ो ौ

5. The first vowel, **अ** *a*, is supposed to be inherent in every consonant; there is, therefore, no necessity for a written medial or final form for this letter.

6. Although **अ** *a* is said to be inherent in every consonant, let not the student suppose that it must be sounded after every consonant that is not accompanied by a vowel. In sanskrit it is always sounded unless its place be taken by some other vowel, or the mark. (`) called *virám* be written after the consonant to indicate a consonantal stop, or the absence of the inherent vowel. In regard to Hindí however, it must be remembered that the inherent **अ** *a*, is generally but not always sounded ; thus, in the word बरसता *barastá* as no vowel is written after the consonants **ब** and **र**, the inherent **अ** is pronounced after them, but it is not pronounced after the **त**, though it is also without any written vowel.

7. The vowels when medial or final are united to the consonants according to the following examples :—

क ka, का ká, कि ki, की kí, कु ku, कू kú, कृ kri, कॄ krí, कॢ klri, कॣ klrí, के ke, कै kai, को ko, कौ kau.

8. In native grammars the initial or full form of a vowel is termed स्वर *swar*, and the medial or final form मात्रा *mátrá*.

PRONUNCIATION OF THE VOWELS, उच्चारण *uchcháran*.

9. **अ** *a*, short, pronounced as *a* in *woman;* as, अटल *atal*, 'immoveable.' This vowel, as has been said, differs from the others in having no medial or final form ; it is inherent in every consonant and though not written it is generally pronounced.

10. When one consonant is joined to another so as to form
with it a compound consonant, the inherent श *a* of the first consonant is dropped; at the end of a word also it is usually silent, except in poetry, when, for the sake of the metre or euphony, it is
frequently sounded; thus, चिट्ठी *chiṭṭhí* 'a letter,' not *chiṭaṭhí*;
गुण *guṇ*, 'a quality,' not *guṇa*.

आ *á*, the preceding letter lengthened; pronounced as *a* in
ah! art; thus, आग *ág*, 'fire,' लाल *lál*, 'red.'

इ *i*, short, as *i* in *wit, pin*. Observe that the medial or final
form of this vowel is always written *before* the letter which it
follows in pronunciation; as कितना *kitná*, 'how many?' इति *iti*,
'this much.'

ई *í*, long, the preceding letter lengthened; pronounced like
i in *police*. Observe that the medial or final form of this vowel
is always written *after* the letter which it follows in pronunciation;
as, जीव *jív*, 'life,' नारी *nárí*, 'woman.'

उ *u*, short, like *u* in *cushion*. The medial or final form of
this vowel resembles a comma, and is written *below* the letter
which it follows in pronunciation, except when it follows the consonant र *r*, for it then assumes a peculiar form and position; thus,
पुकारना *pukárná*, 'to call aloud,' तरुण *taruṇ*, 'a young man,' कुमेरु
kumeru, 'the south pole.'

ऊ *ú*, long, the preceding vowel lengthened; pronounced like *u*
in *rule*. The medial or final form of this vowel is always written
below the letter after which it is pronounced; as, खजूर *khajúr*,
'a date tree.' Like the preceding short vowel when written after
the consonant र *r* it has a peculiar position somewhat within the
letter; thus, रूप *rúp*, 'form,' 'shape.'

ऋ *ri*, sounded like *ri* in such words as *river, rich;* it takes for its medial or final form written under the consonant it follows, and is thus combined, तृण *trin*, 'grass,' पृथिवी *prithivi*, 'the earth,' अमृत *amrit*, 'ambrosia,' 'immortality,' कृपा *kripá* 'favor,' 'pity.'

ॠ *rí*, the preceding vowel lengthened; pronounced like *ree* in *reed*. This and the two following letters need not at first occupy the time of the student, as they are retained from the Sanskrit alphabet and are found only in words of that language. There is as yet scarcely a word in Hindí to represent any of them.

ऌ *lri*, or *li*, but generally pronounced as *li* in *lily*.

ॡ *lrí*, or *lí*, the preceding letter lengthened; pronounced as *lee* in *leek*.

ए *e*, long; pronounced like *e* in *they*, or the first *e* in *there*. The medial or final form of this letter is always written *above* the letter after which it is pronounced; as, एक *ek*, 'one,' केवल *kewal*, 'only,' 'merely.'

ऐ *ai*, long; pronounced like *ai* in *aisle;* medial or final form always written *above* the letter it follows in pronunciation; thus, ऐंचना *ainchná*, 'to draw,' जैसा *jaisá*, 'as,' 'such as.'

ओ *o*, long; pronounced like *o* in *go, note*. The medial or final form is always written, *after* or to the right of the letter it follows in pronunciation; as, ओढ़ना *orhná*, 'to put on' [clothes,] 'a sheet,' 'mantle,' कोना *koná*, 'a corner,' 'angle.'

औ *au*, long; pronounced like *ou* in *our*. The medial or final form like that of the preceding letter is written *after*, or to the right of the letter it follows in pronunciation; thus, और *aur*, 'and,' 'other,' गौरिया *gauriyá*, 'a sparrow.'

11. With the vowels are generally enumerated the nasal symbol (ˊ) *anuswár* and the vowel aspirate (:) *visarg*.

Observe that the *anuswár* is never initial, and that it is sounded after an inherent or written vowel, and is placed over the vowel when it is written. It has, generally, the sound of the *n* in the French *ton*, but it is frequently used for one or another of the five nasals, and then assumes the sound of the nasal for which it stands.

12. The following examples illustrate its uses:—कंगाल *Kangál*, 'poor,' 'indigent,' चंदा *chandá*, 'an assessment,' 'contribution,' गंभीर *gambhír*, 'deep,' 'thoughtful'; (notice, that in the foregoing instances the *anuswár* is not pronounced immediately after the consonant over which it is written, but after the short *a* inherent in it.) कांपना *kámpná*, 'to tremble'; here, because it precedes a labial, the *anuswár* has the sound of *m*.

13. "*Anuswár* is properly the nasal of the semivowels (य *y*, र *r*, ल *l*, व *v*,), sibilants (श *s*, ष *sh*, स *s*,), and the aspirate (ह *h*)," and with them it is expressed by the English *n*; as संसार *sansár*, 'the world,' संशय *sansay*, 'doubt,' 'anxiety, वंश *vans*, 'race,' 'lineage,' (popularly pronounced '*bans*').

14. The soft or vowel aspirate *visarg* is used to give a slight aspiration to the vowel, written or inherent, after which it is written; thus, दुःख *duhkh*, 'pain,' 'grief,' निःशेष *nihsesh*, 'complete.' In these instances the aspiration is very slight, in other cases it is almost imperceptible, and, frequently, the presence of the *visarg* seems to indicate but an abrupt shortening of the preceding vowel, as in अन्तःकरण *antahkaran*, 'the understanding.'

PRONUNCIATION OF THE CONSONANTS.

15. The consonants differ from the vowels in having but one form, whether initial, medial, or final; they are like them in having but one fixed and invariable sound.

16. The only exception to this is the letter ष *sh*, which, according to some grammarians, ought to be pronounced like *kh*.

क *k*, pronounced like the English *k*, as in *king*, *kind*; thus काला *kálá*, 'black,' कुलकुला *kulkulá*, 'gargling.'

ख *kh*, the preceding letter aspirated; pronounced like *kh* in *ink-horn*, but there should be no hiatus between the *k* and the *h*, both letters should be pronounced together; as, खाल *khál*, 'a hide', खोखला *khokhlá*, 'hollow,' 'excavated.'

ग *g*, always hard as in *go*, *gone*; never soft like the *g* in *George*; as, गली *galí*, 'a lane,' गंगा *Gangá*, 'the river Ganges.'

घ *gh*, the preceding letter aspirated, and like it always hard, as *gh* in *log-house*; thus, घंटा *ghanṭá*, 'a bell' or 'gong,' 'an hour,' घास *ghás*, 'grass,' 'hay.'

ङ *ṅ*, the guttural nasal pronounced like the *n* in *sing*; as अङ्गीकार *aṅgíkár*, 'an agreement,' 'promise,' दङ्गा *daṅgá*, 'wrangling,' 'confusion.'

च *ch*, pronounce like *ch* in *church*, but never hard like *ch* in *chemistry*, *choir*; as, चलना *chalná*, 'to move,' चर्चा *charchá*, 'mention.'

छ *chh*, the preceding letter aspirated; pronounced like *ch-h*, in the phrase *watch-him*; as, छापना *chhápná*, 'to print,' छिदना *chhidná*, 'to be pierced.'

ज *j*, pronounced like the English *j* in *jar*; as, जगत *jagat*, 'the world,' जांचना *jánchná*, 'to examine.'

झ or झ़ *jh*, the preceding letter aspirated, with the *h* distinctly sounded; as, झूठा *jhúṭhá*, 'false,' 'defiled,' झोंपड़ी *jhompṛí*, 'a cottage,' 'a hut.'

ञ *ñ*, the palatal nasal, pronounced like *n* in *plunge*; as, चञ्चल *chañchal*, 'unsteady,' 'fickle,' काञ्चन *káñchan*, 'gold,' 'golden.'

ट *ṭ*, this letter and the following ड *ḍ*, together with their as-pirates can be pronounced only by striking the tip of the tongue on the palate; as, टट्टू *ṭaṭṭú*, 'a pony,' टटोलना *ṭaṭolná*, 'to feel for,' 'grope.' It is important to observe that neither ट nor त, ड nor द, nor their aspirates ought to be pronounced like an Eng-lish *t* or *d*; they have no exact representatives in the English al-phabet and it quite misleads to give examples of their pronuncia-tion from our words.

ठ *ṭh*, the preceding letter aspirated; the aspiration should be sensibly and closely uttered as one letter with the *ṭ*; thus, ठग *ṭhag*, 'a robber,' ठठेरा *ṭhaṭherá*, 'a brazier,' 'a tinker.'

ड *ḍ*, this letter can be uttered only by striking the tip of the tongue on the palate; as, डसना *ḍasná*, 'to bite,' 'to sting,' डालना *ḍálná*, 'to throw down.' When medial or final this letter has frequently the sound of *r* in the French *eternel*, or of *r* in the English *bur*; it is then written with a dot placed under it; as बड़ा *baṛa*, 'large,' 'great,' पेड़ *peṛ*, 'a tree.'

ढ *ḍh*, the preceding letter sensibly aspirated; as, ढकना *ḍhak-ná*, 'to cover,' ढारस *ḍháras*, 'firmness of mind.' This letter is also frequently pronounced like the French *r* in *eternel* aspirated; it is then written with a dot below it; thus, पढ़ना *paṛhná*, 'to read,' बढ़ना *baṛhná*, 'to increase,' 'to advance.'

ण *ṇ*, the cerebral nasal, uttered by placing the tip of the tongue back on the palate; as, गिनत *gaṇit*, 'counted,' 'numbered,' मुण्डना *muṇḍná*, 'to be shaved.' This letter has no equivalent in English.

त *t*, this and the following three letters must be uttered somewhat softly, the tip of the tongue being pressed against the roots of the front upper teeth; तांबा *támbá*, 'copper,' गीत *gít*, 'a song.'

थ *th*, the preceding letter aspirated; as, था *thá*, 'was,' थान *thán*, 'a piece of cloth.'

द *d*, to be uttered softly by pressing the tip of the tongue against the roots of the upper front teeth; as, दबाना *dabáná*, 'to press down,' दादा *dádá*, 'a paternal grandfather.'

ध *dh*, the preceding letter aspirated; as, आंधी *ándhí*, 'a storm,' धोखा *dhokhá*, 'deceit,' 'trickery.'

न *n*, pronounced as *n* in *nay*; as, नंगा *nangá*, 'naked,' नाना *náná*, 'various,' 'many.'

प *p*, pronounced like the English *p*, as in *pound*; thus पचास *pachás*, 'fifty,' पाप *páp*, 'sin,' 'crime.'

फ *ph*, the preceding letter aspirated; pronounced like *ph* in *hop-house*; as, फल *phal*, 'fruit,' 'result,' फूल *phúl*, 'flower,' 'blossom.'

ब *b*, pronounced like the English *b*; as, बचन *bachan*, 'a word,' बबूल *babúl*, 'the acacia tree.' This letter is frequently interchanged with व *v*, or *w*; some native authorities maintain that in Hindí the two letters are, in most cases, optionally interchangeable, and in native books the same word is sometimes spelt with the one, and sometimes with the other letter; as बिचार *bichár* or विचार *vichár*, 'thought,' वन *van*, or बन *ban*, 'a wood,' 'a forest.' One system of spelling should be adhered to; and, as a rule, the Sanskrit should be followed.

भ *bh*, the preceding letter aspirated; pronounced like *bh* in *hob-house*, but without any hiatus between the *b* and the *h*. They must be uttered as one letter with the aspiration clearly given; as, भला *bhalá*, 'good,' अभिमान *abhimán*, 'pride,' 'haughtiness.'

म *m*, pronounced like the English *m*; as मद्दा *mahá*, 'great,' मेमना *memná*, 'a kid.'

य *y* or *j*, this is properly the Sanskrit *y*, but in Hindí the sound of *j* is frequently given to it by even learned natives; as, युग *yuj*, or *jug*, 'an age of the world,' यन्त्र *yantra*, or *jantra*, 'a machine in general.'

र *r*, must be fully and distinctly sounded like *r* in *rod*, *river*, but is never pronounced like the anomalous English *r* in such words as *hard*, *hearth*; as, राजा *rájá*, 'a king,' 'a ruler,' पारवार *párwár*, 'on both sides' (of a river), 'quite through.' This letter is often interchanged with ल *l* and ड *ḍ*; as, डालना *ḍálná* or डारना *ḍárná*, 'to throw down'; it interchanges in a few cases with ड़ *ṛ*; as, बाड़ी *báṛí* or बारी *bárí*, 'a garden,' 'an orchard.'

ल *l*, pronounced like *l* in *lane*, *law*, but never as *l* in *hold*; as लेना *lená*, 'to take,' लालच *lálach*, 'longing,' 'covetousness.' ल *l* and न *n* frequently interchange; as, नील *níl*, or लील *líl*, 'indigo,' 'blue.'

व *v* or *w*, pronounced as in English; thus, विकल्प *vikalp*, 'error,' 'doubt,' बनवासी *banwásí*, or *banwásí*, 'one who lives in a wood,' 'a hermit.' When compounded with any consonant but र *r*, as the last letter of the compound, व is usually pronounced *w*; as, ग्वाला *gwálá*, 'a cowherd,' द्वार *dwár*, 'a door,' 'a gate.'

श *s*, a palatal sibilant; pronounced with a slight aspiration as in the word *sure*; as, शरीर *sarír*, 'the body,' पशु *pasu*, 'an animal in general.'

ष *sh*, a cerebral sibilant; pronounced with a stronger aspiration than that of the preceding letter, as *sh* in *shut*; thus, दोष *dosh*, 'fault,' 'sin,' भाषा *bháshá*, 'speech,' 'language.' The sound of *kh* is given to this letter by many.

स *s*, a dental sibilant; pronounced like the ordinary English *s*, as in *sin*; thus, सनातन *sanátan*, 'eternal,' ससुर *sasur* 'father-in-law.' This letter is sometimes interchanged with श *s*; as, आसा *ásá*, or आशा *ásá*, 'hope,' 'dependence.'

ह *h*, pronounced as in English, but clearly expressed ; as, हलका *halká*, 'light,' हांकना *hánkná*, 'to drive.' *

CLASSIFICATION OF THE LETTERS.

17. Native grammarians divide the consonants into the classified, वर्गीय *vargíya*, and the unclassified, अवर्गीय, *avargíya*. In the former are included all the consonants, excepting the semi-vowels, the sibilants, and the aspirate ह, and they form five classes, corresponding with the first five rows of consonants in the usual order of the alphabet, each row having five letters. Each class derives its name from the first letter in it; thus, क-वर्ग *ka-varg*, or the k-class, includes the five letters, क, ख, ग, घ, ङ; च-वर्ग *cha-varg*, or the ch-class, includes the five letters, च, छ, ज, झ, ञ; etc.

---

* No positive rule can be laid down with regard to the interchange of letters in pronunciation, as a great variety in the usage may be observed in different parts of the country. Sikhs will commonly say, *vachan, vastr, vaḍá;* whereas, in the North Western Provinces, generally, and, more especially, in Behar, those words are pronounced *bachan, bastr, baṛá.* In Benares *sanyam* is generally the pronunciation for what nearer Bengal is called *sanjam.*

The following observations are all that can with any degree of certainty be said on this point :—

व *v*, initial, is frequently pronounced as ब *b*, especially in the provinces bordering on Bengal.

य *y*, initial and double, is often pronounced like ज *j*. At and near the end of words, व *v* is frequently pronounced as "o" or "ú," and य *y* as "e."

The distinction between श *s* and स *s*, ण *ṇ* and न *n*, क्ष *ksh* and छ *chchh*, is frequently disregarded in common usage; but these are irregularities for which no rule can be laid down.

(12)

18. The consonants thus classified are named also from the organ by which they are pronounced, the k-class being Gutturals, the ch-class Palatals, the ṭ-class Cerebrals, the t-class Dentals, and the p-class Labials.

19. It will be seen from the following tables, which exhibit a full classification of the Hindí alphabet, that all the letters, whether vowels, semi-vowels, or consonants, may be arranged under one or other of the five great classes, according to the organ by which mainly they are uttered.

20. They may be arranged, according to another principle of classification, into the two classes of hard and soft letters. This arrangement is also exhibited in the tables given below, which should be carefully studied, the student distinguishing between the aspirated and the unaspirated consonants, observing the hard with their corresponding soft letters, and carefully noting to which class of letters the five nasals respectively belong; thus, ख *kh*, is the aspirate of क *k*, and छ *chh* of च *ch*; ग *g* is the soft letter of क *k*, and घ *gh* of ख *kh*; ङ *ṅ* is the guttural nasal, and ञ *ñ* the palatal nasal, etc.

21.   VOWELS CLASSIFIED.

	Short ह्रस्व *hrasv.*	Long दीर्घ *dírgh.*	
Gutturals कंठ *kanthya,*	अ a	आ á	ए e
Palatals तालव्य *tálavya,*	इ i	ई í	ऐ ai
Cerebrals मूर्द्धन्य *múrddhanya,*	ऋ ri	ॠ rí	औ au
Dentals दन्त्य *dantya,*	ऌ lri	ॡ lrí	
Labials ओष्ठ्य *oshṭhya,*	उ u	ऊ ú	ओ o

Class, वर्ग *varj.* (applies to the first five letters only in each row.)	Hard consonants, अघोष *aghosh.*		Soft consonants, घोष *ghosh.*				Hard consonants.	
	Unaspirated, अल्पप्राण *alpaprán.*	Aspirated, महाप्राण *maháprán.*	Unaspirated.	Aspirated.	Nasals, अनुनासिक *anunásik.*	Semi-vowels, अन्तस्थ *antasth.*	Sibilants and aspirate, ऊष्म *úshm.*	
कवर्ग (क-class)	क	ख	ग	घ	ङ		ह	Gutturals.
चवर्ग (च-class)	च	छ	ज	झ	ञ	य	श	Palatals.
टवर्ग (ट-class)	ट	ठ	ड	ढ	ण	र	ष	Cerebrals.
तवर्ग (त-class)	त	थ	द	ध	न	ल	स	Dentals.
पवर्ग (प-class)	प	फ	ब	भ	म	व		Labials.

COMPOUND CONSONANTS, संयुक्त व्यञ्जन *sanyukt vyanjan.*

23.	Hindí derives its compound letters, as well as its simple vowels and consonants, from the Sanskrit.

In that language the short vowel अ *a* is supposed to be inherent in every consonant, and it is, therefore, never written, unless at the beginning of a word ; if, then, two simple consonants occur in a word, with no written vowel between them, the vowel अ *a* must be supplied, unless the mark ् *virám* be placed under the first consonant to indicate that its inherent vowel is dropped.

Thus the word स्वामी would be pronounced *sawámí*; there being no vowel between स and व, the inherent vowel of the स is sounded, and आ *á*, being written after व, takes the place of its inherent vowel. But if we wish to write, not *sawámí*, but *swámí*, so as to exclude the inherent vowel of स, we must combine the स with the following consonant व, thus forming the compound consonant स्व *sw*, and the word becomes स्वामी *swámí*, 'a master,' 'a husband.'

24. This is the theory of compound consonants in Sanskrit, and from it may be perceived the necessity and use of them. This theory, however, is not in every respect applicable to Hindí, for there are numerous instances in which the supposed inherent अ *a* is not sounded in Hindí, even when no *virám* is written, and no other vowel takes the place of the inherent अ *a*; thus in सुनता *suntá*, न and त do not form a compound letter, nor is there any vowel written between them, yet no vowel is sounded after the न. So with compounded words, as, भेड़साला *bheṛsálá*, 'a sheepfold.'

25. The usual method of combining consonants is to write one above the other, the first to be pronounced being above; as, क्त = क+त. They are sometimes written one after the other, the perpendicular line being omitted in all but the last; thus, ब्व = ब+व. Frequently the first member of a compound is more or less changed in form, whilst the second remains unchanged, but as often the reverse of this takes place; thus, न्म = न+म. क्र = क+र. In some cases the form of each letter is so altered as to be scarcely traceable in the compound; this is especially so in the three compounds that follow; क्ष = क+ष, त्र = त+र, ज्ञ = ज+ञ.

The letter र *r*, when it occurs as the first letter of a compound, is written above the other letter in the form of a small crescent; thus, पर्वत *parvat*, 'a mountain;' when it forms the second member of a compound, it is written below the other letter in the form of a stroke drawn to the left; thus, प्रताप *pratáp*, 'splendour.'

27.   In most compounds there are but two letters, but there may be more ; the component parts of them will in most cases be readily traced by the student who has become familiar with the forms of the simple letters.

28.   In forming compounds let it be remembered that the following letters, ङ *ṅ*, छ *chh*, ट *ṭ*, ठ *ṭh*, ड *ḍ*, ढ *ḍh*, are written in full when used as the first member of a compound; all the other consonants undergo some change of form when in that position.

29.   Observe, further, with regard to compounds, that two aspirated letters cannot follow each other in the same compound ; if it be necessary to double an aspirated letter, the first must be changed into the unaspirated letter of the same class or *varg*.

30.   Each of the five *vargs* has its own nasal letter ; in forming compounds remember that the nasals can combine only with classified letters of their own class ; they may combine with the unclassified, or those that do not belong to either of the five *vargs ;* thus, ङ *ṅ* may be combined with क *k*, or with any of the gutturals, but it cannot enter into a compound with च *ch*, or with any of the palatals, for with them the palatal nasal, ञ, *ñ* must be used.   The nasals combine with the unclassified letters ; thus, न्व *nv,* म्य *my,* न्ह *nh,* म्ह *mh,* are correct compounds.

31.   The *anuswár* or nasal symbol (˙) may be used with any class of letters, the pronunciation of the nasal of the class with which it may be united being assumed by it.

32.   The following are among the most common and useful of the compound consonants.

I. DOUBLED LETTERS.

OBSERVE.—When an aspirated letter is doubled, the first must assume the unaspirated form of the letter.

क्क kka,　क्ख kkha,　ग्ग gga,　ग्घ ggha;　च्च chcha,

च्छ chchha,　ज्ज jja,　ज्झ jjha;　ट्ट ṭṭa,　ट्ठ ṭṭha,

ड्ड ḍḍa,　ड्ढ ḍḍha;　त्त tta,　त्थ ttha,　द्द dda,

द्ध ddha,　न्न nna;　प्प ppa,　प्फ ppha,　ब्ब bba,

भ्भ bbha,　म्म mma;　य्य yya,　ल्ल lla,　श्श śśa,

ष्ष shsha,　स्स ssa.

II. NASALS IN COMBINATION.

OBSERVE.—Nasals combine only with classified letters of their own class, but they may combine with letters that do not belong to either of the five *vargs*. *Anuswár* may take the place of any nasal.

ङ्क ṅka,　ङ्ख ṅkha,　ङ्ग ṅga,　ङ्घ ṅgha;　ञ्च ṅcha,

ञ्छ ṅchha,　ञ्ज ṅja,　ञ्झ ṅjha;　ण्ट ṇṭa,　ण्ठ ṇṭha,

ण्ड ṇḍa,　ण्ढ ṇḍha,　ण्म ṇma,　ण्व ṇwa,　ण्य ṇya;

न्त nta,　न्थ ntha,　न्द nda,　न्ध ndha,　न्व nwa,

न्य nya;　म्प mpa,　म्फ mpha,　म्ब mba,　म्भ mbha,

म्म mma,　म्य mya.

III. SIBILANTS IN COMBINATION.

श्च ścha,　श्न śna,　श्य śya,　श्र śra,　श्ल śla,

श्व śwa;　ष्क shka,　ष्ट shṭa,　ष्ठ shṭha,　ष्ण shṇa,

ष्प shpa,　ष्म shma,　ष्य shya,　ष्व shwa;　स्क ska,

स्ख skha,　स्त sta,　स्थ stha,　स्न sna,　स्प spa,

स्फ spha,　स्म sma,　स्य sya,　स्र sra,　स्व swa.

IV. Semi-vowels य and व added to other Letters.

क्न kna,	क्म kma,	क्य kya,	क्र kra,	क्ल kla,
क्व kwa;	ख्य khya,	ख्व khwa;	ग्न gna,	ग्म gma,
ग्य gya,	ग्र gra,	ग्ल gla,	ग्व gwa;	घ्न ghna,
घ्य ghya,	घ्र ghra,	घ्व ghwa;	ज्म jma,	ज्य jya,
ज्र jra,	ज्व jwa;	त्न tna,	त्म tma,	त्य tya,
त्र tra,	त्ल tla,	त्व twa;	थ्न thna,	थ्य thya,
थ्व thwa;	द्न dna,	द्म dma,	द्य dya,	द्र dra,
द्व dwa;	ध्न dhna,	ध्म dhma,	ध्य dhya,	ध्र dhra,
ध्व dhwa;	प्न pna,	प्म pma,	प्य pya,	प्र pra,
प्ल pla,	प्व pwa;	भ्य bhya,	भ्र bhra,	भ्व bhwa;
ह्न hna,	ह्म hma,	ह्य hya,	ह्र hra,	ह्ल hla,
ह्व hwa.				

V. Miscellaneous Compounds.

क्त kta,	क्थ ktha,	ग्द gda,	ग्ध gdha,	ग्ब gba,
ग्भ gbha,	ग्ह gha,	ड्ग dga,	ड्भ dbha,	त्क tka,
त्ख tkha,	त्प tpa,	त्फ tpha,	त्स tsa,	द्ग dga,
द्घ dgha,	द्भ dbha,	न्प npa,	न्फ npha,	न्ध ndha,
न्श nśa,	प्त pta,	प्थ ptha,	प्स psa,	ब्द bda,
ब्ध bdha,	ल्क lka,	ल्ग lga,	ल्त lta,	ल्प lpa,
ल्भ lbha,	ल्ह lha,	व्झ vjha,	र्क rka,	र्च rcha,
र्ण rṇa,	र्त rta,	र्प rpa,	र्म rma,	र्य rya,
र्व rva,	र्श rśa,	र्श rsha,	र्ह rha.	

VI. Combination of three Letters.

क्त्य ktya,	क्त्र ktra,	क्त्व ktwa,	क्ष्म kshma,	क्ष्य kshya,
ग्न्य gnya,	ग्भ्य gbhya,	त्त्व ttwa,	र्य्य ryya,	स्त्र stra,
त्स्थ tstha,	त्स्म tsma,	न्त्र ntra,	न्त्व ntwa,	न्त्स ntsa,
म्प्य mpya,	म्प्र mpra,	ल्प्त lpta,	र्त्त rtta,	र्ग्य rgya,
र्म्य rmya,	र्त्य rtya,	र्ब्ब rbba,	ल्क्य lkya,	ल्ग्य lgya,
ल्प्य lpya,	स्त्य stya,	स्त्व stwa,	स्थ्य sthya,	स्म्य smya.

CHAPTER II.

The Euphonic Permutations of Letters (सन्धि *sandhi*).*

33.   Euphonic changes in declension and conjugation, and in the formation of compound words, take place in most languages; but they form a main peculiarity of the Sanskrit, their influence being felt throughout the entire scheme of its grammar.

According to its laws of euphony, not only letters, but also syllables and words, and even sentences, are combined for the purpose of securing harmony in pronunciation.

34.   As nine-tenths or more of the entire Hindí vocabulary is derived from Sanskrit, a large proportion of the words being compounds, it is obvious that a knowledge of the laws of Sanskrit euphony is indispensable to the student of Hindí.   Without it the forms that many words assume will not be understood, nor will the numerous compounds that exist in the language be readily reduced to their elements; in fact, derivation, which is essential to a correct and comprehensive knowledge of the words, cannot be studied apart from a knowledge of *Sandhi*.

The more useful of the rules of *Sandhi* are given below with examples of their application.

35.   Native grammarians generally divide *Sandhi* into,—

I. स्वरसन्धि *swarsandhi*, or the changes that vowels in combination with vowels undergo.

II. हलसन्धि *halsandhi*, or the changes that consonants in combination with vowels or consonants undergo.

---

* In going through the grammar for the first time it will be well, perhaps, to omit this chapter altogether; when some progress in the language has been made, the subject will be more readily comprehended, and the student will then perceive the importance of *Sandhi* in giving exactness to his knowledge.

III. विसर्गसन्धि *visargsandhi*, or the changes that *visarg* in combination with vowels and consonants undergoes.

I. THE PERMUTATIONS OF VOWELS.

36. The changes that vowels undergo in combining with vowels are of four kinds; termed, गुण *gun*, or 'qualification'; वृद्धि *vriddhi*, or 'increase'; दीर्घ *dírgh*, or 'long'; अन्तर्गत *antargat*, or 'internal.'

1. GUN CHANGES.

37. A final अ or आ coming in contact with any initial and dissimilar vowel causes the change termed गुण. By this change ए is substituted for इ and ई, ओ for उ and ऊ, अर् for ऋ and ॠ, and अल् for ऌ.

38. The subjoined table will now explain itself.

When a word ending in	combines with one beginning with	the final and initial vowels blend into	EXAMPLES.	
			SIMPLE WORDS.	COMPOUNDS.
अ or आ	इ	ए	देव+इन्द्र *deva+Indra*,	देवेन्द्र *dévendra*, the god Indra.
	ई	ए	परम+ईश्वर *parama+Íswar*,	परमेश्वर *parameśwar*, the supreme Lord, God.
,,	उ	ओ	हित+उपदेश *hita+upadeś*,	हितोपदेश *hitopadeś*, friendly instruction.
,,	ऊ	ओ	महा+ऊर्मि *mahá+úrmmi*,	महोर्मि *mahormmi*, a great wave.
,,	ऋ	अर्	महा+ऋषि *mahá+rishí*,	महर्षि *maharshí*, a great rishí or sage.

2. Vriddhi Changes.

39. A final अ or आ coming in contact with any of the diphthongs ए, ऐ, ओ, औ, causes the change termed वृद्धि; अ or आ blends with ए or with ऐ into ऐ; and with ओ or औ into औ. These changes are exemplified in the adjoined table.

40.

When a word ending in	combines with one beginning with	the final and initial vowels blend into	EXAMPLES	
			SIMPLE WORDS.	COMPOUNDS.
अ	अ	ऐ	एक+एकम् *eka+ekam*,	एकैकम् *ekaikam*, each, every.
or आ	„	„	तथा+एव *tathá+ev*,	तथैव *tathaiv*, in like manner.
„	ऐ	ऐ	देव+ऐश्वर्य *deva+aiswarya*,	देवैश्वर्य *devaiswarya*, divine majesty.
„	„	„	महा+ऐश्वर्य *mahá+aiswarya*,	महैश्वर्य *mahaiswarya*, great majesty.
„	ओ	औ	अल्प+ओजस *alpa+ojas*,	अल्पौजस *alpaujas*, little energy.
„	„	„	महा+ओषधि *mahá+oshadhi*,	महौषधि *mahaushadhi*, a sort of plant, a great remedy.
„	औ	औ	ज्वर+औषध *jwara+aushadh*,	ज्वरौषध *jwaraushadh*, fever medicine.
„	„	„	महा+औदार्यम् *mahá+audáryam*,	महौदार्यम् *mahaudáryam*, great munificence.

3. Dírgh Changes.

41. When a vowel comes in contact with a similar vowel they coalesce into one long similar vowel, thus causing the change termed दीर्घ.

42.

When a word ending in	combines with one beginning with	the final and initial vowels blend into	EXAMPLES.	
			Simple words.	Compounds.
अ or आ	अ or आ	आ	देव+आलय *deva+álay,*	देवालय *deválay,* abode of the gods, heaven.
इ or ई	इ or ई	ई	अधि+ईश्वर *adhi+íswar,*	अधीश्वर *adhíswar,* an emperor.
उ or ऊ	उ or ऊ	ऊ	विधु+उदय *vidhu+uday,*	विधूदय *vidhúday,* the rise of the moon.
ऋ or ॠ	ऋ or ॠ	ॠ	भ्रातृ+ऋद्धि *bhrátri+riddhi,*	भ्रातृद्धि *bhrátriddhi,* a brother's wealth.

4. Antargat Changes.

43. Any final vowel, except अ and आ, coming in contact with any initial dissimilar vowel, causes the change termed अन्तर्गत. By this change इ, उ, ऋ, short or long, give place to their kindred semi-vowels; viz., इ or ई to य; उ or ऊ to व; ऋ or ॠ to र; also when ए or ओ comes before अ it remains unchanged, and अ is dropped; but when ए or ओ comes before any other vowel than अ, then ए is changed to अय, and ओ to अव. These changes are exemplified in the annexed table.

EXAMPLES.

When a word ending in	combines with one beginning with any dissimilar vowel, as	the final and initial vowels blend into	SIMPLE WORDS.	COMPOUNDS.
इ	आ	या	इति+आदि *iti+ádi*,	इत्यादि *ityádi*, and so forth, et cetera.
इ	अ	य	यदि+अपि *yadi+api*,	यद्यपि *yadyapi*, although.
इ	ए	ये	प्रति+एक *prati+ek*,	प्रत्येक *pratyek*, singly, one by one.
इ	उ	यु	अति+उत्तम *ati+uttam*,	अत्युत्तम *atyuttam*, very good, superior.
उ	अ	व	अनु+अय *anu+ay*,	अन्वय *anway*, lineage, order.
उ	आ	वा	सु+आगत *su+ágat*,	स्वागत *swágat*, welcome.
उ	ए	वे	अनु+एषण *anu+eshaṇ*,	अन्वेषण *anweshaṇ*, research.
ऋ	आ	रा	मातृ+आनन्द *mátri+ánand*,	मात्रानन्द *mátránand*, a mother's joy.
ऋ	आ	रा	कृ+आन्ति *kri+ánti*,	क्रान्ति *kránti*, the ecliptic.
ऐ	अ	आय	नै+अक *nai+ak*,	नायक *náyak*, a guide, a leader.
औ	अ	आव	पौ+अक *pau+ak*,	पावक *pávak*, a purifier.

45. The annexed table gives a complete view of the system of vowel combinations, and will be found convenient as it admits of quick and easy reference.

Final vowels \ Initial vowels	अ	आ	इ	ई	उ	ऊ	ऋ	ॠ	ए	ऐ	ओ	औ
अ	आ	आ	ए	ए	ओ	ओ	अर	अर	ऐ	ऐ	औ	औ
आ	आ	आ	ए	ए	ओ	ओ	अर	अर	ऐ	ऐ	औ	औ
इ	य	या	ई	ई	यु	यू	यृ	यॄ	ये	यै	यो	यौ
ई	य	या	ई	ई	यु	यू	यृ	यॄ	ये	यै	यो	यौ
उ	व	वा	वि	वी	ऊ	ऊ	वृ	वॄ	वे	वै	वो	वौ
ऊ	व	वा	वि	वी	ऊ	ऊ	वृ	वॄ	वे	वै	वो	वौ
ऋ	र	रा	रि	री	रु	रू	ॠ	ॠ	रे	रै	रो	रौ
ॠ	र	रा	रि	री	रु	रू	ॠ	ॠ	रे	रै	रो	रौ
ए	अय	अया	अयि	अयी	अयु	अयू	अयृ	अयॄ	अये	अयै	अयो	अयौ
ऐ	आय	आया	आयि	आयी	आयु	आयू	आयृ	आयॄ	आये	आयै	आयो	आयौ
ओ	अव	अवा	अवि	अवी	अवु	अवू	अवृ	अवॄ	अवे	अवै	अवो	अवौ
औ	आव	आवा	आवि	आवी	आवु	आवू	आवृ	आवॄ	आवे	आवै	आवो	आवौ

In referring to this table, the final vowel, say ई, will be found in the first perpendicular column, headed, 'Final vowels;' and the initial vowel, say ए, will be found in the first horizontal line, headed 'Initial vowels;' the result of the combination of those two vowels, viz., ये, will be found at the junction of the perpendicular column and horizontal line.

II. Permutations of Consonants and *Anuswár*.

46. The changes that take place when consonants combine with consonants, or consonants with vowels, are termed हल् संधि.[*] These changes and the laws which govern them are very numerous, and the exceptional cases so many, that the subject is exceedingly complicated. It will suffice to indicate here only such consonantal changes as the student of Hindí is likely to meet with; the following rules will include most of them.

a. In combination with a soft or nasal letter, semi-vowel, or vowel, क् is softened to ग्; as दिक्+गज=दिग्गज *diggaj*, 'one of the elephants said to support the globe;' वाक्+दत्त=वाग्दत्त *vágdatt*, 'betrothed;' दिक्+अम्बर=दिगम्बर *digambar*, 'naked,' 'a mendicant that wears no clothes.'

b. In the same position च is usually softened to ज; ट to ड or ड़; and प to ब: as, षट्+दर्शन=षड्दर्शन *khardarian*, 'the six systems of Hindu philosophy.'

c. When क् combines with म they become ग्; and ज with न becomes ज्ञ; thus, पराक्+मुख=पराङ्मुख *parámukh*, 'having the face averted;' यज्+न=यज्ञ *yagya*, 'a sacrifice.'

d. When a word ending with a short vowel (and sometimes even with a long one) combines with a word beginning with छ, the छ becomes च्छ; as, परि+छेद=परिच्छेद *parichchhed*, 'segment,' 'division.' This rule is not, however, always observed in Hindí.

e. The changes that न and ष undergo in combination are numerous, and of frequent occurrence in Hindí. Several of them are given in the following table.

---

[*] The name *hal sandhi* is given, because, unless a consonant has the *hal* indicating a consonantal ending, it is considered to be followed by the inherent vowel, the permutations of which have been described.

47.

When a word ending in	combines with one beginning with	the two consonants combined become	EXAMPLES.
त् or द्	च	च्च	सत्+चिदानन्द=सच्चिदानन्द *sachchidánand,* 'an epithet of God.'
"	छ	च्छ	उत्+छिन्न=उच्छिन्न *uchchhinn,* 'ruined,' 'laid waste.'
"	ज	ज्ज	उत्+ज्वल=उज्ज्वल *ujjwal,* 'bright,' 'luminous.'
"	न	न्न	जगत्+नाथ=जगन्नाथ *jagannáth,* ' lord of the world,' 'name of a god.'
"	म	न्म	सत्+मान=सन्मान *sanmán,* 'respect,' 'esteem,' 'regard.'
"	ल	ल्ल	उत्+लंघन=उल्लंघन *ullanghan,* 'breach of law or custom.'
"	श	च्छ	उत्+शिष्ट=उच्छिष्ट *uchchhisht,* 'left' (as food).
"	ह	द्ध	उत्+हार=उद्धार *uddhár,* 'deliverance.' *

f. In combination with ग घ द ध ब भ य र व, or a vowel, त् is softened to द्; as,

पश्चात्+गामी=पश्चाद्गामी *paschádgámí,* 'a follower.'

* उत्+धार=उद्धार *uddhár,* 'debt.'

उत्+योग=उद्योग *udyog,* 'exertion,' 'endeavour.'

भविष्यत्+वाणी=भविष्यद्वाणी *bhavishyadvání,* ' prophecy.'

सत्+असत्=सदसत् *sadasat,* 'real and unreal,' 'good and bad.'

सच्चित्+आनन्द=सच्चिदानन्द, *sachchidánand,* ' an epithet of God.'

* The student will observe that उद्धार is given twice and with two different derivations and meanings. The derivations are correct, notwithstanding the peculiarity, which is worthy of notice.

जगत्+ईश=जगदीश *jagadís*, 'lord of the world,' 'name of a god.'

g. त and थ following ष become, respectively, ट and ठ; as, प्रविष्+त=प्रविष्ट *pravisht*, 'entered upon,' 'engaged in.'

षष्+थ=षष्ठ *shashṭh*, 'sixth.'

h. When न, preceded by a short vowel, ends a word, and that word is combined with another, beginning with a vowel, the न is doubled; as, सृजन्+ईश्वर=सृजन्नीश्वर *srijanníswar*, 'God the creator.'

i. As *anuswár* in many positions becomes म, both may be included in one remark. In combination with a semivowel, a sibilant, or ह, म becomes *anuswár*, and *anuswár* remains unchanged; thus,—

सं or सम्+युक्त=संयुक्त *saṅyukt*, 'joined with,' 'connected.'

सं or सम्+वाद=संवाद *saṅwád*, 'information,' 'news.'

सं or सम्+हार=संहार *saṅhár*, 'destruction,' especially 'of the world.'

j. Combined with any other letter, म may become *anuswár*, and *anuswár* remain unchanged; or, optionally, either of these may be changed into the nasal of the class to which the other letter belongs; thus,—

सं or सम्+कल्प=संकल्प or सङ्कल्प, *sankalp* or *saṅkalp*, 'resolve,' 'design.'

अहं or अहम्+कार=अहंकार or अहङ्कार, *ahankár* or *ahaṅkár*, 'pride,' 'conceit.'

किं or किम्+चित=किंचित or किञ्चित, *kinchit* or *kiñchit*, 'a little,' 'somewhat.'

सं or सम्+तोष=सन्तोष *santosh*, 'joy,' 'satisfaction.'

सं or सम्+बन्ध=संबन्ध or सम्बन्ध, *saṁbandh* or *sambandh*, ' connexion.'

Irregularities, however, in regard to this rule occur not unfrequently in Hindí writing.

III. Permutations of *Visarg*.

48. *a.* *Visarg* in combination with क ख प फ may remain unchanged, or become a sibilant ; as,—

अन्तः+करण=अन्तःकरण or अन्तस्करण, *antaḥkaraṇ*, or *antaskaraṇ*, ' the heart or seat of the affections,' 'the understanding.'

निः+फल=निःफल or निष्फल, *niḥphal* or *niṣhphal*, ' fruitless.'

निः+कपट=निःकपट or निस्कपट, *niḥkapaṭ* or *niṣkapaṭ*, ' artless,' ' sincere.'

निः+पत्ति=निःपत्ति or निष्पत्ति, *niḥpatti* or *niṣhpatti*, ' termination,' ' completion.'

b. In combination with च छ ट ठ त थ, or a sibilant, *visarg* is changed to a sibilant ; as,—

निः+चल=निश्चल *niśchal*, ' immoveable,' ' fixed.'

निः+चिन्त=निश्चिन्त *niśchint*, ' thoughtless,' ' inconsiderate.'

धनुः+टङ्कार=धनुष्टङ्कार *dhanushṭaṅkár*, ' the twang of a bow.'

निः+सन्देह=निस्सन्देह *nissandeh*, ' without doubt.'

The above rules are not strictly observed in Hindí ; such forms as निर्फल, निःसन्देह, occur.

c. When *visarg*, preceded by the inherent vowel अ, is followed by a word beginning with any of the following letters, ग, ग घ, ज झ, ड ढ, द ध, ब भ, र ज ण न म, य र ल व, ह, it becomes ओ ; as,—

मनः+गुप्त=मनोगुप्त *manogupt,* 'concealed in the mind.'

मनः+नीत = मनोनीत *manonít,* 'chosen,' 'preferred.'

मनः+हर=मनोहर *manohar,* 'captivating.'

तेजः+मय=तेजोमय *tejomay,* 'luminous,' 'energetic,' 'famous.'

d. When *visarg* is preceded by अ, and followed by any other vowel than अ; or when it is preceded by आ, and followed by any of the above consonants, or by a vowel, it is simply elided.

e. When *visarg* is preceded by any other vowel than अ or आ, and followed by any of the above consonants except र, or by any vowel, it is changed into र; as,—

वहिः+देश=वहिर्देश *vahirdeś,* 'a foreign country.'

निः+धन=निर्धन *nirdhan,* 'without wealth,' 'poor.'

निः+भय=निर्भय *nirbhay,* 'fearless,' 'undaunted.'

f. When *visarg* is preceded by any other vowel than अ or आ, and followed by र, it is dropped, and the preceding vowel, if short, is lengthened; as,

निः+रस=नीरस *níras,* 'insipid,' 'dry.'

निः+रोग=नीरोग *nírog,* 'free from disease,' 'healthy.'

CHAPTER III.

Parts of Speech.

49. In all purely native grammars of the Hindí language the entire body of words is divided into three parts of speech; viz., nouns, संज्ञा *sangyá,* verbs, क्रिया *kriyá,* and particles, or indeclinable words, अव्यय *avyaya.*

a. Under the noun are included all words that admit of declension, as substantives, or words that are names of things; adjectives, words that are names of qualities ; and pronouns, words that may be used instead of substantives and adjectives.

b. Under the verb are included all words that may be conjugated, and that declare what a thing is, does, or suffers.

c. Under the particles are included all words that are neither declined nor conjugated ; viz., adverbs, prepositions, interjections, and conjunctions.

Of Nouns, संज्ञा *Sangyá.*

50. Of nouns, as distinguished from adjectives and pronouns, native grammarians reckon three kinds ; viz., जातिवाचक *játivá-chak,* or common nouns ; व्यक्तिवाचक *vyaktiváchak,* or proper nouns ; भाववाचक *bhávaváchak,* or abstract nouns.

51. There are but two genders in Hindí, the masculine, पुल्लिङ्ग *pulliṅg,* and the feminine, स्त्रीलिङ्ग *striliṅg.*

52. There are two numbers, the singular, एकवचन *ekvachan,* and the plural, बहुवचन *bahuvachan.*

53. There are eight cases, कारक *kárak.*

1. The Nominative, कर्त्ता *karttá,* or the case which a noun or pronoun takes when it names the author or source of an action.

2. The Agent or Instrumental, करण *karaṇ,* or the case which denotes by whom anything *has been done.* This case is but another form of the nominative that must be employed with the past tenses of all transitive verbs, as will be hereafter explained.[*]

---

[*] 'Instrumental' is a name that is sometimes given to this case, but incorrectly. It is never used to denote the means or instrument by which an agent performs an action. करण, the Sanskrit term for the instrumental case, is retained as the Hindí name for the case of the Agent in the absence of a more distinctive term.

3. The Genitive, सम्बन्ध *sambandh*, the case which denotes connexion generally, whether arising from origin or possession.

4. The Dative, सम्प्रदान *sampradán*, or the case of the recipient, in which the word is put which represents that in which the object of an action rests.

5. The Accusative, कर्म *karm*, or the case in which that is put which expresses the immediate object of an action.

6. The Ablative, अपादान *apádán*, or the case which denotes the means or instrument by which, or the manner in which, a thing is done.

7. The Locative, अधिकरण *adhikaran*, or the case which indicates the place or time in which any thing is done.

8. The Vocative, संबोधन *sambodhan*, or the case that is used in calling attention, or in addressing an object.

54. There are two declensions, विभक्ति *vibhakti*, corresponding with the two genders.

Of Gender, लिंग liṅg.

55. There is no neuter gender in Hindí; all the substantives of the language, animate or inanimate, and of whatever termination, are regarded as either masculine or feminine.

56. The gender of animate nouns having a sexual distinction is easily ascertained ; for all males, as well as all words that may be applied to males only, are of the masculine gender ; and all females, and words that may be applied to females only, are feminine.

57. It is not so easy to determine the gender of things without life, for there is nothing in Hindí grammar apparently more arbitrary or unaccountable than the gender of inanimate objects.

The best rules that can be laid down for distinguishing gender are not always a safe guide, because of the numerous exceptions that come under them. This is one of the few real difficulties of Hindí grammar (which, for the most part, is very regular and simple) to which the careful attention of the student must be given from the commencement. It is impossible to speak or write in Hindí with accuracy unless the gender of the nouns be known, because of the action of the gender of the noun on the verb. The best, and, indeed, the only way to overcome the difficulty is to learn and remember the gender of each substantive that may be met with.

With an ordinarily retentive memory this will not prove so difficult a task as the reader, now unacquainted with the language, may suppose ; and in it the ear will prove a great help if each noun be associated with a masculine or feminine form of some verb, according to its gender, and the ear be accustomed to the sound.

58. A few general rules may be given and may prove useful ; but in any case of doubt as to the gender of a noun, observe, that it is considered far less culpable to err in favour of the masculine than of the feminine.

59. In leaning to the masculine, moreover, there is a greater chance of being right, than in supposing the gender to be feminine, for the greater number of the substantives in Hindí are taken from the Sanskrit which has three genders, masculine, feminine, and neuter, and nearly all nouns that are either masculine or neuter in Sanskrit are masculine in Hindí.

To distinguish Masculine Nouns.

60. Nouns ending in श्रा *á*, or in any consonant but न *t*, are, for the most part, masculine ; as, बच्चा *bachichá*, 'the young of any animal;' पाप *páp*, 'sin ;' जाल *jál*, 'a net ;' ज्ञान *gyán*, 'knowledge.'

To distinguish Feminine Nouns.

61. Nouns ending in ई *i*, and त *t* are generally feminine ; as, मोरी *morí*, 'a drain,' 'a ditch ;' नथनी *nathní*, 'a ring worn in the nose ;' जुगत *jugat*, 'cleverness ;' बात *bát*, 'a word,' 'saying.'

62. The most noticeable exceptions to the rule regarding feminine nouns in ई *i* are the following ; घी *ghí*, 'clarified butter ;' जी *jí*, 'life ;' पानी *pání*, 'water ;' मोती *motí*, 'a pearl ;' दही *dahí*, 'curdled milk.'

63. Feminine nouns are formed from masculines in various ways ; as :—

a. By changing long आ *á* into long ई *í* ; as,

MASCULINE.	FEMININE.
घोड़ा *ghorá*, 'a horse,'	घोड़ी *ghorí*, 'a mare,'
बिल्ला *billá*, 'a male cat,'	बिल्ली *billí*, 'a female cat,'
गधा *gadhá*, 'a male donkey,'	गधी *gadhí*, 'a female donkey,'
साला *sálá*, 'a brother-in-law,'	साली *sálí*, 'a sister-in-law,'
चचा *chachá*, 'uncle,'	चची *chachí*, 'aunt,'
भांजा *bhánjá*, 'nephew,'	भांजी *bhánjí*, 'niece,'
चेला *chelá*, 'a male disciple,'	चेली *chelí*, 'a female disciple,'
बेटा *betá*, 'a son,'	बेटी *betí*, 'a daughter.'

b. Masculines ending in a consonant form their feminines in many cases by adding ई *í* ; thus,—

MASCULINE.	FEMININE.
अहीर *ahír*, 'a cowherd,'	अहीरी *ahírí*, 'a cowherdess,'
देव *dev*, 'a god,'	देवी *deví*, 'a goddess,'
बन्दर *bandar*, 'a male monkey,'	बन्दरी *bandarí*, 'a female monkey,'
ब्राह्मण *bráhman*, 'a brahman,'	ब्राह्मणी *bráhmaní*, 'a brahman's wife,'

तरुण *tarun,* 'a young man,'   तरुणी *taruni,* 'a young woman,'
दास *dás,* 'a man servant,'   दासी *dásí,* 'a woman servant,'
मेषपाल *meshpál,* 'a shepherd,'   मेषपाली *mcshpálí,* 'a shepherdess,'
पुत्र *putra,* 'a son,'   पुत्री *putrí,* 'a daughter,'
नागर *nágar,* 'a knowing man,'   नागरी *nágarí,* 'a knowing woman.'

c. Names of occupations, professions, and trades, form the feminine by adding इन *in*; but if the masculine end in आ *á* or ई *i* it is dropped before adding इन *in;* thus :—

<table>
<tr><td>MASCULINE.</td><td>FEMININE.</td></tr>
</table>

सोनार *sonár,* 'a goldsmith,'   सोनारिन *sonárin,* 'a goldsmith's wife,'

कसेरा *kaserá,* 'a brazier,'   कसेरिन *kaserin,* 'a brazier's wife,'

लोहार *lohár,* 'a blacksmith,'   लोहारिन *lohárin,* 'a blacksmith's wife,'

कलवार *kalwár,* 'a distiller,'   कलवारिन *kalwárin,* 'a distiller's wife,'

मोदी *modí,* वेपारी *vaipárí,* } 'a merchant,'   मोदिन *modin,* वेपारिन *vaipárin,* } 'a merchant's wife,'

दूल्हा *dúlhá,* 'a bridegroom,'   दूल्हिन *dúlhin,* 'a bride,'

माली *málí,* 'a gardener,'   मालिन *málin,* 'a gardener's wife,'

धोबी *dhobí,* 'a washerman,'   धोबिन *dhobin,* 'a washerwoman,'

तेली *telí,* 'an oilman,'   तेलिन *telin,* 'an oilwoman,'

बढ़ई *barhaí,* 'a carpenter,'   बढ़िन *burhain,* 'a carpenter's wife,'

बारी *bárí,* 'a torch-bearer,'   बारिन *bárin,* 'a torch-bearer's wife,'

नाई *náí,* 'a barber,'   नाइन *náin,* 'a barber's wife,'

तम्बोली *tambolí,* 'a seller of betel,'   तम्बोलिन *tambolin,* 'a betel seller's wife.'

d. Words that were originally titles, but have been corrupted and are now used as family names, form the feminine from the masculine by adding वादिन *dín* ; but if the vowel of the first syllable be चा *á*, ई *í*, or ऊ *ú*, it must be changed for its corresponding short vowel ; as :—

MASCULINE.	FEMININE.
चौबे *chaube*,	चौबादिन *chaubdín*,
तिवारी *tiwárí*,	तिवरादिन *tiwardín*,
दूबे *dúbe*,	दुबादिन *dubáin*,
पांड़े *pánṛe*,	पड़ादिन *paṛdín*,
मिश्र *miśr*,	मिशरादिन *miśrdín*,
ओझा *ojhá*,	ओझरादिन *ojhdín*.

e. The feminine of a few is formed by adding नी *ní* to the masculine ; as,—

सिंह *siṅha*, 'a lion,'	सिंहनी *siṅhaní*, 'a lioness,'
बाघ *bágh*, 'a tiger,'	बाघनी *bághní*, 'a tigress,'
मोर *mor*, 'a peacock,'	मोरनी *morní*, 'a peahen,'
करि *kari*, 'an elephant,'	करिनी *kariní*, 'a female elephant,'
अहि *ahi*, 'a serpent,'	अहिनी *ahiní*, 'a female serpent.'

f. The feminines of many nouns are words quite distinct from the masculines ; as,—

पुरुष *purush*, 'a man,'	स्त्री *strí*, 'a woman,'
पिता *pitá*, 'a father,'	माता *mátá*, 'a mother,'
भाई *bhái*, 'a brother,'	बहिन *bahin*, 'a sister,'
राजा *rájá*, 'a king,'	रानी *rání*, 'a queen,'
बैल *bail*, 'an ox,'	गाय *gáe*, 'a cow.'

64. OBSERVE.—Compounds take the gender of the last member of the compound : thus the word स्त्रीलिंग *stríliṅg* is masculine, because *ling* is, though the first word, *strí*, is feminine, and the idea conveyed by the compound is feminine.

Of number, सङ्ख्या *saṅkhyá.*

65. There are two numbers, the singular and the plural. The nominative singular and the nominative plural are alike in all masculine nouns that end in any letter but आ *á.* Masculine nouns that end in आ *á* form their nominative plural by changing आ *á* into ए *e ;* * thus, बेटा *beṭá,* 'a son,' बेटे *beṭe,* 'sons.'

66. The nominative plural of feminine nouns, ending in ई *í* is formed by adding आं *áṅ,* or यां *yáṅ* to the nominative singular; if the termination यां be adopted, the preceding vowel must be shortened; thus, बेटीआं *beṭíáṅ,* or बेटियां *beṭiyáṅ,* 'daughters.'

67. The nominative plural of feminine nouns, ending in any letter but ई *í* or ऊ *ú,* is formed by adding एं *eṅ* to the nominative singular; thus, बात *bát,* 'a word,' बातें *báteṅ,* 'words.'

68. As the nominative plural of most nouns is the same in form as the nominative singular, words indicative of number or quantity are often used to shew that the plural is intended; thus, सेवक *sevak,* as a nominative, may mean one 'servant' or more than one, but सेवक लोग *sevak log* gives the idea of 'servants iu general.' This use of लोग *log,* 'people,' is highly idiomatic; the word is not confined, like the word 'people,' to rational beings, but is commonly used in speaking of irrational as well as rational objects; thus, गाय लोग घास खातीं *gáe log ghás kátíṅ,* ' cows eat grass ;' पशु लोगों में भी एक प्रकार की बोली होती है *paśu logoṅ meṅ bhí ek prakár kí bolí hotí hai,* ' among animals also there is a kind of language.'

69. The word गण *gaṇ,* 'a multitude,' 'a troop,' is frequently added to nouns to denote the plural; as, देवगण *devgaṇ,*

---

* All proper names aud words expressive of relationship, such as गंगा *Gaṅgá,* 'the river Ganges'; पिता *pitá;* 'a father,' are exceptions; they do not change their terminations in the plural.

'the gods,' ग्रहगण *grahgaṇ*, 'the planets.' The word जाति *játi* is similarly used to indicate a class or species; thus, मनुष्यजाति *manushyajáti*, 'mankind'; स्त्रीजाति *strijáti*, 'womankind'; प्राणीजाति *práníjáti*, 'the animal kingdom.'

70. When a noun is preceded by an adjective expressive of number or quantity it does not always take a plural termination in the nominative case; but if the noun be in an oblique case the plural termination is usually employed; thus, पांच स्त्री वहां थीं *pánch strí wahán thín*, 'five women were there'; दो स्त्रियां पीसती थीं *do striyán písti thín*, 'two women were grinding'; पांच स्त्रियों में *pánch striyon men*, 'among five women.'

71. The plural termination, ओं, of the oblique cases is idiomatically used in the nominative plural of large numbers to signify their indefinite multiplication; as, लाखों बरस *lákhon baras*, 'hundreds of thousands of years'; सैकड़ों पुरुष *saikron purush*, 'hundreds of men.'

OF CASE, कारक kárak.

72. There are eight cases as already mentioned.

The nominative is the form of the word as given in Hindí dictionaries; the other cases are formed by certain particles written after the word, and, therefore, called postpositions, certain changes being also made usually in the form of the word.

73. The postpositions are the same in both numbers; they are ;—

For the Agent,..................ने *ne*, 'by.'
* Genitive, ...का, के, की, *ká*, *ke*, or *kí*, 'of,' 's.
* Dative,   }
* Accusative,   }........को *ko*, 'to.'
* Ablative,................से *se*, 'from.'
* Locative, ...में, पर, तक, *men*, *par*, or *tak*, 'in,' 'upon,' ' up to.'

74. The vocative differs from the other oblique cases in not taking a postposition ; it is generally preceded by some interjection, such as हे *he,* हो *ho,* अरे *are,* अबे *abe,* अजी *ají,* रे *re.*

These often indicate the feeling entertained towards the person addressed; e. g., अरे, अबे, contempt or anger; अजी, familiarity or friendship; हे, respect.

75: It is of importance to remember that the accusative is often identical in form with the nominative.

76. All the cases, with the exception of the agent and the genitive, are simple in their form and application and will be readily understood.

77. The case of the agent is never used except with the past-tenses of transitive verbs ; we shall therefore delay a fuller consideration of it till we come to the verb.

78. There are three ways of forming the genitive in Hindí ; it is of the greatest importance that the student should clearly understand and distinguish between them.

79. Observe, then, that in forming the genitive there are two words to be considered ; the word that governs, and the word that is governed ; or, we may term them, for the sake of distinction, the 'governing noun,' and the 'genitive noun.' For instance, in the sentence, ब्राह्मण का पुत्र *bráhman ká putra,* 'a brahman's son,' the word पुत्र is the 'governing noun,' and ब्राह्मण is the 'genitive noun.'

80. *Rule* 1. When the 'governing noun' is masculine and in the nominative case singular, or in the accusative case, that case having the nominative form, the genitive is formed with का *ká ;* thus, पेड़ का फल *per ká phal,* 'fruit of a tree'; द्वार का ताला खोलो *dwár ká tálá kholo,* 'open the lock of the door.'

81. *Rule* 2. When the 'governing noun' is masculine, but

in any other case or number than those mentioned in the preceding rule, the genitive is formed with के *ke*. Also when the genitive is governed by a preposition it takes के *ke*. Ex. gr. राजा के घोड़े पर *rájá ke ghore par*, 'on the king's horse'; नदी के जल से *nadí ke jal se*, 'from the water of the river'; घर के सामने *ghar ke sámhne*, 'in front of the house.'

82. *Rule* 3. When the 'governing noun' is feminine, in whatever number or case it may be, the genitive is always formed with की *kí*; thus, पण्डित की स्त्री *pandit kí strí*, 'the pandit's wife'; मित्र की सहायता से *mitra kí saháyatá se*, 'through the assistance of a friend'; कवि की चार बेटियां *kavi kí chár betiyán* 'the four daughters of the poet.'

The following additional examples will enable the student to understand still more clearly the foregoing important rules :—

83. अक्षर का रूप *akshar ká rúp*, 'the shape of a letter'; the genitive formed with का, because रूप, the 'governing noun,' is masculine and in the nominative case singular. For a similar reason, 'the shape of the earth' would be, पृथिवी का रूप *prithiví ká rúp*, and not, पृथिवी की रूप *prit'hiví kí rúp*, though पृथिवी be feminine ; shewing that the genitive sign, whether *ká, ke*, or *kí*, does not at all depend upon the noun itself which is put in the genitive, but upon the noun by which it is governed.

84. मछुवे का जाल लाओ *machhwe ká jál láo*, 'bring the fisherman's net;' in this instance, जाल is in the accusative case, but as it has the nominative form, it governs the genitive in का as if it were a real nominative. If the accusative form with को *ko* were used, the genitive would be formed with के *ke*, and the sentence would stand thus, मछुवे के जाल को लाओ. 'From the man's son' would be, मनुष्य के पुत्र से *manushya ke putra se*, because पुत्र, the 'governing noun,' though masculine, is in the ablative case, the genitive must therefore take के *ke*. 'The man's horses' would

be, मनुष्य के घोड़े *manushya ke ghore*, because the 'governing noun,' घोड़े, though masculine and in the nominative case, is not in the nominative singular, the genitive therefore must take के *ke*.

85. वैद्य की बेटी *vaidya ki beṭi*, 'the physician's daughter'; रानी की सहेलियां *ráni ki saheliyáṅ*, 'the queen's female companions'; रानी की सहेलियों में *ráni ki saheliyoṅ meṅ*, 'among the female companions of the queen'; and so in every case when the 'governing noun' is feminine, the genitive is invariably formed with की *ki*.

Of Declension, विभक्ति *vibhakti*.

86. There is, strictly speaking, only one declension of nouns in Hindí; but, as a matter of convenience, and as an aid to memory, all the substantives of the language may be arranged under two declensions. As the simplest principle of division is the natural one, we shall include in the first declension all masculine nouns, and in the second declension all feminine nouns.

First Declension :—*All masculine nouns.*

87. The nouns of the first declension are divided into two classes :—

Class I. All masculine nouns that end in आ *á*.

    " II. All masculine nouns that end in any letter but आ *á*.

88. OBSERVE :—Nouns of the first class, or those that end in आ *á*, are subject to change in their terminations before they receive the postpositions; nouns of the second class, ending in any letter but आ *á*, are not subject to any change of termination.

CLASS I.

89. Masculine nouns ending in आ *á* change their termination to ए *e* in all the oblique cases of the singular and in the nominative plural; and to ओं *oṅ* in the oblique cases of the plural, with the exception of the vocative which ends in ओ *o*, the *anuswár* being rejected.

लड़का *laṛká*, 'a boy.'

90.   SINGULAR, एकवचन *ekvachan*.

Nom.   लड़का *laṛká*, a boy.
Agent.   लड़के ने *laṛke ne*, by a boy.
Gen.   लड़के का, के, की, *laṛke ká, ke*, or *kí*, of a boy.
Dat.   लड़के को *laṛke ko*, to a boy.
Acc.   लड़का, लड़के को, *laṛká*, or *laṛke ko*, a boy.
Abl.   लड़के से *laṛke se*, from a boy.
Loc.   लड़के में *laṛke meṅ*, in a boy.
Voc.   हे लड़के *he laṛke*, O boy.

PLURAL, बहुवचन *bahuvachan*.

Nom.   लड़के *laṛke*, boys.
Agent.   लड़कों ने *laṛkoṅ ne*, by boys.
Gen.   लड़कों का, के, की, *laṛkoṅ ká, ke*, or *kí*, of boys.
Dat.   लड़कों को *laṛkoṅ ko*, to boys.
Acc.   लड़के, लड़कों को, *laṛke*, or *laṛkoṅ ko*, boys.
Abl.   लड़कों से *laṛkoṅ se*, from boys.
Loc.   लड़कों में *laṛkoṅ meṅ*, in boys.
Voc.   हे लड़को *he laṛko*, O boys.

91. In a similar manner are declined all masculine nouns ending in आ *á*, with the following exceptions :—पिता *pitá*, 'a

father'; राजा *rájá*, 'a king'; लाला *lálá*, 'a writer,' 'a school-master,' 'Sir'; दाता *dátá*, 'a giver,' 'a benefactor'; देवता *devtá*, 'a god'; आत्मा *átmá*, 'soul,' 'spirit';[*] कर्त्ता *karttá*, 'a maker,' 'author,' 'agent'; काका *káká*, 'a paternal uncle'; वक्ता *vaktá*, 'a speaker'; and most proper names and words expressive of relationship that end in आ *á;* these do not change their terminations but are declined like masculine nouns of the second class.

With regard to nouns of this class the following rule may be laid down :—

92. All masculine nouns in आ *á* derived from the Sanskrit, *and retaining their original Sanskrit form,* are not inflected in the oblique cases: as, श्रोता *srotá*, 'a hearer,' 'a listener'; युवा *yuvá,* 'a youth,' 'young man'; etc.

CLASS II.

93. All masculine nouns that do not end in आ *á* belong to this class; their terminations remain unchanged throughout the singular and in the nominative plural, the postpositions being added to the nominative form of the word. In the oblique cases of the plural ओं *oṅ* is inserted before adding the postpositions, except in the vocative, which in the plural always ends in ओ *o*, rejecting the *anuswár.*

जल *jal*, 'water.'

94.   SINGULAR, एकवचन *ek vachan.*

Nom.	जल *jal*, water.	
Ag.	जल ने *jal ne*, by water.	
Gen.	जल का, के, की, *jal ká, ke,* or *kí,* of water.	
Dat.	जल को *jal ko*, to water.	

---

[*] देवता and आत्मा are properly feminine nouns, but when used as masculines they follow the usage assigned to them above.

F

Acc.   जल, जल को, *jal*, or *jal ko*, water.

Abl.   जल से *jal se*, from water.

Loc.   जल में *jal men*, in water.

Voc.   हे जल *he jal*, O water.

PLURAL, बहुवचन *bahuvachan.*

Nom.   जल *jal*, waters.

Ag.   जलों ने *jalon ne*, by waters.

Gen.   जलों का, के, की, *jalon ká, ke*, or *kí*, of waters.

Dat.   जलों को *jalon ko*, to waters.

Acc.   जल, जलों को, *jal*, or *jalon ko*, waters.

Abl.   जलों से *jalon se*, from waters.

Loc.   जलों में *jalon men*, in waters.

Voc.   हे जलो *he jalo*, O waters.

The following are examples of masculine nouns ending in a vowel other than आ *á.*

माली *máli*, 'a gardener.'

95.   SINGULAR.

Nom.   माली *máli*, a gardener.

Ag.   माली ने *máli ne*, by a gardener.

Gen.   माली का, के, की, *máli ká, ke*, or *kí*, of a gardener.

Dat.   माली को *máli ko*, to a gardener.

Acc.   माली, माली को, *máli*, or *máli ko*, a gardener.

Abl.   माली से *máli se*, from a gardener.

Loc.   माली में *máli men*, in a gardener.

Voc.   हे माली *he máli*, O gardener.

PLURAL.

Nom.   माली *máli*, gardeners.

Ag.   मालियों ने *máliyon ne*, by gardeners.

Gen.   मालियों का, के, की, *máliyon ká, ke*, or *kí*, of gardeners.

Dat.   मालियों को *máliyon ko*, to gardeners.

Acc.	मालो, मालियों को,	*málí,* or *máliyoṅ ko,* gardeners.
Abl.	मालियों से	*máliyoṅ se,* from gardeners.
Loc.	मालियों में	*máliyoṅ meṅ,* in gardeners.
Voc.	हे मालियो	*he máliyo,* O gardeners.

96. OBSERVE:—When masculine nouns end in a long vowel, as, माली, they form the oblique cases of the plural with ओं *oṅ,* or with यों *yoṅ;* but if with the latter, the preceding vowel must be shortened. Some native grammarians shorten the vowel in the oblique cases of the plural before ओं *oṅ* as well as before यों *yoṅ.* If the vowel be short, it remains unchanged throughout the singular and plural; as,—

साधु *sádhu,* 'a religious person,' 'a mendicant.'

97. SINGULAR.

Nom.	साधु	*sádhu,* a mendicant.
Ag.	साधु ने	*sádhu ne,* by a mendicant.
Gen,	साधु का, के, की,	*sádhu ká, ke,* or *kí,* of a mendicant.
Dat.	साधु को	*sádhu ko,* to a mendicant.
Acc.	साधु, साधु को,	*sádhu,* or *sádhu ko,* a mendicant.
Abl.	साधु से	*sádhu se,* from a mendicant.
Loc.	साधु में	*sádhu meṅ,* in a mendicant.
Voc.	हे साधु	*he sádhu,* O mendicant.

PLURAL.

Nom.	साधु	*sádhu,* mendicants.
Ag.	साधुओं ने	*sádhuoṅ ne,* by mendicants.
Gen.	साधुओं का, के, की,	*sádhuoṅ ká, ke,* or *kí,* of mendicants.
Dat.	साधुओं को	*sádhuoṅ ko,* to mendicants.
Acc.	साधु, साधुओं को,	*sádhu,* or *sádhuoṅ ko,* mendicants.
Abl.	साधुओं से	*sádhuoṅ se,* from mendicants.
Loc.	साधुओं में	*sádhuoṅ meṅ,* in mendicants.
Voc.	हे साधुओ	*he sádhuo,* O mendicants.

SECOND DECLENSION :—*All feminine nouns.*

98. OBSERVE.—Feminine nouns of whatever termination differ from masculine nouns of the second class, that is from masculine nouns that do not end in आ *á*, in the nominative plural only ; in all other respects they are identical as regards the formation of the cases.

99. The nouns of the second declension, like those of the first, are divided into two classes :—

Class. I. All feminine nouns that terminate in ई *í* or इ *i*.

II. All feminine nouns that terminate in any letter but ई *í* or इ *i*.

CLASS I.

100. All feminine nouns that terminate in ई *í* or इ *i* form their nominative plural by changing ई *í* or इ *i* into इयां *iyán* ; as,—

पुत्री *putrí,* 'a daughter.'

101.   SINGULAR.

Nom.	पुत्री *putrí,*	a daughter.
Ag.	पुत्री ने *putrí ne,*	by a daughter.
Gen.	पुत्री का, के, की, *putrí ká, ke,* or *kí,*	of a daughter.
Dat.	पुत्री को *putrí ko,*	to a daughter.
Acc.	पुत्री, पुत्री को, *putrí,* or *putrí ko,*	a daughter.
Abl.	पुत्री से *putrí se,*	from a daughter.
Loc.	पुत्री में *putrí meṅ,*	in a daughter.
Voc.	हे पुत्री *he putrí,*	O daughter.

PLURAL.

Nom.	पुत्रियां *putriyáṅ*,	daughters.
Ag.	पुत्रियों ने *putriyoṅ ne*,	by daughters.
Gen.	पुत्रियों का, के, की, *putriyoṅ ká, ke*, or *kí*,	of daughters.
Dat.	पुत्रियों को, *putriyoṅ ko*,	to daughters.
Acc.	पुत्रियां, पुत्रियों को, *putriyáṅ*, or *putriyoṅ ko*,	daughters.
Abl.	पुत्रियों से *putriyoṅ se*,	from daughters.
Loc.	पुत्रियों में *putriyoṅ meṅ*,	in daughters.
Voc.	हे पुत्रियो *he putriyo*,	O daughters.

Similarly are declined लड़की *laṛkí*, a girl ; बुद्धि *buddhi*, knowledge, intellect ; घोड़ी *ghoṛí*, a mare ; and all feminine nouns ending in ई or उ.

CLASS II.

102. All feminine nouns that terminate in any letter but ई or उ form their nominative plural by adding ें to the nominative singular ; as,—

बात *bát*, ' a word.'

103. SINGULAR.

Nom.	बात *bát*,	a word.
Ag.	बात ने *bát ne*,	by a word.
Gen.	बात का, के, की, *bát ká, ke*, or *kí*,	of a word.
Dat.	बात को *bát ko*,	to a word.
Acc.	बात, बात को, *bát*, or *bát ko*,	a word.
Abl.	बात से *bát se*,	from a word.
Loc.	बात में *bát meṅ*,	in a word.
Voc.	हे बात *he bát*,	O word.

PLURAL.

Nom.	बातें *báten*,	words.
Ag.	बातों ने *báton ne*,	by words.
Gen.	बातों का, के, की, *báton ká, ke*, or *ki*,	of words.
Dat.	बातों को *báton ko*,	to words.
Acc.	बातें, बातों को, *báten*, or *báton ko*,	words.
Abl.	बातों से *báton se*,	from words.
Loc.	बातों में *báton men*,	in words.
Voc.	हे बातो *he báto*,	O words.

104. OBSERVE.—जोरू *jorú*, 'a wife,' is anomalous in the formation of its nominative plural; generally जोरूयां *jorúán* is given, but जोरू *jorú* is also made the nominative plural by some native grammarians. गैया *gaiyá*, 'a cow,' makes in the nominative plural गैयां *gaiyán*; similarly ठिलिया *thiliyá*, 'a waterpot,' makes ठिलियां *thiliyán*.

105. There is often in practice an elision of the sign of the nominative plural of feminine nouns, perhaps, for the sake of euphony; this has led to the declension of some feminine nouns without any change in the nominative plural : as,—

माता *mátá*, 'a mother.'

106. SINGULAR.

Nom.	माता *mátá*,	a mother.
Ag.	माता ने *mátá ne*,	by a mother.
Gen.	माता का, के, की, *mátá ká, ke*, or *ki*,	of a mother.
Dat.	माता को *mátá ko*,	to a mother.
Acc.	माता, माता को, *mátá*, or *mátá ko*,	a mother.
Abl.	माता से *mátá se*,	from a mother.
Loc.	माता में *mátá men*,	in a mother.
Voc.	हे माता *he mátá*,	O mother.

PLURAL.

Nom.	माता *mátá*, mothers.
Ag.	माताओं ने *mátáoṅ ne*, by mothers.
Gen.	माताओं का, के, की, *mátáoṅ ká, ke*, or *kí*, of mothers.
Dat.	माताओं को *mátáoṅ ko*, to mothers.
Acc.	माता, माताओं को, *mátá*, or *mátáoṅ ko*, mothers.
Abl.	माताओं से *mátáoṅ se*, from mothers.
Loc.	माताओं में *mátáoṅ meṅ*, in mothers.
Voc.	हे माताओ *he mátáo*, O mothers.

In a similar manner are declined धेनु *dhenu*, 'a milch cow,' झाड़ू *jháṛú*, 'a broom,' and a few more.

CHAPTER IV.

Of Adjectives, गुणवाचक *guṇaváchak*.

107. In Hindí adjectives have no system of declension peculiar to them; when used as concrete nouns, and therefore declinable, they follow the model of substantives; thus, बड़ों की मति पर चला चाहिये *baṛoṅ kí mati par chalá cháhiye*, 'we ought to act on the opinion of the great'; बुरों की संगति से अकेला रहना अच्छा है *buroṅ kí sangati se akelá rahná achchhá hai*, 'to live alone is better than the companionship of the wicked.'

108. As a rule, adjectives are placed immediately before the nouns they qualify, as in English; and, unless they end in the long vowel आ *á*, they do not change their terminations to agree with their nouns, in whatever gender, number, or case they may be; thus, पवित्र ब्राह्मण *pavitra bráhman*, 'a pure brahman'; पवित्र स्त्री *pavitra strí*, 'a pure woman'; पवित्र वस्तु *pavitra vastu*, 'a pure thing'; पवित्र लड़कियां *pavitra laṛkiyáṅ*, 'pure girls.'

109. Adjectives that end in आ *á*, like काला *kálá*, 'black,'
ऊंचा *únchá*, 'high,' भला *bhalá*, 'good,' change their terminations
to ए *e*, or ई *i*, by rules similar to those by which the sign of the
possessive, का, is changed to के or की.

a. An adjective ending in आ *á* and qualifying a noun in
the *masculine gender and nominative case singu'ar*, or the *accusative
in the nominative form*, does not alter its termination; thus, उजला
तारा *ujlá tárá*, 'a bright star'; काला वस्त्र पहिनो *kálá vastra pahino*,
'wear black raiment.'

b. An adjective ending in आ *á* and qualifying a *masculine
noun in any case but the nominative singu'ar, or accusative in the nominative form*, must change its termination to ए *e*; thus, बड़े घर
में *bare ghar men*, 'in a large house'; ऊंचे पर्बत पर *únche parb-
bat par*, 'on a high mountain'; चौड़े फाटक से *chaure phátak se*,
'through a broad gate'; बड़े लड़के *bare larke*, 'big boys'; अच्छे
दासों को *achchhe dásoṅ ko*, 'to good servants'; मोटे घोड़ों पर *mote
ghoroṅ par*, 'on stout horses.'

c. Adjectives ending in आ *á* and qualifying feminine nouns
must change their terminations to ई *i*, whatever may be the
case or number of the noun; thus, गोरी लड़की *gorí larkí*, 'a fair
girl'; लम्बी रस्सी लाओ *lambí rassí lao*, 'bring a long string';
हरी घास में, *harí ghás men*, 'in the green grass'; मीठी बातें *míthí
báteṅ*, 'sweet words.'

110. Adjectives when used to qualify nouns in the plural
number do not take the plural terminations : if the adjective follow the noun, which is rare, the plural termination may be given ;
but such usage is very unfrequent, and almost confined to poetry.

111. The particle सा *sá*, (*se, sí.*) expressive of similitude or
intensity, is treated in all respects like an adjective ending in
आ *á*. It may be used with an adjective, a noun, or pronoun; when

used with an adjective it generally renders its meaning more inten-
sive, but it may have the effect of weakening the meaning; thus,
बड़ा सा घर *baṛá sá ghar*, may mean, 'a very large house', or, 'a
largeish house.'   When सा *sá* is used with a noun there is an
ellipsis of the noun to avoid its unpleasant repetition; thus,
हाथी का सा मुंह *háthí ká sá munh*, 'a face like that of an elephant,'
the full form of this expression would be, हाथी का मुंह सा मुंह;
similarly, मेरी सी दशा *merí sí dasá*, 'a condition like mine'; which
without the ellipsis would be, मेरी दशा सी दशा.

112. Observe.—In the preceding and all similar cases
the sign of the genitive and the termination of सा are made to
agree with the word indicating the thing said to resemble the other.

113. सा when used with nouns is represented by some as
governing them in the genitive case; thus, बन्दर का सा हाथ
bandar ká sá háth, 'a hand like that of a monkey'; बन्दर having, as it is said, the sign of the genitive through the government of
सा. This explanation, however, cannot be correct; for if सा in such
cases governed the noun it would always be in the inflected form
with के, as when governed by समान, आगे, etc.   The true explanation is that given above, viz., that there is an ellipsis of the
noun before सा to avoid an unpleasant repetition of it.

114.   Care must be taken not to confound से, the inflected
form of the particle of resemblance or intensity, with से, the sign
of the ablative case.   The particle सा expresses likeness, but
never direct comparison, which is always indicated by the ablative.

115.   The sign of the plural, ओं *oṅ*, is frequently used with
numeral adjectives to denote definiteness; thus, तीन बरस *tín
baras*, would be any 'three years;' but तीनों बरस *tínoṅ baras*,
would signify 'the three years.'   This observation does not hold
good when the number is large; for with large numbers ओं has

the opposite effect, being used idiomatically to express indefinite multiplication ; as, लाखों बरस *lákhoṅ baras*, 'hundreds of thousands of years ;' करोड़ों मनुष्यों में *karoṛoṅ manushyoṅ meṅ*, 'among tens of millions of men.' See 71.

116. The ordinal numbers, पहिला *pahilá*, 'first,' दूसरा *dúsrá*, 'second,' तीसरा *tísrá*, 'third,' and चौथा *chauthá*, 'fourth,' all ending in आ, are subject to the same changes as adjectives ending in that vowel ; thus, पहिला घोड़ा *pahilá ghoṛá*, 'the first horse ;' दूसरी घोड़ी *dúsrí ghoṛí*, 'the second mare ;' तीसरे खेत में *tísre khet meṅ*, 'in the third field ;' and चौथे पर्ब में *chauthe parbb meṅ*, 'in the fourth chapter.'

117. After the fourth the ordinals are formed by adding वां *wáṅ* to the cardinals. This termination is changeable to वें *weṅ* and वीं *wíṅ* by the rule according to which adjectives in आ are made to agree with their substantives.

COMPARISON OF ADJECTIVES.

118. There is no regular system of inflections for the comparison of adjectives in Hindí ; this defect of the language is supplied in various simple ways which will be fully explained when we enter upon the syntax of adjectives.

119. The most common method of expressing comparison may be indicated here. When two objects are to be compared the noun or pronoun compared takes the nominative case, the noun or pronoun with which it is compared is put in the ablative case, and the adjective is used in its simple form ; or, which is the same thing, the adjective may be said to govern the noun in the ablative case. For instance, if we wish to say, 'wisdom is better than wealth,' we put 'wisdom,' the object compared, in the nominative case, and 'wealth,' with which it is compared, in the ablative case, and use the positive adjective 'good ;' the sentence

then stands, ज्ञान धन से अच्छा है *gyán dhan se achchhá hai,* literally, 'wisdom than wealth is good.'

120. The following are other examples :—

लकड़ी पत्थर से हलकी है *lakṛí patthar se halkí hai,* 'wood is lighter than stone'; लकड़ी से पत्थर भारी है *lakṛí se patthar bhárí hai,* 'stone is heavier than wood'; यमुना गंगा से छोटी है *Yamuná Gangá se chhoṭí hai,* 'the Jumna is smaller than the Ganges'; लड़की लड़के से सुन्दर है *larkí larke se sundar hai,* 'the girl is more beautiful than the boy'; इन दोनों में से कौन भला है *in donoṅ meṅ se kaun bhalá hai,* 'of these two which is the best?' बुद्धिमान शत्रु बुद्धिहीन मित्र से उत्तम है *buddhimán śatru buddhihín mitra se uttam hai,* 'a wise enemy is better than a foolish friend.'

121. The superlative degree in Hindí is formed in precisely the same manner as the comparative, the comparison being made, not with one object, but with all of the class, by means of सब से *sab se,* the ablative case of सब ; thus, यह सब से अच्छा लड़का है *yah sab se achchhá larká hai,* 'this is the best boy'; वह सब से चौड़ा खेत है *wah sab se chaurá khet hai,* 'that is the broadest field'; मनुष्य सब जन्तुओं से ज्ञानी है *manushya sab jan-tuoṅ se gyání hai,* 'man is wiser than all animals.'

122. The Sanskrit method of forming the degrees of comparison, viz., the comparative by adding तर *tar,* and the superlative by adding तम *tam* to the positive, is sometimes employed in Hindí ; but the ordinary usage is that explained above. The following are examples of the formation of the comparative and superlative according to the Sanskrit model ;—

कोमल *komal,* 'mild'; कोमलतर *komaltar,* 'milder'; कोमलतम *komaltam,* 'mildest.'

शिष्ट *śishṭ,* 'docile'; शिष्टतर *śishṭatar,* 'more docile'; शिष्टतम *śishṭatam,* 'most docile.'

प्रिय *priya*, 'dear'; प्रियतर *priyatar*, 'dearer ;' प्रियतम *priyatam*, 'dearest,' 'most beloved.'

उत *ut*, 'up'; उत्तर *uttar*, 'higher'; उत्तम *uttam*, 'highest.'

In the last instance the comparative and superlative are formed from the inseparable preposition उत.

Such words as धर्म्मिष्ठ *dharmmishṭh*, 'most virtuous'; पापिष्ठ *pápishṭh*, 'most sinful' ; श्रेष्ठ *śreshṭh*, 'best,' found in this form in the Hindí dictionaries, are superlative in meaning and in form, having the Sanskrit superlative termination इष्ठ.

CHAPTER V.

Of Pronouns, सर्वनाम *Sarvanám*.

123. The declension of pronouns in Hindí differs essentially from that of nouns, though in some respects resembling it. Pronouns have but one form for the two genders ; any pronoun may therefore be masculine or feminine, according to the gender of the noun which it represents. They have separate forms for the singular and plural, and for the first, second, and third persons.

PERSONAL PRONOUNS,
नामवाचक सर्वनाम *námváchak sarvanám*.
First person, उत्तम पुरुष *uttam purush*.

मैं *maiṅ*, I.

124.   SINGULAR.

N. मैं *maiṅ*, I.
Ag. मैं ने *maiṅ ne*, by me.
G. मेरा, रे, री, *merá*, *mere*, or *merí*, my, of me.

D. Ac.　मुझ को, मुझे, *mujh ko*, or *mujhe*, to me, me.
Ab.　मुझ से *mujh se*, from me.
L.　मुझ में *mujh men*, in me.

PLURAL.

N.　हम *ham*, we.
Ag.　हम ने, हमों ने, *ham ne*. or *hamon ne*, by us.
G.　हमारा, रे, री, *hamárá, hamáre,* or *hamári,* our, of us.
D. Ac.　हम को, हमें, हमों को, *ham ko, hamen,* or *hamon ko,* to us, us.
Ab.　हम से, हमों से, *ham se,* or *hamon se,* from us.
L.　हम में, हमों में, *ham men,* or *hamon men,* in us.

Second person, मध्यम पुरुष *madhyam purush.*

तू *tú*, thou.

125.　　　　　　SINGULAR.

N.　तू *tú*, thou.
Ag.　तू ने *tú ne*, by thee.
G.　तेरा, रे, री, *terá, tere,* or *teri,* thy, of thee.
D. Ac.　तुझ को, तुझे, *tujh ko,* or *tujhe,* to thee, thee.
Ab.　तुझ से *tujh se*, from thee.
L.　तुझ में *tujh men*, in thee.
V.　हे तू *he tú*, O thou.

PLURAL.

N.　तुम *tum*, you, ye.
Ag.　तुम ने, तुम्हों ने, *tum ne,* or *tumhon ne,* by you.
G.　तुम्हारा, रे, री, *tumhárá, tumháre,* or *tumhári,* your, of
　　you.
D. Ac.　तुम को, तुम्हें, तुम्हों को, *tum ko, tumhen,* or *tumhon ko,*
　　to you, you.

Ab.　तुम से, तुम्हों से, *tum se*, or *tumhoṅ se*, from you.

L.　तुम में, तुम्हों में, *tum meṅ*, or *tumhoṅ meṅ*, in you.

V.　हे तुम *he tum*, O ye.

Third person, अन्य पुरुष *anya purush*.

वह *wah*, he, she, it; that.

126.　　　　　　　SINGULAR.

N.　वह *wah*, he, she, it; that.

Ag.　उस ने *us ne*, by him, etc.

G.　उस का, के, की, *us ká, ke*, or *kí*, his, of him, etc.

D. Ac.　उस को, उसे, *us ko*, or *use*, to him, him, etc.

Ab.　उस से *us se*, from him, etc.

L.　उस में *us meṅ*, in him, etc.

PLURAL.

N.　वे *we*, they, those.

Ag.　उन ने, उन्हों ने, *un ne*, *unhoṅ ne*, by them, etc.

G.　उन का, के, की, *un ká, ke*, or *kí*, of them, etc.

D. Ac.　उन को, उन्हें, उन्हों को, *un ko*, *unheṅ*, or *unhoṅ ko*, to them, them, etc.

Ab.　उन से, उन्हों से, *un se*, or *unhoṅ se*, from them, etc.

L.　उन में, उन्हों में *un meṅ*, or *unhoṅ meṅ*, in them, etc.

OBSERVATIONS ON THE PERSONAL PRONOUNS.

127.　In the *first* and *second* personal pronouns the sign of the agent, ने *ne*, is used with the nominative or uninflected forms, मैं *maiṅ*, तू *tú*, etc., and not with the oblique or inflected forms, मुझ *mujh*, तुझ *tujh*.

128.　Such expressions however, as मुझ ब्राह्मण ने *mujh bráhman ne,* 'by me a brahman,' तुझ निर्बुद्धि ने *tujh nirbuddhi ne,* 'by you senseless,' are sometimes found, in which the oblique forms are used with ने.   The rule with regard to such usage is, that when no noun is expressed with a pronoun, the pronoun takes the sign of the case ; but when there is a noun expressed, the noun takes it, and the inflected form of the pronoun is used before the noun.

129.   In the *third* personal pronoun the case of the agent always assumes the inflected forms उस *us,* उन *un,* and is never formed with वह *wah,* or वे *we.*

130.   The first and second personal pronouns differ further from the third in taking रा, रे, री, in the singular, and आरा, आरे, आरी, in the plural, as signs of the genitive, instead of का, के, की, which are the signs of the genitive in the third personal pronoun, which follows, in this respect, the analogy of nouns.

131.   Observe :—The rule for the use of the signs of the genitive of the personal pronouns is the same as that already stated for the use of का, के, की, in the declension of nouns, or for adjectives ending in आ changeable to ए and ई. See 80-83.

132.   The forms मेरा *merá,* तेरा *terá,* of the first and second persons are almost always used for the genitive case singular ; but the regular oblique forms मुझ *mujh* and तुझ *tujh* with का, के, or की, are occasionally employed, especially in poetic license. The principle that regulates this usage is the same as that stated above in reference to the case of the agent, viz., that when no noun is expressed with a pronoun, the pronoun takes the sign of the case ; but when there is a noun expressed, the noun takes it, and the inflected form of the pronoun is used before the noun.   Thus, '*my condition,*' would be मेरी दशा *merí dašá,* there being no noun

expressed with the pronoun ; but, 'the condition of me a wretch' would be, मुझ अधम की दशा *mujh adham kí daśá*, in which the noun has the sign of the case, and the inflected form of the pronoun is used before it.

133. The dative and accusative cases are alike in both numbers, and they have each two distinct forms ; those of the singular ending in को *ko* and ए *e*, and those of the plural in को *ko* and एं *eṅ*. These forms are indiscriminately used in common conversation, but the best writers prefer को, as a termination, to ए or एं, as more respectful.

134. When an accusative and dative occur in juxtaposition, in order to avoid the disagreeable repetition of the same termination, को may be used in one case, and ए or एं in the other ; thus मैं उसे तुम को देता हूं *maiṅ use tumko detá húṅ*, 'I give it to you.'

135. In the oblique cases of the plural ओं *oṅ* may be inserted before the postpositions ; thus, in the dative plural of the first person we have, besides the two forms हम को, हमें, a third form, हमों को. As the plural forms of the pronouns are frequently used in Hindí for the singular, to indicate respect or honor, in the same manner as in English *you* is used for *thou*, it is in accordance with correct native usage to insert ओं *oṅ* when a real plural is meant, and to omit it when the plural is employed merely out of respect, for the singular ; thus, हम को, or हमें would mean, ' to me,' but हमों को would be the real plural, ' to us.'

136. The locative case is generally formed with the postposition में *meṅ*, 'in,' 'among;' but it may take other postpositions, such as, पर *par*, or पै *pai*, 'on,' 'upon,' 'at;' तक *tak*, or तलक *talak*, 'to,' ' up to;' लों *loṅ*, 'till,' ' to.'

Demonstrative Pronouns.

निश्चयवाचक सर्वनाम *niśchayváchak sarvanám.*

137. The third personal pronoun also supplies the place of the demonstrative in Hindí. For this purpose it has two forms; यह *yah*, 'this,' for the near demonstrative; and वह *wah*, 'that,' for the remote demonstrative.

138. यह and वह are the same for both genders; the connection in which they are used alone determines whether they are to be regarded as masculine or feminine. The former is used of an object that is near, or in reference to the last of two objects mentioned in conversation; the latter is used of what is more remote, or as referring to the first named object.

The declension of वह has already been given: यह is declined as follows :—

139.

SINGULAR.

N.	यह *yah*,	this.
Ag.	इस ने *is ne*,	by this.
G.	इस का, के, की, *is ká, ke,* or *kí,*	of this.
D. Ac.	इस को, इसे, *is ko,* or *ise,*	to this, this.
Ab.	इस से *is se*,	from this.
L.	इस में *is meṅ*,	in this.

PLURAL.

N.	ये or यह, *ye,* or *yah,*	these.*
Ag.	इन ने, इन्हों ने, *in ne,* or *inhoṅ ne,*	by these.

---

* यह and वह are occasionally used for the plural as well as for the singular by the best writers and speakers. This usage, however, may sometimes prove confusing. It were well if they were confined to the singular.

H

G. इन का, इन्हों का, के, की, *in ká*, or *inhoṅ ká*, etc., of these.

D. Ac. इन को, इन्हें, इन्हों को, *in ko, inheṅ*, or *inhoṅ ko*, to these, these.

Ab. इन से, इन्हों से, *in se*, or *inhoṅ se*, from these.

L. इन में, इन्हों में, *in meṅ*, or *inhoṅ meṅ*, in these.

140. Observe that the near and remote demonstratives are similarly declined; यह becomes इस in the oblique cases of the singular, and the nominative plural, ये, becomes इन in the oblique cases of the plural. Similarly, वह is changed to उस in the oblique cases of the singular, and the nominative plural, वे, is changed to उन in the oblique cases of the plural. The terminations that are added to these bases are identical in the two demonstratives.

141. The rule laid down, (see 128, 132) in regard to personal pronouns is applicable to the demonstratives also, viz., that when no noun is expressed, the pronoun takes the sign of the case; but when there is a noun expressed, the noun takes it, and the inflected form of the pronoun is used before the noun ; thus, इस में *is meṅ*, 'in this'; इस घर में *is ghar meṅ*, 'in this house'; इन को *in ko*, 'to these'; इन मनुष्यों को *in manushyoṅ ko*, 'to these men'; उन से *un se*, 'from those'; उन खेतों में *un khetoṅ meṅ*, 'in those fields.'

142. Observe, then, that when यह and वह are used in the oblique cases as personal pronouns they take the postpositions; but when they are used as demonstratives the noun takes them ; thus, 'of his household' would be, उस के परिवार का *us ke pariwár ká ;* but, 'of that household' would be, उस परिवार का *us pariwár ká.*

143. The genitives, singular and plural, of the personal and demonstrative pronouns, viz., मेरा, तेरा, हमारा, तुम्हारा, इस का, उस का, इन का, उन का, are constantly used as pronominal adjectives answering the purpose of possessive pronouns.

THE POSSESSIVE AND REFLEXIVE PRONOUN, आप *áp*.

144. With the exception of the genitives of the personal and demonstrative pronouns given above, the only possessive in the language is the word आप, which may be used instead of any of them, but is of most frequent use for the second person in an honorific sense. It is one of the most useful and comprehensive pronouns in Hindí, serving the purpose of a common reflexive, a possessive, and an honorific pronoun, for both genders.

145. When used as a common reflexive or possessive, आप is declined as follows :—

N.	आप *áp*,	self, myself, thyself, etc.
G.	अपना, ने, नी, *apná*, *apne*, or *apní*,	own, of self, etc.
D. Ac.	अपने को, आप को, *apne ko*, or *áp ko*,	to self, self, etc.
Ab.	अपने से, आप से, *apne se*, or *áp se*,	from self, etc.
L.	अपने में, आप में, *apne men*, or *áp men*,	in self, etc.

146. The phrase आपस में *ápas men*, an irregularly formed locative plural, signifying, 'among ourselves,' 'among yourselves,' 'among themselves,' etc., is of frequent use ; thus, आपस में बांटलो *ápas men bánt lo*, 'divide it among yourselves ;' ये लोग आपस में नित्य झगड़ा करते हैं *ye log ápas men nitya jhagrá karte hain*, 'these people are continually quarrelling among themselves.'

147. The pronoun आप, as declined above, is applicable to the first, second, and third persons and to both numbers. Its genitive is in constant use as a substitute for the possessive pronouns, 'my,' 'thy,' 'his,' 'her,' 'our,' 'your,' 'their,' *when they are connected with, or represent the same person as the nominative of the sentence ;* thus, मैं अपने लोगों में रहूंगा *main apne logon men rahúngá*, 'I will stay among my own people'; वे अपने देश को चले गये *we apne des ko chale gaye*, 'they went to their own country ;'

वे अपना पाठ सीखते हैं *we apná páṭh síkhte haiṅ*, 'they are learning their lesson.'

148. When the pronouns, 'my,' 'thy,' 'his,' 'her,' 'our,' 'your,' 'their,' are not connected with, and do not represent the same object as the nominative of the sentence in which they stand, they cannot be expressed by अपना, the genitive of the personal pronoun must then be used; thus, 'I came into his house' would be, मैं उस के घर में आया *maiṅ us ke ghar meṅ áyá*; 'they went into his garden,' वे उस की बारी में गये *we us kí bárí meṅ gaye*; 'they are learning his lesson,' वे उस का पाठ सीखते हैं *we us ká páṭh síkhte haiṅ*.

आप, when employed as an honorific pronoun, is declined as follows :—

149.

N.	आप *áp*,	sir, your honor, etc.
Ag.	आप ने *áp ne*,	by you, sir, by your honor.
G.	आप का, के, की, *áp ká, ke*, or *kí*, of you, sir, of your honor.
D. Ac.	आप को *áp ko*,	to you, sir, your honor.
Ab.	आप से *áp se*,	from you, sir, from your honor.
L.	आप में *áp meṅ*,	in you, sir, in your honor.

150. As thus declined, आप may represent any word denoting respect or honor; as, 'Sir,' 'Your Honor,' 'Your Highness,' 'Your Majesty,' etc. It is commonly applied to the second person but may be used of the third person also in the presence of the individual intended, the direction in which the speaker is looking, or the motion of his hand indicating that the third and not the second person is intended.

151. When used in an honorific sense आप requires the adjective or verb with which it may be connected to be in the plural

number ; thus, आप उन से बच्चे हैं *áp un se achchhe haiń,* 'You, Sir, are better than they ;' आप कब चलेंगे *áp kab chaleńge,* 'when will Your Highness go ?'

152. When it is necessary to indicate that the real honorific plural is meant, the word लोग *log,* 'people,' is commonly used after आप; in the oblique cases it becomes लोगों *logoń,* and in accordance with a rule already stated takes the postposition, आप without a postposition being placed before it ; thus, आप लोग *áp log,* ' Sirs,' ' Your Honors ;' आप लोगों से *áp logoń se,* 'from you, Sirs,' etc. See 128, 132.

153. The learner must be careful to distinguish between आप as a reflexive or possessive pronoun and the same word when used as an honorific pronoun.

THE RELATIVE PRONOUN,

सम्बन्धवाचक सर्वनाम *sambandhwáchak sarvanám.*

154.   SINGULAR.

N.   जो, जौन, *jo,* or *jaun,* who, which, that.
Ag.   जिस ने *jis ne,* by whom, by which, etc.
G.   जिस का, के, की, *jis ká, jis ke,* or *jis kí,* of whom, of
           which, etc.
D. Ac.   जिस को, जिसे, *jis ko,* or *jise,* to whom, whom, etc.
Ab.   जिस से *jis se,* from whom, from which, etc.
L.   जिस में *jis meń,* in whom, in which, etc.

                        PLURAL.

N.   जो, जौन, *jo* or *jaun,* who, which, that.
Ag.   जिन ने, जिन्होंं ने, *jin ne,* or *jinhoń ne,* by whom, etc.
G.   जिन का, जिन्होंं का, के, की, *jin ká,* or *jinhoń ká,* etc.
           of whom.

D. Ac.　जिन को, जिन्हें, जिन्हों को, *jin ko, jinhen,* or *jinhon ko,* to whom, whom.

Ab.　जिन से, जिन्हों से, *jin se,* or *jinhon se,* from whom.

L.　जिन में, जिन्हों में, *jin men,* or *jinhon men,* in whom.

155.　The correlatives of जो and जौन are सो and तौन, respectively. The correlative is declined exactly like the relative, substituting त for ज in the oblique cases; thus, Nom: सो or तौन; Ag: तिसने; Gen: तिस का, etc.

156.　As a rule, in Hindí the relative clause of a sentence precedes the correlative clause, and the latter has in it the correlative or demonstrative pronoun answering to the relative in the former clause; thus, जो लड़का रोगी था सो चंगा हुआ *jo laṛká rogí thá so changá huá,* 'the boy who was sick has recovered;' जो वृक्ष यहाँ था वह काटा गया *jo vriksh yahán thá wah káṭá gayá,* 'the tree that was here has been cut down.'

157.　The preceding statement is equally true of the pronouns derived from the relative and correlative, or demonstrative, as जैसा *jaisá,* तैसा *taisá,* or वैसा *waisá;* जितना *jitná,* तितना *titná,* or उतना *utná;* thus, जैसा मैं चाहता था वैसा घर बन गया *jaisá main cháhtá thá waisá ghar ban gayá,* 'as I desired so the house was made.'

158.　When the relative refers to a personal pronoun it follows it; as, तू जो लड़के को मारता है कौन है *tú jo laṛke ko mártá hai kaun hai,* 'who are you that are beating the boy?'

INTERROGATIVE PRONOUNS,

प्रश्नवाचक सर्वनाम *praśnaváchak sarvanám.*

159.　The interrogatives are कौन *kaun,* and क्या *kyá;* the former is declined exactly like the relative जो, substituting क for ज in the oblique cases; thus :—

160. SINGULAR.

N.   कौन *kaun*, who? which?

Ag.   किस ने *kis ne*, by whom?

G.   किसका, के, की, *kis ká, ke*, or *kí*, whose?

D. Ac.   किस को, किसे, *kis ko*, or *kise*, to whom? whom?

Ab.   किस से *kis se*, from whom?

L.   किस में *kis men*, in whom?

PLURAL.

N.   कौन *kaun*, who? which?

Ag.   किन ने, किन्हों ने, *kin ne*, or *kinhon ne*, by whom?

G.   किन का, किन्हों का, के, की, *kin ká*, or *kinhon ká*, etc., of whom?

D. Ac.   किन को, किन्हें, किन्हों को, *kin ko, kinhen*, or *kinhon ko*, to whom? whom?

Ab.   किन से, किन्हों से, *kin se*, or *kinhon se*, from whom?

L.   किन में, किन्हों में, *kin men*, or *kinhon men*, in whom?

क्या is said to be declined as follows :—

161.   SINGULAR AND PLURAL.

N. Ac.   क्या *kyá*, what?

G.   काहे का, के, की, *káhe ká, ke*, or *kí*, of what?

D.   काहे को *káhe ko*, to or for what?

Ab.   काहे से *káhe se*, from what?

L.   काहे में, *káhe men*, in what? See 164.

162. The interrogative कौन is used of both persons and things; when used alone it almost invariably applies to persons; thus, कौन है *kaun hai*, 'who is there?' किस का है *kis ká hai*, 'whose is it?' किन ने किया *kin ne kiyá*, 'by whom was it done?' In the preceding instances, no substantive being expressed, the

interrogative is understood to refer to persons, and it takes the sign of the case; but if a substantive be expressed with कौन, the substantive will take the sign of the case, and the inflected form of कौन. will be used before it; thus, किस बरतन में *kis bartan meṅ*, 'in what vessel?' किस दिन को *kis din ko*, 'on what day?' किन लोगों में *kin logoṅ meṅ*; 'among what people?'

163. When used adjectively, कौन may have reference to either persons or things; as, किस मनुष्य को *kis manushya ko*, 'to what man?' किस उपाय से *kis upáy se*, 'by what means?'

164. The form काहे has been given as coming from क्या;—but क्या is said by native grammarians to be indeclinable, and the form काहे they regard as a corruption. Such, very probably, it was; but काहे is now so frequently used in writing as well as in conversation, that it is convenient to regard it as forming the basis of the oblique cases of क्या. The use of the form, however, is limited, and before a noun it generally becomes कौन; thus, अनाज काहे में रखा है *anáj káhe meṅ rakhá hai*, 'in what have you put the grain?' with a noun expressed would be, अनाज कौन टोकरे में रखा है *anáj kaun ṭokre meṅ rakhá hai*, 'in what basket,' etc.

165. Notice that in the last sentence, and in many instances, कौन, by an idiomatical irregularity, is used with an inflected noun.

166. There is no separate plural form for क्या; it is applied to inanimate objects of both numbers; thus, क्या है *kyá hai*, 'what is it?' क्या हैं *kyá haiṅ*, 'what are they?'

167. As an exclamation of surprise or wonder, क्या may be used of persons; as, क्या चोर *kyá chor*, 'what a thief!' क्या योद्धा *kyá yoddhá*, 'what a warrior!'

168. It may also be used of persons, discriminately, or as a conjunction; thus, क्या राजा क्या प्रजा *kyá rájá kyá prajá*, 'whe-

ther king or subject;' क्या जल में क्या थल में *kyá jal men kyá thal men,* 'whether in water or on land.'

169. The repetition of क्या expresses either variety or distribution; as, वे क्या क्या लाये हैं *we kyá kyá láe hain,* which might, according to circumstances, denote variety, 'what various things have they, in the aggregate, brought?' or distribution, 'what in particular has each of them brought?'

170. With a noun expressed the repetition of क्या usually denotes a simple exclamation; as, बारी में क्या क्या फूल हैं *bárí men kyá kyá phúl hain,* 'what flowers there are in the garden!'

INDEFINITE PRONOUNS,

अनिश्चयवाचक सर्वनाम *aníschayváchak sarvanám.*

171. There are several words that partake, more or less, of a pronominal signification, and may be conveniently classed under the head of indefinites. The most common and useful of them are, कोई *koí,* 'any one,' 'some one,' and कुछ *kuchh,* 'any thing,' 'something.' They are declined as follows :—

172.

N.	कोई *koí,*	any one, some one.
Ag.	किसी ने *kisí ne,*	by any one, by some one.
G.	किसी का, के, की, *kisí ká, ke,* or *kí,*	of any one, etc.
D. Ac.	किसी को *kisí ko,*	to any one, any one, etc.
Ab.	किसी से *kisí se,*	from any one, etc.
L.	किसी में *kisí men,*	in any one, etc.

173.

N.	कुछ *kuchh,*	any thing, something.
Ag.	किसू ने *kisú ne,*	by any thing, etc.
G.	किसू का, के, की, *kisú ká, ke,* or *kí,*	of any thing, etc.

D. Ac. किसू को *kisú ko*, to any thing, etc.
Ab. किसू से *kisú se*, from any thing, etc.
L. किसू में *kisú men*, in anything, etc. See 179.

174.

कोई and कुछ, the nominative forms, are also used for the accusative, when they do not refer to a person; and none of the cases but the nominative and the accusative, in the nominative form, are used in the plural.

175. In native books as well as in common conversation कोई and कुछ are indiscriminately used; but when any distinction in their use is made, the former is applied to animate, and the latter to inanimate objects. When used adjectively no distinction is observed. The following sentences exemplify their use :— कोई है *koí hai*, 'is any one (present)?' कुछ है *kuchh hai*, 'is there any thing?' कोई बात *koí bát*, 'any word,' or 'affair'; कुछ लोग *kuchh log*, 'some people'; किसी नगर में *kisí nagar men*, 'in some town'; कुछ दिन से *kuchh din se*, 'for some days.'

176. कोई is frequently used in the sense of the English article, *a, an;* thus, किसी गांव में *kisí gánw men*, 'in a village'; किसी धनी के घर में *kisí dhaní ke ghar men*, 'in the house of a rich man.'

177. The repetition of कोई and कुछ conveys the idea of fewness, littleness; as, कोई कोई हैं *koí koí hain*, 'there are some,' or 'there are a few'; कुछ कुछ है *kuchh kuchh hai*, 'there is a little.'

178. कुछ has sometimes the force of an adverb; as, यह भेद कुछ जाना नहीं जाता *yah bhed kuchh jáná nahín játá*, 'this secret is not at all known.'

179. We have declined कुछ giving it the form किसू in the oblique cases; but native grammarians regard it as indeclinable,

like क्या, and the form किसू they treat as a corruption of किसी, the inflected form of कौन. Probably किसू, like कौने, was originally a corruption; but it cannot be treated as such now, for it has entered into the literature of the language. The use of the form is, however, limited; for, though in many cases it seems to be used indiscriminately as the inflected form of कौन or of कुछ, yet it cannot always be used where किसी, the regular inflected form of कौन, is admissable.

180. कुछ, like कौन, by an idiomatical irregularity, is used with inflected nouns; as, कुछ खाने में *kuchh khâne meñ*, 'in some food'; कुछ कपड़े को *kuchh kapṛe ko*, 'for some cloth.'

181. The following words are used with a pronominal and indefinite signification and take the case endings after them; एक *ek*, 'one,' also used in the sense of 'a,' 'an'; दूसरा *dûsrâ*, 'another,' 'other'; दोनों *donoñ*, 'both'; और *aur*, 'other,' 'different'; सब *sab*, 'all,' 'every.'

182. The word कई *kaî*, used as a pronoun, 'how many?' and as an adjective, 'several,' is not declined. कई एक *kaî ek*, 'several,' is declined; but though plural in meaning it cannot take ओं *oñ* in the oblique cases of the plural. सब frequently changes the अ into भ in the oblique cases of the plural; thus, सब ने कहा *sab ne kahâ*, or सभों ने कहा *sabhoñ ne kahâ*, 'all said.' एक is frequently followed by दूसरा to express opposition or contrariety; thus, एक जाता है और दूसरा आता है *ek jâtâ hai aur dûsrâ âtâ hai*, 'one is going and another is coming.' They are also used in immediate succession to indicate reciprocity; as, एक दूसरे की सहायता क्यों नहीं करते *ek dûsre kî sahâyatâ kyoñ nahiñ karte*, 'why do ye not help one another?'

183. Most of the adjective pronouns admit of being compounded. Each member of the compound may be inflected, if the

simple forms are capable of it ; or but one member may be inflected. The postpositions are attached to the second member only. The following are among the most useful compounds :—जो कोई *jo koí*, 'whoever,' जो कुछ *jo kuchh*, 'whatever,' और कोई *aur koí*, 'some one else'; और कुछ *aur kuchh*, 'something else'; सब कोई *sab koí*, 'every one'; सब कुछ *sab kuchh*, 'every thing'; कोई और *koí aur*, 'some other'; कुछ और *kuchh aur*, 'some more'; कोई न कोई *koí na koí*, 'some one or other'; कुछ न कुछ *kuchh na kuchh*, 'something or other.'

184. There are cases, but they are infrequent, of pronouns repeated distributively but not compounded; as, किसका किसका कपड़ा यहां धरा है *kiskā kiskā kaprá yahán dhará hai*, 'whose (plur :) clothes are placed here ?'

185. Observe:—By changing the final letter, स, of इस, उस, किस, जिस, तिस, (the inflected forms of the demonstrative, relative, and interrogative pronouns) into तना, the following adjectives expressive of number or quality are formed:—इतना *itná*, 'so many,' 'this much'; उतना *utná*, 'so many,' 'that much'; कितना *kitná*, 'how many?' 'how much?' जितना *jitná*, 'as many,' 'as much'; तितना *titná*, 'so many,' 'so much.'

186. The following are also formed from the demonstrative, relative, and interrogative pronouns :—ऐसा *aisá*, 'thus'; कैसा *kaisá* 'how?' जैसा *jaisá*, 'as'; तैसा *taisá*, 'so'; वैसा *waisá*, 'so.' These are the meanings when the words are used adverbially ; when used adjectively, their meanings are, respectively, 'such,' 'of what kind?' 'such as,' 'such,' 'such.'

CHAPTER VI.

Of the Verb, क्रिया *kriyá.*

187. The verb in Hindí is extremely simple and regular in its formation. It is of two kinds, Transitive or Active, and Intransitive or Neuter : they differ only in the tenses formed from the past participle.

188. There is but one conjugation, the terminations of the tenses of which never vary in any verb ; so that, with the exception of a few words whose past participles are formed somewhat irregularly, (though perfectly regular as regards the terminations of their tenses) all verbs may be regarded as perfectly regular.

189. There are two voices, the Active and the Passive. There are four moods, the indicative, the subjunctive, the imperative, and the infinitive. The potential is usually expressed by compounding the root of the verb with सकना *sakná*, 'to be able.'

190. The commonly used tenses are nine in number, in addition to which there are six other tenses, but, as they are seldom used, they need not burden the memory of the student in learning the conjugation for the first time ; they will be hereafter separately explained.

191. Of the nine commonly used tenses, there are but three that have distinct personal terminations, viz., those derived from the root; the remaining six tenses have only one form for the three persons.

192. Verbs have two genders, the masculine and the feminine, and have separate terminations for each in all the tenses, with the exception of those formed from the root, and the present tense of the auxiliary verb होना *honá*, 'to be,' which have but one form for the masculine and feminine.

193. The tenses that have distinct inflections for the masculine and feminine follow the gender of their governing nouns. The characteristic termination of the masculine singular throughout the conjugation is आ *á*; of the feminine singular ई *í*; of the masculine plural ए *e*; and of the feminine plural ईं *ín*, or इयाँ *iyán*. Any other termination may be masculine or feminine.

194. There are two numbers, the singular and the plural, and in each number there are three persons.

ON THE CONJUGATION OF THE VERB.

195. In conjugating Hindí verbs there are two points to be considered; viz., the root of the verb and the inflexional endings of the moods and tenses. The root contains the fundamental form and idea of the verb and must enter into every part of the conjugation: the inflexional endings being added to the root express the main idea of the verb in the variations of tense, number, gender, and person.

196. As the infinitive, which always ends in ना *ná*, is the form in which verbs are given in the Hindí Dictionary, it will be most convenient to begin with it in explaining the structure of the conjugation.

197. Observe, then, carefully the following rules :—

1. The root of the verb, which is also the second person singular of the imperative, is found by rejecting ना *ná* of the infinitive; thus, infinitive खोलना *kholná*, 'to open'; root and second singular imperative, खोल *khol*, 'open.'

2. By adding ता *tá* to the root the present participle is formed; thus, root खोल, present participle, खोलता *kholtá*, ' opening.'

3. By adding आ *á* to the root the past participle is formed; thus, root खोल, past participle खोला *kholá*, 'opened.'

198. If the root end in a vowel (आ *á*, ओ *o*, or ए *e*) the letter य *y* is, for the sake of euphony, inserted before आ *á* in forming the past participle; and व *w* is optionally inserted before the terminations ए *e*, एं *eṅ* ओ *o*; thus, गाना *gáná*, 'to sing,' makes the past participle गाया *gáyá*, 'sang;' plural गाये or गाय; बुलाना *buláná*, 'to call,' makes 3rd singular imperative, बुलाय or बुलावे, *buláe* or *buláwe*; 1st plural imperative बुलायं *buláeṅ*, or बुलावें *buláweṅ*; 2nd plural imperative बुलाओ *buláo*, or बुलावो *buláwo*.

199. From the three principal parts of the verb, viz., the root, the present participle, and the past participle, with the present and past tenses of the verb होना *honá*, 'to be,' as auxiliaries, all the moods and tenses of the conjugation are formed.

1. From the Root are formed,—

a. The Prospective Conditional, *b.* The Future, *c.* The Imperative.

2. From the Present Participle are formed,—

a. The Retrospective Conditional and Present Indefinite, *b.* The Present Definite, *c.* The Imperfect.

3. From the Past Participle are formed,—

a. The Historical Past, *b.* The Perfect, *c.* The Pluperfect.

The two following tenses which enter as auxiliaries into the conjugation of every verb, must be carefully committed to memory.

200.   PRESENT TENSE.

SINGULAR.	PLURAL.
मैं हूँ *maiṅ húṅ*, I am.	हम हैं *ham haiṅ*, we are.
तू है *tú hai*, thou art.	तुम हो *tum ho*, you are.
वह है *wah hai*, he, she, or it is.	वे हैं *we haiṅ*, they are.

201.   Past Tense.

मैं था *maiṅ thá*, I was.   हम थे *ham the*, we were.

तू था *tú thá*, thou wast.   तुम थे *tum the*, you were.

वह था *wah thá*, he *or* it was.   वे थे *we the*, they were.

Fem. मैं थी *maiṅ thí*, etc.   Fem. हम थीं *ham thíṅ*, etc. *

202.   Native grammarians follow the natural order of time in the conjugation of verbs, treating first the past tenses, then the present, and last of all the future : it will be more convenient, as an aid to memory, if we take the principal parts of the verb in order, giving under each of them the tenses formed from it.

Conjugation of a Transitive Verb.

203.   Active Voice.

Observe.—The root may end in a consonant or in a vowel : if in a consonant, the verb will be conjugated like देखना *dekhná*, 'to see'; if in a vowel, like पाना *páná*, 'to find.' Remember that the only difference between them is, that when the root ends in a consonant, the past participle is formed by adding आ *á* to it; but when the root ends in a vowel, the past participle is generally formed by adding या *yá* to it.

Model verb, देखना *dekhná*, 'to see.'

204.   Principal parts.

Root, ...देख *dekh*, see.

Present Participle,............देखता *dekhtá*, seeing.

Past Participle, ...देखा *dekhá*, seen.

---

* These two tenses are generally referred to the verb होना and are represented as anomalous forms of it. It is, however, probable, that हूँ is from the Sanskrit अहं, i. e., अहम्, 'I'; and था from the Sanskrit root स्था *sthá*, 'to remain.' They are used, not only as auxiliaries to other verbs, but also alone, as substantive verbs for the expression of simple existence.

205. 1. *Three tenses are formed from the root,* देख.

a. THE PROSPECTIVE CONDITIONAL.

'If I see,' *etc.*

SINGULAR.	PLURAL.
मैं देखूं *main dekhún,* if I see.	हम देखें *ham dekhen,* if we see.
तू देखे *tú dekhe,* if thou see.	तुम देखो *tum dekho,* if you see.
वह देखे *wah dekhe,* if he see.	वे देखें *we dekhen,* if they see.

b. THE FUTURE.

'I shall *or* will see,' *etc.*

मैं देखूंगा *main dekhúngá.*	हम देखेंगे *ham dekhenge.*
तू देखेगा *tú dekhegá.*	तुम देखोगे *tum dekhoge.*
वह देखेगा *wah dekhegá.*	वे देखेंगे *we dekhenge.*
Fem. मैं देखूंगी *main dekhúngí,* etc.	Fem. हम देखेंगीं *ham dekhengín,* etc.

c. THE IMPERATIVE.

'Let me see,' 'see thou,' *etc.*

मैं देखूं *main dekhún.*	हम देखें *ham dekhen.*
तू देख *tú dekh.*	तुम देखो *tum dekho.*
वह देखे *wah dekhe.*	वे देखें *we dekhen.*

206. 2. *Three tenses are formed from the present participle,* देखता.

a. THE RETROSPECTIVE CONDITIONAL AND PRESENT INDEFINITE.

'If I had seen,' 'I see,' *etc.*

मैं देखता *main dekhtá.*	हम देखते *ham dekhte.*
तू देखता *tú dekhtá.*	तुम देखते *tum dekhte.*
वह देखता *wah dekhtá.*	वे देखते *we dekhte.*
Fem. मैं देखती *main dekhtí,* etc.	Fem. हम देखतीं *ham dekhtín,* etc.

J

(74)

b. THE PRESENT DEFINITE.

'I see *or* am seeing,' *etc.*

मैं देखता हूं *main dekhtá hún.*	हम देखते हैं *ham dekhte hain.*
तू देखता है *tú dekhtá hai.*	तुम देखते हो *tum dekhte ho.*
वह देखता है *wah dekhtá hai.*	वे देखते हैं *we dekhte hain.*
Fem. मैं देखती हूं *main dekhti hún,* etc.	Fem. हम देखती हैं *ham dekhti hain,* etc.

c. THE IMPERFECT.

'I was seeing,' *etc.*

मैं देखता था *main dekhtá thá.*	हम देखते थे *ham dekhte the.*
तू देखता था *tú dekhtá thá.*	तुम देखते थे *tum dekhte the.*
वह देखता था *wah dekhtá thá.*	वे देखते थे *we dekhte the.*
Fem. मैं देखती थी *main dekhti thí,* etc.	Fem. हम देखती थीं *ham dekhti thin,* etc.

207. 3. *Three tenses are formed from the Past Participle,* देखा.

a. THE HISTORICAL PAST.

'I saw,' *or* 'It was seen by me,' *etc.*

मैं ने देखा *main ne dekhá.*	हम ने देखा *ham ne dekhá.*
तू ने देखा *tú ne dekhá.*	तुम ने देखा *tum ne dekhá.*
उस ने देखा *us ne dekhá.*	उन ने, उन्हों ने देखा *un ne, or unhon ne dekhá.*

b. THE PERFECT.

'I have seen,' *or* 'It has been seen by me,' *etc.*

मैं ने देखा है *main ne dekhá hai.*	हम ने देखा है *ham ne dekhá hai.*
तू ने देखा है *tú ne dekhá hai.*	तुम ने देखा है *tum ne dekhá hai.*
उस ने देखा है *us ne dekhá hai.*	उन ने, उन्हों ने देखा है, *un ne, or unhon ne dekhá hai.*

c. THE PLUPERFECT.

'I had seen,' *or* 'It had been seen by me,' *etc.*

मैं ने देखा था *main ne dekhá thá.*	हम ने देखा था *ham ne dekhá thá.*
तू ने देखा था *tú ne dekhá thá.*	तुम ने देखा था *tum ne dekhá thá.*
उस ने देखा था *us ne dekhá thá.*	उन ने, उन्हों ने देखा था, *un ne,* or *unhon ne dekhá thá.* *

Participles.

208.

1. ADJECTIVE PARTICIPLES.

Present, 'Seeing.'

SINGULAR.	PLURAL.
Mas. देखता, देखता हुआ, *dekhtá,* or *dekhtá huá.*	Mas. देखते, देखते हुए, *dekhte,* or *dekhte hue.*
Fem. देखती, देखती हुई, *dekhtí,* or *dekhtí huí.*	Fem. देखतीं, देखती हुईं, *dekhtín,* or *dekhtí huín.*

Past, 'Seen.'

Mas. देखा, देखा हुआ, *dekhá,* or *dekhá huá.*	Mas. देखे, देखे हुए, *dekhe,* or *dekhe hue.*
Fem. देखी, देखी हुई, *dekhí,* or *dekhí huí.*	Fem. देखीं, देखी हुईं, *dekhín,* or *dekhí huín.*

2. CONJUNCTIVE PARTICIPLES.

'Seeing,' 'Having Seen.'

देख *dekh,* देखके *dekhke,* देखकर *dekhkar,* देखकरके *dekhkarke* देखकरकर *dekhkarkar.*

---

* उन ने or उन्हों ने may be used for the third person plural in the tenses of the past participle of transitive verbs; but as उन ने is frequently used for the singular to indicate respect, उन्हों ने is more commonly employed to denote the real plural.

3. ADVERBIAL PARTICIPLE.

देखतेही *dekhtehi,* 'on seeing,' 'in the act of seeing.'

209   NOUN OF AGENCY.

देखनेहारा, देखनेवाला, *dekhnehárá,* or *dekhnewálá,* 'one who sees.'

INFINITIVE OR VERBAL NOUN.

Nom.   देखना *dekhná,* seeing.
Gen.   देखने का *dekhne ká,* of seeing, *etc.*

(Declined like a noun of the 1st Decl., 1st class.)

210.

PRECATIVE OF RESPECTFUL FORMS OF THE IMPERATIVE AND FUTURE.

देखिये *dekhiye,* be you or ye pleased to see.

देखियेगा *dekhiyegá,* you or ye will be pleased to see.

MILD IMPERATIVE. See 215.

* देखियो *dekhiyo,* see you or ye.

211. The student may now observe how the various tenses of the conjugation are formed. The Prospective Conditional is obtained by adding the following terminations to the root :—

---

* The names of some of the tenses as given in the conjugation of देखना differ from those by which they are now generally known. The functions of what is called the 'Aorist' are quite distinct from those of the Greek Aorist, which is strictly an Historical tense and frequently indicative. The so called Aorist in Hindi is not indicative at all, for it never simply asserts, except in ungrammatical *patois.* If the form be not imperative, it always supposes a conjunction preceding, though not always expressed, it always implies a relation to some other action, and, though not invariably, yet very commonly, it is followed by a verb in the future tense, or in the same tense, denoting futurity. Therefore

	SINGULAR.			PLURAL.	
1st Person.	2nd.	3rd.	1st Person.	2nd.	3rd.
ऊँ	ए	ए	एँ	ओ	एँ

The Future is formed directly from the Prospective Conditional by adding गा for the masculine singular, and गी for the feminine; गे for the masculine plural, and गीं for the feminine.

The Imperative is the same in form as the Prospective Conditional, except in the second person singular, which is the same as the root of the verb without any addition.

212. The Retrospective Conditional and Present Indefinite is the same in form as the present participle : the termination changes to ते in the masculine plural, to ती in the feminine singular, and to तीं in the feminine plural.

The Present Definite and the Imperfect are formed by adding the present tense of the auxiliary verb to the present participle for the former, and the past tense for the latter.

213. The Historical Past is the same in form as the past participle : the Perfect is also the same as the past participle with the present auxiliary है, or with हैं, when the object is plural, added to it : the Pluperfect differs from the preceding in taking था, the past tense of the auxiliary, changeable to agree with the object of the verb in gender and number. The peculiarity of construction in

---

the name Prospective Conditional seems to accord more with its nature than Aorist, which is likely to mislead. And so of the form for the Present Indefinite, which conveys quite a different idea from the Present Indefinite of the Indicative mood when a conjunction is used before it, and is generally followed by a verb in some past tense, or in the same tense, pointing to the past. For these reasons it is termed 'Retrospective Conditional and Present Indefinite.'

the tenses formed from the past participle of all transitive verbs
will be explained further on.

214.   The Conjunctive Participle may be the same in form as
the root, or be formed by adding to it one or other of the terminations, के, कर, करके, करकर. There are thus five distinct forms of this
participle, (a sixth, formed with य added to the root, is given in
some grammars, but incorrectly; य added to the root is always
the inflected form of the past participle, except, perhaps, occasionally in poetry by poetical license) they are all indeclinable, have
each the same signification, and are generally employed in connection with the past tenses.

215.   The precative or respectful forms of the imperative and
future are formed by adding इये, इयेगा. to the root; and the mild
form of the imperative by adding इयो. The respectful imperative,
देखिये, is used for both numbers, and, generally, with आप or some
term of respect expressed or understood; it is often also used
impersonally.   The form देखियेगा is also used for both numbers
and differs from the preceding only in the future signification that
is given to it by the addition of the termination गा.   In some
of the grammars देखियो is incorrectly given as the plural of
देखिये, which is itself constantly used for the plural as well as
for the singular.   It is rather a distinct form, a mild form of the
imperative, but not respectful like देखिये.

216.   It is of the greatest importance to clearly understand and
remember the peculiarity of construction in *the tenses formed from
the past participle of all transitive verbs.*   A full explanation of this
matter will be given in the Syntax; let it now suffice to say that, in
*the historical past, the perfect, and the pluperfect of transitive verbs
only,* a kind of passive construction is adopted, the nominative
is changed into the case of the agent with ने, and the verb is made
to agree with the object if it be in the nominative form.   But if the

object take को, the sign of the accusative, or if the object be part
of a sentence, the verb must be used impersonally and always in
the third masculine singular. The following sentences shew the
application of the preceding principles :—

लड़के ने घोड़ा देखा *larke ne ghoṛá dekhá*, 'the boy saw the horse';
लड़के ने घोड़ी देखी *larke ne ghoṛí dekhí*, 'the boy saw the mare':
लड़की ने घोड़ा देखा *larkí ne ghoṛá dekhá*, 'the girl saw the horse';
मनुष्य ने घोड़े देखे *manushya ne ghoṛe dekhe*, 'the man saw the horses';
उस ने लड़कियां देखीं *us ne larkiyán dekhín*, 'he saw the girls.'

217.   Observe that in the foregoing instances को does not accompany the object; consequently, the verb and object are made to
agree in gender and number: in the following instances the accusative form with को is used; the verb is therefore employed impersonally, in the form of the third person masculine singular.

पिता ने पुत्र को पाया *pitá ne putra ko páyá*, 'the father found
the son'; किसान ने घोड़ों को बेचा है *kisán ne ghoṛon ko bechá hai*
'the husbandman has sold the horses'; उन्हों ने दास को भेजा था
unhon ne dás ko bhejá thá, 'they had sent a servant'; रानी ने अपनी
एक सहेली को बुलाया *rání ne apní ek saheli ko buláyá*, 'the queen
called one of her attendants.'

218.   Conjugation of a Transitive Verb, Active Voice.

Root ending in a Vowel.

Remember that transitives whose root ends in a vowel differ
form those whose root ends in a consonant by inserting य *y*
before आ *á* in forming the past participle, and in optionally inserting व *w* before the terminations ए *e*, एं *en*, ओ *o*. See
198.

Model verb, पाना *páná*, 'to find.'

219.   PRINCIPAL PARTS.

Root,........................ पा *pá*, find.
Present Participle,............... पाता *pátá*, finding.
Past Participle,...... .... पाया *páyá*, found.

220.   1. *Three tenses are formed from the root,* पा.

a. THE PROSPECTIVE CONDITIONAL.

'If I find,' *etc.*

SINGULAR.	PLURAL.
मैं पाऊं *main paún*.	हम पाएं, पावें, *ham páen*, or *páwen*.
तू पाए, पावे, *tú páe*, or *páwe*.	तुम पाओ, पावो, *tum páo*, or *páwo*.
वह पाए, पावे, *wah páe*, or *páwe*.	वे पाएं, पावें, *we páen*, or *páwen*.

b. THE FUTURE.

'I shall *or* will find,' *etc.*

SINGULAR.	PLURAL.
मैं पाऊंगा *main páúngá*.	हम पाएंगे, पावेंगे *ham páenge*, or *páwenge*.
तू पाएगा, पावेगा, *tú páegá*, or *páwegá*.	तुम पाओगे, पावोगे *tum páoge*, or *páwoge*.
वह पाएगा, पावेगा, *wah páegá*, or *páwegá*.	वे पाएंगे, पावेंगे *we páenge*, or *páwenge*.
Fem. मैं पाऊंगी *main páúngí*, etc.	Fem. हम पाएंगी *ham páengín*, etc.

c. THE IMPERATIVE.

'Let me find,' 'find thou,' *etc.*

SINGULAR.	PLURAL.
मैं पाऊं *main páún*.	हम पाएं, पावें *ham páen*, or *páwen*.
तू पा *tú pá*.	तुम पाओ, पावो *tum páo*, or *páwo*.
वह पाए, पावे *wah páe*, or *páwe*.	वे पाएं, पावें *we páen*, or *páwen*.

221.   2. *Three tenses are formed from the present participle,* पाता.

(81)

a. THE RETROSPECTIVE CONDITIONAL AND PRESENT INDEFINITE.

'If I found,' 'I find,' *etc.*

मैं पाता *main pátá.*	हम पाते *ham páte.*
तू पाता *tú pátá.*	तुम पाते *tum páte.*
वह पाता *wah pátá.*	वे पाते *we páte.*
Fem. मैं पाती *main pátí,* etc.	Fem. हम पातीं *ham pátín,* etc.

b. THE PRESENT DEFINITE.

'I find *or* am finding,' *etc.*

मैं पाता हूँ *main pátá hún.*	हम पाते हैं *ham páte hain.*
तू पाता है *tú pátá hai.*	तुम पाते हो *tum páte ho.*
वह पाता है *wah pátá hai.*	वे पाते हैं *we páte hain.*
Fem. मैं पाती हूँ *main pátí hún,* etc.	Fem. हम पातीं हैं *ham pátí hain,* etc.

c. THE IMPERFECT.

'I was finding,' *etc.*

मैं पाता था *main pátá thá.*	हम पाते थे *ham páte the.*
तू पाता था *tú pátá thá.*	तुम पाते थे *tum páte the.*
वह पाता था *wah pátá thá.*	वे पाते थे *we páte the.*
Fem. मैं पाती थी *main pátí thí,* etc.	Fem. हम पातीं थीं *ham pátí thín,* etc.

222. 3. *Three tenses are formed from the past participle,* पाया.

a. THE HISTORICAL PAST.

'I found,' *or* 'It was found by me,' *etc.*

मैं ने पाया *main ne páyá.*	हम ने पाया *ham ne páyá.*
तू ने पाया *tú ne páyá.*	तुम ने पाया *tum ne páyá.*
उस ने पाया *us ne páyá.*	उन ने, उन्हों ने पाया, *un ne, or unhon ne páyá.*

K

b. The Perfect.

'I have found,' *or* 'It has been found by me,' *etc.*

मैं ने पाया है *maiṅ ne páyá hai.*
तू ने पाया है *tú ne páyá hai.*
उस ने पाया है *us ne páyá hai.*

हम ने पाया है *ham ne páyá hai.*
तुम ने पाया है *tum ne páyá hai.*
उन ने, उन्हों ने पाया है, *un ne, or unhoṅ ne páyá hai.*

c. The Pluperfect.

'I had found,' *or* 'It had been found by me,' *etc.*

मैं ने पाया था *maiṅ ne páyá thá.*
तू ने पाया था *tú ne páyá thá.*
उस ने पाया था *us ne páyá thá.*

हम ने पाया था *ham ne páyá thá.*
तुम ने पाया था *tum ne páyá thá.*
उन ने, उन्हों ने पाया था, *un ne, or unhoṅ ne páyá thá.*

223.　　　　*Participles.*

1. Adjective Participles.

Present, 'Finding.'

Singular.	Plural.
Mas. पाता, पाता हुआ, *pátá,* or *pátá huá.*	Mas. पाते, पाते हुए, *páte,* or *páte hue.*
Fem. पाती, पाती हुई, *pátí,* or *pátí huí.*	Fem. पातीं, पाती हुईं, *pátíṅ,* or *pátí huíṅ.*

Past, 'Found.'

Mas. पाया, पाया हुआ, *páyá,* or *páyá huá.*	Mas. पाये, पाये हुए, *páye,* or *páye hue.*
Fem. पाई, पाई हुई, *páí,* or *páí huí.*	Fem. पाईं, पाई हुईं, *páíṅ,* or *páí huíṅ.*

2. Conjunctive Participles.

'Finding,' 'having found.'

पा *pá,* पाके *páke,* पाकर *pákar,* पाकरके *pákarke,* पाकरकर *pákarkar.*

(83)

3. ADVERBIAL PARTICIPLE.

पातेही *pátehí*, on finding, in the act of finding.

224. NOUN OF AGENCY.

पानेहारा, पानेवाला, *pánehárá*, or *pánewálá*, one who finds.

INFINITIVE OR VERBAL NOUN.

Nom. पाना *páná*, finding.
Gen. पाने का, *páne ká*, of finding, *etc.*

225. PRECATIVE OR RESPECTFUL FORMS OF THE IMPERATIVE
AND FUTURE.

पाइये *páiye*, be you or ye pleased to find.
पाइयेगा *páiyegá*, you or ye will be pleased to find.

MILD IMPERATIVE.

पाइयो *páiyo*, find you, or find ye.

CONJUGATION OF AN INTRANSITIVE OR NEUTER VERB.

Root ending in a Consonant.

226. The root may end in a consonant or in a vowel : if in
a consonant, the verb will be conjugated like देखना, except the
tenses formed from the past participle ; if in a vowel, the verb
will be conjugated like पाना, except in the tenses formed from
the past participle. Remember that the only difference between
intransitives whose root ends in a consonant, and intransitives
whose root ends in a vowel, is, that the past participle of the former is obtained by adding आ *á* to the root ; and of the latter
by adding या *yá*; the latter also optionally insert व *w* before
the terminations ए *e*, एं *eṅ*, ओ *o*. See 198.

227. Model verb, रहना *rahná*, 'to remain.'

PRINCIPAL PARTS.

Root, ... रह *rah*, remain.
Present Participle, ... रहता *rahtá*, remaining.
Past Participle, ... रहा *rahá*, remained.

228. 1. *Three tenses are formed from the root,* रह.

a. THE PROSPECTIVE CONDITIONAL,
b. THE FUTURE,
c. THE IMPERATIVE,

} Formed exactly like the corresponding tenses of देखना.

229. 2. *Three tenses are formed from the present participle,* रहता.

a. THE RETROSPECTIVE CONDITION-
   AL AND PRESENT INDEFINITE,
b. THE PRESENT DEFINITE,
c. THE IMPERFECT,

} Formed exactly like the corresponding tenses of देखना.

230. 3. *Three tenses are formed from the past participle,* रहा.

a. THE HISTORICAL PAST.

' I remained,' *etc.*

SINGULAR.	PLURAL.
मैं रहा *maiṅ rahá.*	हम रहे *ham rahe.*
तू रहा *tú rahá.*	तुम रहे *tum rahe.*
वह रहा *wah rahá.*	वे रहे *we rahe.*
Fem. मैं रही *maiṅ rahí*, etc.	Fem. हम रहीं *ham rahíṅ*, etc.

b. THE PERFECT.

' I have remained,' *etc.*

मैं रहा हूँ *maiṅ rahá húṅ.*	हम रहे हैं *ham rahe haiṅ.*
तू रहा है *tú rahá hai.*	तुम रहे हो *tum rahe ho.*
वह रहा है *wah rahá hai.*	वे रहे हैं *we rahe haiṅ.*
Fem. मैं रही हूँ *main rahí húṅ*, etc.	Fem. हम रही हैं *ham rahí haiṅ*, etc.

c. THE PLUPERFECT.

'I had remained,' *etc.*

मैं रहा था *main rahá thá.*	हम रहे थे *ham rahe the.*
तू रहा था *tú rahá thá.*	तुम रहे थे *tum rahe the.*
वह रहा था *wah rahá thá.*	वे रहे थे *we rahe the.*
Fem. मैं रही थी *main rahí thí,* etc.	Fem. हम रही थीं *ham rahí thíṅ.* etc.

231. The remainder of the conjugation is formed exactly like the corresponding parts of the model verb देखना.

CONJUGATION OF AN INTRANSITIVE OR NEUTER VERB.

Root ending in a Vowel.

Model verb, आना *áná,* 'to come.'

232. PRINCIPAL PARTS.

Root, ... आ *á,* come.
Present Participle, ... आता *átá,* coming.
Past Participle, ... आया *áyá,* came.

233. *Three tenses are formed from the root,* आ.

a. THE PROSPECTIVE CONDITIONAL,
b. THE FUTURE, } Formed exactly like the cor-
c. THE IMPERATIVE, responding tenses of पाना.

234. 2. *Three tenses are formed from the present participle,* आता.

a. THE RETROSPECTIVE CONDITION-
AL AND PRESENT INDEFINITE, } Formed exactly like the cor-
b. THE PRESENT DEFINITE, responding tenses of पाना.
c. THE IMPERFECT,

235. 3. *Three tenses are formed from the past participle,* आया.

a. THE HISTORICAL PAST.

'I came,' *etc.*

मैं आया *main áyá.*	हम आये *ham áye.*
तू आया *tú áyá.*	तुम आये *tum áye.*
वह आया *wah áyá.*	वे आये *we áye.*
Fem. मैं आई *main áí,* etc.	Fem. हम आईं *ham áín,* etc.

b. THE PERFECT.

'I have come,' *etc.*

मैं आया हूँ *main áyá hún.*	हम आये हैं *ham áye hain.*
तू आया है *tú áyá hai.*	तुम आये हो *tum áye ho.*
वह आया है *wah áyá hai.*	वे आये हैं *we áye hain.*
Fem. मैं आई हूँ *main áí hún,* etc.	Fem. हम आईं हैं *ham áí hain,* etc.

c. THE PLUPERFECT.

'I had come,' *etc.*

मैं आया था *main áyá thá.*	हम आये थे *ham áye the.*
तू आया था *tú áyá thá.*	तुम आये थे *tum áye the.*
वह आया था *wah áyá thá.*	वे आये थे *we áye the.*
Fem. मैं आई थी *main áí thí,* etc.	Fem. हम आईं थीं *ham áí thín,* etc.

236. The remainder of the conjugation is formed exactly like the corresponding parts of the model verb पाना.

THE PASSIVE VOICE.

237. The passive voice is formed by compounding the past participle of the active verb with the neuter verb जाना *jáná,* 'to go.'

The past participle when thus employed is changed in its termination to agree with a feminine or with a plural nominative, but it is not conjugated; जाना is conjugated throughout.

238. Notice that the roots of verbs also are frequently prefixed to the tenses of आना to form compound verbs which have not necessarily a passive signification; thus, बैठ आना *baiṭh jáná,* 'to sit down'; उठ आना *uṭh jáná,* 'to rise up'; खा आना *khá jáná,* 'to eat'; डर आना *ḍar jáná,* 'to fear'; etc. See 273. The passive voice can be formed only by placing the tenses of आना after a past participle.

239. Notice also that आना is one of the only six verbs in the language that form their past participles somewhat irregularly; it takes for its past participle, not आया *jáyá,* but गया *gayá;* fem. गई *gaí;* mas. pl. गये *gaye;* fem. pl. गईं *gaíṅ.*

Model verb, देखा आना *dekhá jáná,* 'to be seen.'

240.   Principal Parts.

Imperative, ...देखा आ *dekhá já,* be thou seen.
Present Participle,.......देखा आता *dekhá játá,* being seen.
Past Participle,... ...... देखा गया *dekhá gayá,* been seen.

241.   1. *Three tenses are formed from the root,* आ.

a. The Prospective Conditional.

'If I be seen,' *etc.*

Singular.	Plural.
मैं देखा जाऊं *maiṅ dekhá jáúṅ.*	हम देखे आवें, आंय, *ham dekhe jáweṅ,* or *jáṅe.*
तू देखा आवे, आय, *tu dekhá jáwe,* or *jáe.*	तुम देखे आवो, आचे, *tum dekhe jáwo,* or *jáo.*
वह देखा आवे, आय, *wah dekhá jáwe,* or *jáe.*	वे देखे आवें, आंय, *we dekhe jáweṅ,* or *jáṅe.*
Fem. मैं देखी आऊं *maiṅ dekhí jáúṅ,* etc.	Fem. हम देखी आवें *ham dekhí jaweṅ,* etc.

b. THE FUTURE.

'I shall *or* will be seen,' *etc.*

मैं देखा जाऊंगा *main dekhá jáúṅgá.*

तू देखा जावेगा, जायगा, *tú dekhá jáwegá,* or *jáegá.*

वह देखा जावेगा, जायगा, *wah dekhá jáwegá,* or *jáegá.*

Fem. मैं देखी जाऊंगी *main dekhí jáúṅgí,* etc.

हम देखे जावेंगे, जायेंगे, *ham dekhe jáweṅge,* or *jáyeṅge.*

तुम देखे जावोगे, जाओगे, *tum dekhe jáwoge,* or *jáoge.*

वे देखे जावेंगे, जायेंगे,* *we dekhe jáweṅge,* or *jáyeṅge.*

Fem. हम देखी जावेंगीं *ham dekhí jáweṅgíṅ,* etc.

c. IMPERATIVE.

'Let me be seen,' 'be thou seen,' *etc.*

मैं देखा जाऊं *main dekhá jáúṅ.*

तू देखा जा *tú dekhá já.*

वह देखा जावे, जाय, *wah dekhá jáwe,* or *jáe.*

Fem. मैं देखी जाऊं *main dekhí jáúṅ,* etc.

हम देखे जावें, जांय, *ham dekhe jáweṅ,* or *jáṅe.*

तुम देखे जावो, जाओ, *tum dekhe jáwo,* or *jáo.*

वे देखे जावें, जांय, *we dekhe jáweṅ,* or *jáṅe.*

Fem. हम देखी जावें *ham dekhí jáweṅ,* etc.

242. 2. *Three tenses are formed from the present participle,* जाता.

a. THE RETROSPECTIVE CONDITIONAL AND PRESENT INDEFINITE.

'I am seen,' 'If I had been seen,' *etc.*

मैं देखा जाता *main dekhá játá.*

तू देखा जाता *tú dekhá játá.*

वह देखा जाता *wah dekhá játá.*

Fem. मैं देखी जाती *main dekhí játí,* etc.

हम देखे जाते *ham dekhe játe.*

तुम देखे जाते *tum dekhe játe.*

वे देखे जाते *we dekhe játe.*

Fem. हम देखी जातीं *ham dekhí játíṅ,* etc.

---

* Some Pandits prefer the form जायगे *jáṅege,* for the 1st and 3rd persons plural of this tense. Observe that य *y* in the above and other cases when it occurs at or near the end of a word, is pronounced like *e.* See the note on page 11.

b. THE PRESENT DEFINITE.
'I am being seen,' *etc.*

मैं देखा जाता हूं *main dekhá játá   *   हम देखे जाते हैं *ham dekhe játe*
    hún.   [*hai.*   *hain.*   [*ho.*

तू देखा जाता है *tú dekhá játá*   तुम देखे जाते हो *tum dekhe játe*

यह देखा जाता है *wah dekhá játá*   वे देखे जाते हैं *we dekhe játe*

    hai.   [*játí hún,* etc.   *hain.* [*dekhí játí hain,* etc.

Fem. मैं देखी जाती हूं *main dekhí*   Fem. हम देखी जाती हैं *ham*

c. THE IMPERFECT.
'I was seen *or* being seen,' *etc.*

मैं देखा जाता था *main dekhá játá*   हम देखे जाते थे *ham dekhe játe*
    thá.   [*thá.*   *the.*   [*the.*

तू देखा जाता था *tú dekhá játá*   तुम देखे जाते थे *tum dekhe játe*

यह देखा जाता था *wah dekhá*   वे देखे जाते थे *we dekhe játe the.*

    játá thá. [*dekhí játí thí,* etc.   Fem. हम देखी जाती थीं *ham*

Fem. मैं देखी जाती थी *main*   *dekhí játí thín,* etc.

243   3.   *Three tenses are formed from the past participle,* गया.

a. THE HISTORICAL PAST.
'I was seen, *etc.*

मैं देखा गया *main dekhá gayá.*   हम देखे गये *ham dekhe gaye.*

तू देखा गया *tú dekhá gayá.*   तुम देखे गये *tum dekhe gaye.*

यह देखा गया *wah dekhá gayá.*   वे देखे गये *we dekhe gaye.*

Fem. मैं देखी गई *main dekhí gaí,*   Fem. हम देखी गईं *ham dekhí*

    etc.   *gaín,* etc.

b. THE PERFECT.
'I have been seen,' *etc.*

मैं देखा गया हूं *main dekhá gayá*   हम देखे गये हैं *ham dekhe gaye*
    hún.   [*hai.*   *hain.*   [*ho.*

तू देखा गया है *tú dekhá gayá*   तुम देखे गये हो *tum dekhe gaye*

वह देखा गया है *wah dekhá gayá hai.* [*gaí húṅ, etc.* | वे देखे गये हैं *we dekhe gaye haiṅ.* [*gaí haiṅ, etc*
Fem. मैं देखी गई हूँ *maiṅ dekhí* | Fem. तुम देखी गई हैं *ham dekhí.*

c. THE PLUPERFECT.

'I had been seen,' *etc.*

मैं देखा गया था *maiṅ dekhá gayá thá.* [*thá.* | हम देखे गये थे *ham dekhe gaye the.*
तू देखा गया था *tú dekhá gayá* | तुम देखे गये थे *tum dekhe gaye the.*
वह देखा गया था *wah dekhá gayá thá.* [*gaí thí, etc.* | वे देखे गये थे *we dekhe gaye the.*
Fem. मैं देखी गई थी *maiṅ dekhí* | Fem. हम देखी गई थीं *ham dekhí gaí thíṅ, etc.*

244.   *Participles.*

1. ADJECTIVE PARTICIPLES.

Present, 'Being seen.'

SINGULAR.	PLURAL.
Mas. देखा जाता, देखा जाता हुआ, *dekhá játá,* or *dekhá játá huá.*	Mas. देखे जाते, देखे जाते हुए, *dekhe játe,* or *dekhe játe hue.*
Fem. देखी जाती, देखी जाती हुई, *dekhí játí,* or *dekhí játí huí.*	Fem. देखी जातीं, देखी जाती हुईं, *dekhí játíṅ,* or *dekhí játí huíṅ.*

Past, 'Been seen.'

Mas. देखा गया, देखा गया हुआ, *dekhá gayá,* or *dekhá gayá huá.*	Mas. देखे गये, देखे गये हुए, *dekhe gaye,* or *dekhe gaye hue.*
Fem. देखी गई, देखी गई हुई, *dekhí gaí,* or *dekhí gaí huí.*	Fem. देखी गईं, देखी गई हुईं, *dekhí gaíṅ,* or *dekhí gaí huíṅ.*

2. CONJUNCTIVE PARTICIPLE.

'Being seen,' 'having been seen.'

देखा जा *dekhá já,* देखा जाके *dekhá jáke,* देखा जाकर *dekhá jákar,* देखा जाकरके *dekhá jákarke,* देखा जाकरकर *dekhá jákurkar.*

3. ADVERBIAL PARTICIPLE.

देखे जातेही *dekhe játehí,* 'on being seen,' 'in the act of being seen.'

245. NOUN OF AGENCY.

देखा जानेहारा, देखा जानेवाला, *dekhá jánehárá,* or *dekhá jánewálá,* 'one who is seen.'

INFINITIVE OR VERBAL NOUN.

Nom. देखा जाना, *dekhá jáná,* 'being seen.'
Gen. देखे जानेका, *dekhe jáneká,* etc., 'of being seen,' *etc.*

246. PRECATIVE OR RESPECTFUL FORMS OF THE IMPERATIVE AND FUTURE.

देखे जाइये *dekhe jáiye,* be you or ye pleased to be seen.
देखे जाइयेगा *dekhe jáiyegá,* you or ye will be pleased to be seen.

MILD IMPERATIVE.

देखे जाइयो *dekhe jáiyo,* be you or ye seen.

247. It has already been stated that verbs in Hindí are perfectly regular, with the exception of six words that are slightly anomalous in the formation of their past participles. Four of the six take the termination जिये *jiye* in the respectful imperative, and जियो *jiyo* in the mild form of the imperative. The six verbs are given below with the anomalous parts tabulated: पाना *páná,* which, though regular in the past participle and its formatives, also takes जिये and जियो in the respectful and mild imperatives, is included.

248.

INFINITIVE.	PAST PARTICIPLES.				RESPECTFUL IMPERATIVE.	MILD IMPERATIVE.]
	Singular.		Plural.			
	Mas.	Fem.	Mas.	Fem.		
होना *honá*, to be	हुआ *huá*	हुई *huí*	हुए *hue*	हुई *huíń*	हूजिये *hújiye*	हूजियो *hújiyo*.
करना *karná*, to do	किया *kiyá*	किई *kií*	किये *kiye*	किई *kiíń*	कीजिये *kíjiye*	कीजियो *kíjiyo*.
देना *dená*, to give	दिया *diyá*	दिई *dií*	दिये *diye*	दिई *diíń*	दीजिये *díjiye*	दीजियो *díjiyo*.
लेना *lená*, to take	लिया *liyá*	लिई *lií*	लिये *liye*	लिई *liíń*	लीजिये *líjiye*	लीजियो *líjiyo*. —
जाना *jáná*, to go	गया *gayá*	गई *gai*	गये *gaye*	गई *gaíń*		
मरना *marná*, to die	मूआ *múá*	मूई *múí*	मूए *múe*	मूई *múíń*		
पीना *píná*, to drink					पीजिये *píjiye*	पीजियो *píjiyo*.

249. भया *bhayá*, an anomalous defective tense or participle with the signification 'was,' or 'became,' is declined like आया *áyá*. Derivation, probably, from the Sanskrit root भू *bhú*, 'being.'

250. The irregularities of three of the six verbs whose past participles are anomalously formed, viz., होना, देना, लेना, are owing entirely to euphony. From the Sanskrit root कृ *kri*, 'doing,' modified into कर *kar* and की *kí*, two Hindí infinitives were derived, viz., करना *karná* and कीना *kíná*, having the same signification. From these infinitives the past participles and respectful imperatives were formed thus :—

करना infinitive, करा past participle, करिये respectful imperative.
कीना   „   किया „   „   कीजिये „   „

Of the former, करा and करिये now but seldom occur, their place being supplied by किया and कीजिये, the corresponding forms from कीना.* The verb जाना comes from the Sanskrit root या *yá*, 'going,' the initial य *y* of the Sanskrit becoming, as a rule, ज *j* in Hindí; but it takes its past participle गया from the root गम् *gam*, having the same signification as या. The form जाया *jáyá*, is used, but only in compounds; as, जाया करना *jáyá karná*, 'to go frequently.' मरना is from the Sanskrit root मृ *mri*, 'dying'; its past participle, मूआ *múá*, may have come through the Prakrit, in which the Sanskrit vowel ऋ *ri* was generally changed into उ *u*. The regular past participle मरा *marú* is also used, and, as the first member of compound verbs, is preferred to मूआ; thus, मरा चाहना *marú cháhná*, 'to wish to die.'

---

* The following is from the Prem Sagar,—हे नाथ तुमने बड़ी कृपा करी जो मेरा गर्ब दूर किया *he náth tum ne baṛí kripá karí jo merá garb dúr kiyá*, 'O lord you have done me a great favor in having removed my pride.'

251. Of the six verbs whose past participles are irregularly formed, three, viz., होना, जाना, मरना, are neuter; and three, viz., करना, देना, लेना, are active, and therefore follow the construction peculiar to active verbs in the tenses formed from the past participle.

252. The verbs लाना *lánâ*, 'to bring'; भूलना *bhúlná*, 'to forget'; बोलना *bolná*, 'to speak'; बकना *baknâ*, '.to chatter'; and, perhaps, लड़ना *larná*, 'to fight,' though they are transitive and may take an object after them, are yet peculiar in not taking the case of the agent before them in the tenses from the past participle. They conform in the conjugation of those tenses to the neuter verb, and govern their objects in the same way as transitives in the present or future tenses generally do.

253. The verb लाना differs from the others; it is an abbreviation of ले आना *le áná*, and therefore follows the usage of आना *áná*, in respect to the nominative, and of ले *le* in respect to the objective. As for the other words, they are often intransitive as well as often transitive verbs; बकना, more especially, is much more frequently intransitive than transitive, though in some cases it appears to have an accusative after it.

254. OBSERVE:—Verbs having a dissyllabic root, with a short vowel in the first and the inherent अ *a* in the second syllable, generally, though not invariably, drop the inherent अ *a* in all such parts of the conjugation as have the last consonant of the root followed by a vowel other than अ *a*. Thus, from समझना *samajhná*, 'to understand,' the past participle is समझा *samjhá*, the 2nd pl. imper. समझो *samjho*: from खुरचना *khurachná*, 'to scrape,' खुरचा *khurchá*, 'scraped'; खुरचो *khurcho*, 'scrape,' etc. As these omissions are simply on the score of euphony, variations in usage will be observed; thus with some the past participle of *nikalná* is *niklá*, with others, *nikalá*; so of *pakarná*, 'to seize,' the two forms, *pakrá* and *pakará*, are in use.

SIX ADDITIONAL TENSES COMMON TO ALL VERBS.

255.   It has been stated that, in addition to the nine tenses formed from the three principal parts of the verb, there are six other but more rarely used tenses common to all verbs: those six tenses are formed by using the prospective conditional, the future, and the retrospective conditional or present indefinite of the verb होना as auxiliaries to the present and past participles of any verb. See 190.

256.   These tenses are given in native grammars and are regarded as distinct parts of the verb; as from their nature they cannot be often required, it will suffice simply to indicate them under the verb रोना *roná*, 'to cry.'

257.   1. *Three tenses are formed from the present participle,* रोता.

a.   PRESENT PROSPECTIVE CONDITIONAL.

'I may be crying,' *etc.*

SINGULAR.	PLURAL.
मैं रोता होऊँ *main rotá houn.*	हम रोते होवें *ham rote howen.*
तू रोता होवे *tú rotá howe.*	तुम रोते होओ *tum rote hoo.*
वह रोता होवे *wah rotá howe.*	वे रोते होवें *we rote howen.*
Fem. मैं रोती होऊँ *main rotí houn,* etc.	Fem. हम रोती होवें *ham rotí howen,* etc.

b.   PRESENT RETROSPECTIVE CONDITIONAL.

'Had I been crying,' *etc.*

मैं रोता होता *main rotá hotá.*	हम रोते होते *ham rote hote.*
तू रोता होता *tú rotá hotá.*	तुम रोते होते *tum rote hote.*
वह रोता होता *wah rotá hotá.*	वे रोते होते *we rote hote.*
Fem. मैं रोती होती *main rotí hotí,* etc.	Fem. हम रोती होतीं *ham rotí hotín,* etc.

(96)

c. PRESENT DUBIOUS.

'I shall be crying,' *etc.*

मैं रोता होऊंगा *main rotá hoúṅgá.*	हम रोते होवेंगे *ham rote howeṅge.*
तू रोता होवेगा *tú rotá howegá.*	तुम रोते होओगे *tum rote hooge.*
वह रोता होवेगा *wah rotá howegá.*	वे रोते होवेंगे *we rote howeṅge.*
Fem. मैं रोती होऊंगी *main rotí hoúṅgí,* etc.	Fem. हम रोती होवेंगी *ham rotí howeṅgíṅ,* etc.

258. 2. *Three tenses are formed from the past participle,* रोया.

a. PAST PROSPECTIVE CONDITIONAL.

'I may have cried,' *etc.*

मैं रोया होऊं *main royá hoúṅ.*	हम रोये होवें *ham roye howeṅ.*
तू रोया होवे *tú royá howe.*	तुम रोये होओ *tum roye hoo.*
वह रोया होवे *wah royá howe.*	वे रोये होवें *we roye howeṅ.*
Fem. मैं रोई होऊं *main roí hoúṅ.* etc.	Fem. हम रोई होवें *ham roí howeṅ,* etc.

b. PAST RETROSPECTIVE CONDITIONAL.

'Had I cried,' *etc.*

मैं रोया होता *main royá hotá.*	हम रोये होते *ham roye hote.*
तू रोया होता *tú royá hotá.*	तुम रोये होते *tum roye hote.*
वह रोया होता *wah royá hotá.*	वे रोये होते *we roye hote.*
Fem. मैं रोई होती *main roí hotí,* etc.	Fem. हम रोई होती *ham roí hotíṅ,* etc.

c. PAST DUBIOUS.

'I shall *or* will have cried,' *etc.*

मैं रोया होऊंगा *main royá hoúṅgá.*	हम रोये होवेंगे *ham roye howeṅge.*
तू रोया होवेगा *tú royá howegá.*	तुम रोये होओगे *tum roye hooge.*
वह रोया होवेगा *wah royá howegá.*	वे रोये होवेंगे *we roye howeṅge.*
Fem. मैं रोई होऊंगी *main roí hoúṅgí,* etc.	Fem. हम रोई होवेंगी *ham roí howeṅgíṅ,* etc.

259. Observe that when the first verb is transitive and preceded by a noun in the case of the agent with ने, the second or auxiliary verb will follow it in agreeing with the object in gender and number, when the object is in the nominative form without को; but if the object have को, which is unusual when it is the name of something inanimate, both the principal and the auxiliary verb must be used impersonally in the third singular masculine gender; thus, जो तुम ने छुरी न दी होती तो लड़के का हाथ न कटता *jo tum ne chhurí na dí hotí to larke káháth na kaṭtá,* 'if you had not given the knife to the boy his hand would not have been cut'; यदि उन्हों ने लड़कों को देखा होता तो क्या नहीं कहते *yadí unhoṅ ne larkoṅ ko dekhá hotá to kyá nahíṅ kahte,* 'if they had seen the boys would they not have said so?'

260. Of the six uncommon tenses the forms मैं रोता होता, etc., मैं रोया होता, etc., are least likely to occur, as their place is usually taken by the simpler form, मैं रोता, etc., of the Retrospective Conditional. The form मैं रोया होऊँगा, etc., is the most frequent.

261. It must not be supposed that of the preceding tenses those that are future in form are so in signification; they rather express uncertainty; thus, वह जाता होगा *wah játá hogá,* would mean, 'perhaps (or, probably,) he is going.' The names Present Dubious, Past Dubious, accord therefore more with their functions, than "Present Future," "Past Future," by which they are sometimes known; such names are paradoxical and can convey no definite idea to a learner's mind.

Of Derivative and Compound Verbs.

1. DERIVATIVES.

262. Derivative verbs abound in Hindí: we shall consider here those only that are derived from other verbs, leaving those

that are formed from nouns and adjectives for the section on derivation in general.

263. By far the most common and useful are actives derived from neuters, and causals, or doubly transitives derived
from actives. The rules for their formation are given below ; let
it be observed that the first is the general rule of which the others
are but modifications, mainly for the sake of euphony.

264. *a.* To form an active or causal from a neuter verb, insert आ *á* between the root and the sign of the infinitive (ना) ;
and to form a doubly causal, or doubly transitive, insert वा *wá* ;
or, which is the same thing, insert व *w* between the root and the
termination आना *ána* of the causal ; thus, बनना *banná,* 'to be
made,' बनाना *banáná,* to make, बनवाना *banwáná,* 'to cause to be
made.' The following are other examples :—

SIMPLE OR NEUTER VERB.	ACTIVE OR CAUSAL.	DOUBLY CAUSAL.
उड़ना *uṛná,* to fly	उड़ाना *uṛáná.*	उड़वाना *uṛwáná.*
उठना *uṭhná,* to rise up	उठाना *uṭháná*	उठवाना *uṭhwáná.*
बचना *bachná,* to be saved	बचाना *bacháná*	बचवाना *bachwáná.*
बजना *bajná,* to be sounded	बजाना *bajáná*	बजवाना *bajwáná.*
बुझना *bujhná,* to be extinguished	बुझाना *bujháná*	बुझवाना *bujhwáná.*
पढ़ना *paṛhná,* to read	पढ़ाना *paṛháná*	पढ़वाना *paṛhwáná.*
रचना *rachná,* to be made	रचाना *racháná*	रचवाना *rachwáná.*
चढ़ना *chaṛhná,* to ascend	चढ़ाना *chaṛháná*	चढ़वाना *chaṛhwáná.*
चलना *chalná,* to move	चलाना *chaláná*	चलवाना *chalwáná.*
छिपना *chhipná,* to be hidden	छिपाना *chhipáná*	छिपवाना *chhipwáná.*
गिरना *girná,* to fall	गिराना *giráná*	गिरवाना *girwáná.*
घुलना *ghulná,* to melt.	घुलाना *ghuláná*	घुलवाना *ghulwáná.*
जलना *jalná,* to burn	जलाना *jaláná*	जलवाना *jalwáná.*
दबना *dabná,* to be pressed down	दबाना *dabáná*	दबवाना *dabwáná.*

दौड़ना *daurná*, to run   दौड़ाना *dauráná*   दौड़वाना *daurwáná.*

पहुंचना *pahunchná*, to arrive   पहुंचाना *pahun-cháná*   पहुंचवाना *pahunch-wáná.*

लगना *lagná*, to be applied   लगाना *lagáná*   लगवाना *lagwáná.*

सुना *sunná*, to hear   सुनाना *sunáná*   सुनवाना *sunwáná.*

मिलना *milná*, to mix, to meet   मिलाना *miláná*   मिलवाना *milwáná.*

हिलना *hilná*, to move   हिलाना *hiláná*   हिलवाना *hilwáná.*

265. Many verbs having a dissyllabic root with a short vowel in the first, and the inherent अ *a* in the second syllable, come under the foregoing rule, but omit the inherent अ *a* of the second syllable in forming the active or causal; as:—(See 254.)

चमकना *chamakná*, to shine   चमकाना *chamkáná*   चमकवाना *chamakwáná.*

परचना *parachná*, to be introduced   परचाना *parcháná*   परचवाना *parachwáná.*

पलटना *palaṭná*, to return   पलटाना *palṭáná*   पलटवाना *palaṭwáná.*

पिघलना *pighalná*, to be melted   पिघलाना *pighláná*   पिघलवाना *pighalwáná.*

बिथरना *bitharná*, to be scattered   बिथराना *bithráná*   बिथरवाना *bitharwáná.*

भटकना *bhaṭakná*, to go astray   भटकाना *bhaṭkáná*   भटकवाना *bhaṭakwáná.*

समझना *samajhná*, to understand   समझाना *samjháná*   समझवाना *samajhwáná.*

सरकना *sarakná*, to be moved   सरकाना *sarkáná*   सरकवाना *sarakwáná.*

लटकना *laṭakná*, to hang   लटकाना *laṭkáná*   लटकवाना *laṭakwáná.*

266. *b.* If the root of the simple or neuter verb be a monosyllable having a long vowel between two consonants, the vowel must

be shortened (श्रा *á* into अ *a*; ई *í*, ए *e*, into इ *i*; and ऊ *ú*, ओ *o*, into उ *u*,) before adding श्रा and वा to form actives and doubly causals; and if the monosyllabic root end in a long vowel, shorten it, and add ला *lá* for the active, and लवा *lwá* for the doubly causal.

घूमना *ghúmná*, to go round	घुमाना *ghumáná*	घुमवाना *ghumwáná*.
रोना *roná*, to cry	रुलाना *ruláná*	रुलवाना *rulwáná*.
जागना *jágná*, to be awake	जगाना *jagáná*	जगवाना *jagwáná*.
जीतना *jítná*, to win, conquer	जिताना *jitáná*	जितवाना *jitwáná*.
झूलना *jhúlná*, to swing	झुलाना *jhuláná*	झुलवाना *jhulwáná*.
डूबना *dúbná*, to be immersed	डुबाना *dubáná*	डुबवाना *dubwáná*.
डोलना *dolná*, to be shaken	डुलाना *duláná*	डुलवाना *dulwáná*.
बोलना *bolná*, to speak	बुलाना *buláná*	बुलवाना *bulwáná*.
भीगना *bhígná*, to be wet	भिगाना *bhigáná*	भिगवाना *bhigwáná*.
भूलना *bhúlná*, to forget, err	भुलाना *bhuláná*	भुलवाना *bhulwáná*.
लेटना *letná*, to lie down	लिटाना *litáná*	लिटवाना *litwáná*.
खाना *kháná*, to eat	खिलाना *khiláná*	खिलवाना *khilwáná*.
पीना *piná*, to drink	पिलाना *piláná*	पिलवाना *pilwáná*.
देना *dená*, to give	दिलाना *diláná*	दिलवाना *dilwáná*.
धोना *dhoná*, to wash	धुलाना *dhuláná*	धुलवाना *dhulwáná*.
सोना *soná*, to sleep	सुलाना *suláná*	सुलवाना *sulwáná*.

267. *a.* Many neuter verbs with a short vowel in the root simply lengthen it to form the active or causal, and form the doubly causal regularly with वा; thus :—

कटना *katná*, to be cut	काटना *kátná*	कटवाना *katwáná*.
खुलना *khulná*, to be opened	खोलना *kholná*	खुलवाना *khulwáná*.
गड़ना *garná*, to be buried	गाड़ना *gárná*.	गड़वाना *garwáná*.
गुथना *guthná*, to be plaited	गूथना *gúthná*.	गुथवाना *guthwáná*.
निकलना *nikalná*, to come out	निकालना *nikálná*.	निकलवाना *nikalwáná*.
पलना *palná*, to be reared	पालना *pálná*.	पलवाना *palwáná*.
बन्धना *bandhná*, to be tied	बांधना *bándhná*	बन्धवाना *bandhwáná*.

मरना *marná*, to die   मारना *márná*   मरवाना *marwáná.*
लदना *ladná*, to be laden   लादना *ládná*   लदवाना *ladwáná.*

268. *d.* Many verbs form their actives and doubly causals anomalously ; as :—

छुटना *chhuṭná*, to be let go   छोड़ना *chhoṛná*   छुड़वाना *chhuṛwáná.*
टूटना *ṭuṭná*, to be broken   तोड़ना *toṛná*   तोड़वाना *toṛwáná.*
फटना *phaṭná*, to be rent   फाड़ना *pháṛná*   फड़वाना *phaṛwáná.*
फूटना *phúṭná*, to be split   फोड़ना *phoṛná*   फुड़वाना *phuṛwáná.*
बिकना *biknä*, to be sold   बेचना *bechná*   बिकवाना *bikwáná.*
रहना *rahná*, to remain   रखना *rakhná*   रखवाना *rakhwáná.*

269. Observe that in the preceding lists there are some verbs that have two forms of the active ; as :—

डूबना to be immersed, has   डुबाना *ḍubáná* or डुबोना *ḍuboná.*
भीगना to be wet   „   भिगाना *bhigáná* „ भिगोना *bhigoná.*
देखना to see   „   दिखाना *dikháná* „ दिखलाना *dikhláná.*
बैठना to sit   „   बैठाना *baiṭháná* „ बिठलाना *biṭhláná.*
सीखना to learn   „   सिखाना *sikháná* „ सिखलाना *sikhláná.*
छुटना to be let go   „   छोड़ना *chhoṛná* „ छुड़ाना *chhuṛáná.*

270. There are also a few that have two forms of the doubly causal, as रखवाना and रखाना 'to cause to place.' A few -in the column headed simple or neuter, are active, such as देना, खाना, भेजना ; by the application of the rule under which they are placed, they are made doubly active or causal.

271. The use and application of the three forms in which the greater number of Hindí verbs are capable of appearing will be apparent from the following examples :—

घर बनता है *ghar bantá hai*, 'the house is being made'; थवई घर बनाता है *thawaí ghar banátá hai*, 'the mason is building a house'; महाजन घर बनवाता है *mahájan ghar banwátá hai*, 'a rich man is having a house built,' or 'is causing a house to be built';

सड़का पढ़ता था *larká parhtá thá,* 'a boy was reading'; पण्डित सड़के को पढ़ाता था *pandit larke ko parhátá thá,* 'a pandit was causing the boy to read,' i. e., was teaching him ; पिता अपने लड़के को पढ़वाता था *pitá apne larke ko parhwátá thá,* 'a father was causing his son to be taught.'

2. Compound Verbs.

272. The number of compound verbs in Hindí is very large as the structure of the language is such that they may be formed almost *ad libitum.* As many as eleven or twelve different kinds have been enumerated ; but, strictly speaking, most of them are rather phrases, or instances of one verb governing another, than compound verbs.

They may be arranged under three classes, 1. those from the root, 2. those from the present participle, 3. those from the past participle.

1. *From the root three kinds are formed by prefixing a verb regularly conjugated to the root of another verb.*

273. *a.* Intensives :—So called because more forcible in signification than a simple verb. The peculiarity of these is that the first member gives its signification to the compound, that of the second intensifying the idea by being merged in it ; thus,—

काट डालना *kát dálná,* ' to cut off.'
खो देना *kho dená,* ' to squander, lose.'
खा जाना *khá jáná,* 'to eat up.'
मार डालना *már dálná,* ' to kill outright.'
ले आना *le áná,* ' to bring.'
ले जाना *le jáná,* ' to take away.'
हो जाना *ho jáná,* ' to become.'
पी जाना *pí jáná,* 'to drink off.
गिरा देना *girá dená,* 'to throw down.'
रख देना *rakh dená,* 'to set down.'

274. *b.* POTENTIALS :—Are formed by adding the root of a verb to सकना *saknà*, 'to be able;' they express ability to perform the action indicated by the verb whose root is used, and serve the purpose of a potential mood. The following are examples :—

चल सकना *chal saknà*, to be able to walk.
चढ़ सकना *charh saknà*, to be able to ascend.
दे सकना *de saknà*, to be able to give.
बोल सकना *bol saknà*, to be able to speak.
लिख सकना *likh saknà*, to be able to write.
ले सकना *le saknà*, to be able to take.

275. *c.* COMPLETIVES :—Express the completion of the action; they are formed by using the root of a verb with चुकना *chuknà*, ' to be finished.' Completives, when used in the future tense, serve the purpose of the future perfect of the verb whose root is employed.

खा चुकना *khà chuknà*, to have done eating.
दे चुकना *de chuknà*, to have done giving.
मार चुकना *màr chuknà*, to have done beating.
सो चुकना *so chuknà*, to have done sleeping.

276. *2. From the present participle are formed what are termed continuatives and statisticals; they are, strictly speaking, not true compound verbs, but forms of expression in which the present participle is used as an adjective or adverb.*

277. *a.* CONTINUATIVES :—Are formed by prefixing a present participle to the verb जाना *jànà*, ' to go,' or to रहना *rahnà* ' to remain.' The participle must agree in gender and number with the nominative; जाना or रहना to which it is added is conjugated throughout.

लिखता जाना *likhtà jànà*, to continue writing.
पढ़ता जाना *parhtà jànà*, to continue reading.

बोलता रहना *boltá rahná*, to continue speaking

आता रहना *játá rahná*, to continue going.

मारते जाते हैं *márte játe hain*, they continue to beat.

पढ़ती रहती है *parhtí rahtí hai*, she continues to read.

278. *b.* STATISTICALS :—Are formed by prefixing a present participle to another verb. The participle is invariably used in the inflected form of the masculine singular.*

रोते चलना *rote chalná*, to go away crying.

गाते आना *gáte áná*, to come singing.

हँसते जाना *hanste jáná*, to go away laughing.

वह रोते आती है *wah rote átí hai*, she comes crying.

वे रोते दौड़ते हैं *we rote daurte hain*, they run weeping.

279. 3. *From the past participle are formed two kinds of compound verbs, frequentatives and desideratives.*

280. *a.* FREQUENTATIVES :—Formed by adding करना *karná*, 'to do,' to the past participle of a verb. The past participle must be in the uninflected form of the masculine singular in whatever number or gender the nominative may be ; thus :—

किया करना *kiyá karná*, to do frequently or habitually.

लिखा करना *likhá karná*, to write frequently.

आया करना *áyá karná*, to come frequently.

आया जाया करना *áyá jáyá karná*, to be in the habit of coming and going.

वह मुझे दिया करता *wah mujhe diyá kartá*, he gives to me frequently.

---

* The inflected form of the participle is accounted for in some of the grammars by " *men*, denoting, ' in the state of,' being understood ;" it is rather an example of the rule that the inflected participle denotes state or condition in itself, and without the aid of a postposition.

281. *b.* DESIDERATIVES :—Expressive of wish, desire, need, are formed by prefixing an uninflected past participle to the verb चाहना *cháhná*, 'to wish,' 'to need,' regularly conjugated.

देखा चाहना *dekhá cháhná*, to wish to see.
बोला चाहना *bolá cháhná*, to wish to speak.
जाया चाहना *jáyá cháhná*, to wish to go.
मरा चाहना *mará cháhná*, to wish to die.
सीखा चाहना *síkhá cháhná*, to wish to learn.

282. Desideratives may also be used to indicate the proximity of an action, or that it is about to take place ; thus :—

वह गिरा चाहता है *wah girá cháhtá hai*, he is about to fall.
वह मरा चाहती है *wah mará cháhtí hai*, she is about to die.
घड़ी बजा चाहती है *gharí bajá cháhtí hai*, the clock is about to strike.

283. As in a true compound the first member should remain unchanged, the latter alone being subject to inflection, it is evident that, of the so-called compounds described above, only five are real ; viz., Intensives, Potentials, Completives, Frequentatives, and Desideratives ; in these the first verb remains unchanged whilst the second is regularly conjugated in all its tenses.

284. A compound verb is considered neuter if the second member of the compound be neuter, though the first member be transitive and convey the main idea of the compound ; thus, लिखना *likhná*, 'to write,' is transitive, but लिख चुकना *likh chukná*, 'to have done writing,' is neuter.

285. The following are instances of one verb governing another in the inflected infinitive rather than examples of compound verbs ; but as they commonly occur it may be well to refer to them here.

INCEPTIVES :—An inflected infinitive followed by the verb, लगना *lagná*, 'to begin' ; as, बोलने लगा *bolne lagá*, 'he began to speak'; चलने लगे *chalne lage*, 'they began to go'; दौड़ने लगी *dauṛne lagí*, 'she began to run.'

PERMISSIVES :—An inflected infinitive followed by the verb देना *dená*, 'to give'; as, मुझे जाने नहीं देता *mujhe jáne nahíṅ detá*, 'he does not allow me to go'; उन को सोने दो *un ko sone do*, 'let them sleep'; उस ने हम को आने न दिया *us ne ham ko áne na diyá*, 'he did not allow us to come.'

ACQUISITIVES :—An inflected infinitive followed by the verb पाना *páná*, 'to get,' 'to obtain'; as, जो मैं आने पाऊँ तो आऊँगा *jo maiṅ áne páúṅ to áúṅgá*, 'if I obtain (leave) to come, then I will come'; जाने पाते हैं *jáne páte haiṅ*, 'they get (leave) to go'; उसे उठने न पावे *use uṭhne na páwe*, 'do not let him get up.'

286. What are termed Nominals are of frequent occurrence : they are formed by uniting a noun or an adjective with a verb; thus, ध्यान करना *dhyán karná*, 'to meditate'; विचार करना *bichár karná*, 'to reflect', 'to consider'; स्नान करना *snán karná*, 'to bathe'; एकट्ठे होना *ekaṭṭhe honá*, 'to be together,' 'to be assembled'; खड़ा होना *khará honá*, 'to be erect,' 'to stand up'; सुध लेना *sudh lená*, 'to take care of'; भय खाना *bhay kháná*, 'to be afraid.'

287. What are called Reiteratives are but instances of the excessive fondness of the Hindús for words and phrases that have a rhyming or jingling sound, such as the English words *topsy-turvy, chit-chat, hurly-burly, helter-skelter, pell-mell.* Two verbs of the same, or nearly the same meaning, especially such as jingle, are strung together in the tenses of the present participle and the conjunctive participle and are conjugated throughout, the auxiliary being added to the last only ; thus, धो धाकर *dho dhákar*, 'having washed'; बोलते चालते हैं *bolte chálte, haiṅ*, 'they chit-chat together'; फुसला फन्दलाकर *phuslá phandlá- kar*, ' having ensnared'; समझा बुझाकर *samjhá bujhákar*, 'having

explained.' In these and all such instances it is obvious that the latter of the two verbs is redundant and can convey no distinct meaning to the mind.

CHAPTER VII.

Of Indeclinable Words, अव्यय *avyaya.*

1. Adverbs, क्रियाविशेषण *kriyávishaṇ.*

The more common and useful adverbs are divisible into four classes as follows :—

288. *a.* Of Time, कालवाचक *kálaváchak.*

अब *ab,* now.

तब *tab,*
तद *tad,* } then.

कब *kab,*
कद *kad,* } when ?

जब *jab,*
जद *jad,* } when.

आज *áj,* to-day.

कल *kal,* yester-day, to-morrow.

आज कल *áj kal,* now-a-days.

नरसों *narson,* four days ago, or to come.

तरसों *tarson,* three days ago, or to come.

परसों *parson,* the day before yesterday, or the day after to-morrow.

प्रतिदिन *pratidin,* every day.

तड़के *tarke,* early, at dawn.

नित्य *nitya,* constantly, continually.

सदा *sadá,*
सर्वदा *sarvadá,* } always, at all times.

कदाचित *kadáchit,*
कदापि *kadápi,* } perhaps, sometimes.

निदान *nidán,* at last, finally.

बारंबार *bárambár,* often, frequently.

तुरन्त *turant,*
सत्काल *tatkál,*
सत्क्षण *tatkshaṇ,* } instantly, immediately.

पश्चात *paśchát,* afterwards.

एकदा *ekdá,* once.

सवेरे *savere,* in the morning, early.

फिर *phir,*
फेर *pher,* } again.

289. *b.* Of Place, स्थानवाचक *sthánaváchak.*

यहां *yahán,* here.

वहां *wahán,* there.

कहां *kahán,* where ?

तिधर *tidhar,* thither.

आसपास *áspás,* around, on all sides.

वरे *ware,* on this side, near.

जहाँ *jahán*, where. परे *pare*, on that side, yonder.

तहाँ *tahán*, there. सर्वत्र *sarvatra*, everywhere.

इधर *idhar*, hither. पार *pár*, over, across, on the other side.

उधर *udhar*, thither.

किधर *kidhar*, whither? निकट *nikaṭ*, near, almost, about.

जिधर *jidhar*, whither. नेरे *nere*, near, beside.

290. c. Of Manner, गुणवाचक *guṇaváchak.*

आकस्मात् *akasmát*, accidentally. यद्यपि *yadyapi*, although.

अचानक *achának*, suddenly, unexpectedly. निपट *nipaṭ*, very, exceedingly.

अति *ati*, very, exceedingly. निरन्तर *nirantar*, constantly, incessantly.

अधिक *adhik*, besides, moreover. शीघ्र *síghra*, quickly, speedily.

अत्यन्त *atyant*, very, very much. वृधा *brithá*, in vain.

अर्थात् *arthát*, that is to say, viz. यूँ *yún*,

केवल *kewal*, only, merely. यों *yon*, } thus, in this manner.

परस्पर *paraspar*, mutually, reciprocally. क्यों *kyon*, how? in what manner?

ज्यों *jyon*, as, in what manner.

पृथक् *prithak*, separately, severally त्यों *tyon*, so, in like manner.

झटपट *jhaṭ-paṭ*, quickly, at once. सचमुच *sachmuch*, truly, indeed.

ठीक *ṭhík*, exactly, properly. सेंत *sent*, } gratis, free of

यथार्थ *yathárth*, properly, suitably. सेंतमेत *sentmet*, } cost.

तथापि *tathápi*, } nevertheless, इत्यादि *ityádi*, et cætera, and so

तदपि *tadapi*, } yet. forth.

291. d. Of Affirmation and Negation.

स्वीकारवाचक *swikárvachak.* निषेधवाचक *nishedhváchak.*

हाँ *hán*, yes, yea. नहीं *nahín*, no, not, nay.

निश्चय *nischay*, surely, certainly. न *na*,

निस्सन्देह *nissandeh*, doubtlessly. ना *ná*, } no, not, nay.

अवश्य *avaśya*, necessarily. मत *mat*, do not.

तो *to*, indeed, in fact. जिन *jin*,

जनि *jani*, } no, do not.

292. The preceding adverbs are, with a few exceptions, simple; by adding to some of them the emphatic affix, ही, or हीं, signifying 'very,' 'indeed,' 'only,' other and more emphatic adverbs may be formed; thus,—

अभी *abhí*, just now.

तभी *tabhí*, just then.   [other.

कभी *kabhí*, ever, some time or

जभी *jabhí*, at the very time.

यूंहीं *yúṅhíṅ*, in this very way.

वोंहीं *woṅhíṅ*, in that very way.

293. By changing the termination वां *áṅ* into एं *íṅ*, the meaning of some becomes more emphatic; as, यहीं *yahíṅ*, exactly here; वहीं *wahíṅ*, exactly there; कहीं *kahíṅ*, anywhere, somewhere.

294. A useful class of compound adverbs is formed by repeating some of the preceding, or by compounding two different adverbs; thus,—

कभी कभी *kabhí kabhí*, sometimes, now and then.

जहां जहां *jaháṅ jaháṅ*, wherever.

बेर बेर *ber ber*, repeatedly, again and again.

धीरे धीरे *dhíre dhíre*, gently, softly.

अब तक *ab tak*, till now, yet.

कब तक *kab tak*, till when ? how long ?

कभी नहीं *kabhí nahíṅ*, never.

वारपार *wárpár*, on both sides, right through.   [so so.

ऐसा वैसा *aisá waisá*, indifferently,

जब कभी *jab kabhí*, whenever.

जहां कहीं *jaháṅ kahíṅ*, wherever.

और कहीं *aur kahíṅ*, elsewhere.

कहीं नहीं *kahíṅ nahíṅ*, nowhere.

यहां तक *yaháṅ tak*, hitherto, to this degree.   [otherwise.

नहीं तो *nahíṅ to*, if not, else,

295. Some adverbs are repeated with the negative particle, न, connecting them, to give universality or indefiniteness to the idea, probably, by ellipsis; as कभी न कभी *kabhí na kabhí*, 'sometime or other;' कहीं न कहीं *kahíṅ na kahíṅ*, 'somewhere or other;' जब न तब *jab na tab*, now and then;' यूं न यूं *yúṅ na yúṅ*, 'somehow or other.' The full expression might be, 'at some time,

(110)

'(if) not, (then) at some (other) time'; 'somewhere, (if) not, somewhere (else);' etc.

296. Adverbs in a great many instances admit the signs of the cases after them; thus, यहां की भूमि अच्छी है *yahán ki bhúmi achchhí hai*, 'the soil of this place is good'; अब की बेर देखूंगा *ab ki ber dekhúngá*, 'I will see this turn;' मैं उधर से आता था *main udhar se átá thá*, 'I was coming from there;' यह आज का काम है कि कल का *yah áj ká kám hai ki kal ká*, 'is this to-day's work or to-morrow's?' कहां को जाओगे *kahán ko jáoge*, 'where will you go?'

297. Many adjectives and pronouns in the inflected form serve as adverbs, and sometimes in the uninflected form likewise ; as, धीरे चलो *dhíre chalo*, 'go gently;' वह बिरले आता है *wah birle átá hai*, 'he seldom comes ;' इस को थोड़े थोड़े सरकाओ *is ko thore thore sarkáo*, 'move this gradually aside;' पेड़ों को सीधे लगाते जाओ *peron ko sídhe lagáte jáo*, 'go on planting the trees straight;' तुम अपना काम कैसे करते हो *tum apná kám kaise karte ho*, 'how are you doing your work?'; जैसा मैं पढ़ता हूं वैसे तुम भी पढ़ो *jaisá main parhtá hún waise tum bhí parho*, 'as I am reading so do you also read;' यह पाठ बड़ा कठिन है *yah páth bará kathin hai*, 'this lesson is very difficult.'

298. Nouns in the ablative case have often an adverbial sense, as in other languages ; thus, वह बड़ी आसकत से काम करता है *wah barí ásakat se kám kartá hai*, 'he works very lazily'; जो राजा बुद्धि से चलता है सो सुख से राज्य करता है *jo rájá buddhi se chaltá hai so sukh se rájy kartá hai*, 'the king that acts wisely reigns happily.' करके *karke* is used with nouns, and even with adjectives and adverbs, with the same effect; as, प्रेम और सत्यता करके व्यवहार करो *prem aur satyatá karke vyavahár karo*, 'act lovingly and ruly'; वह ज्यों त्यों करके निकल गया *wah jyon tyon karke nikal gayá*, 'he, by some means or other, escaped.'

PREPOSITIONS.

उपसर्ग *upasarg.* *

299. The following prepositions are, for the most part, formed from nouns or adjectives, and are used in government with nouns or pronouns causing them to be put in the genitive case masculine form with के *ke.* They are nearly all nouns in the locative case that have dropped the case ending, and hence the के *ke* which precedes them in their government of nouns and pronouns. Thus the nouns आगा *ágá,* 'the front,' 'the forepart,' पीछा *pichhá,* 'the rear,' 'the hinder part,' put in the locative case, become, आगे में *áge men,* पीछे में *pichhe men;* if a noun precede them in the genitive it will regularly take के; as, घर के आगे में *ghar ke áge men,* or dropping the *men, ghar ke áge,* 'in front of the house.' etc.

300. With the exception of बिन or बिना, the prepositions almost invariably follow the nouns they govern. Placing them before the words they govern is an idiom almost confined to Urdu, and to poetry; सहित समाज occurs in the Rámáyaṇ.

आगे *áge,* in front, before, beyond.
पीछे *pichhe,* behind, after, afterwards.
ऊपर *úpar,* above, on, over.
नीचे *niche,* under, beneath.
भीतर *bhitar,* in, within.

सन्मुख *sanmukh,* }
सामने *sámne,* } facing, in front.
साक्षात *sákshát,* before, in presence.
लिये *liye,* for, account of, because.
बिन *bin,* }
बिना *biná,* } without, except, unless.

---

* उपसर्ग *upasarg* is scarcely a correct term for preposition as we understand the word; it is applied in Sanskrit to inseparable prefixes that are added to roots to modify or extend their meaning. See 334. The above prepositions, being in reality, inflected nouns or adjectives, there is no term for them answering exactly to our word ' preposition.'

बाहर *báhar,*
बाहिर *báhir,* } out, without.

बीच, *bích,* in, among, during.

निकट *nikaṭ,*
समीप *samíp,* } near, at hand.

पास *pás,* at the side of, by, with.

संग *sang,*
साथ *sáth,*
समेत *samet,* } with, along with, together.

समान *samán,* like, similar, same.

द्वारा *dwárá,* through, by means of.

विषय *vishay,* relating to, regarding.

बदले *badle,* instead, in exchange.

विरुद्ध *viruddh,* contrary, opposite, averse. [endowed with.

सहित *sahit,* with, possessed of,

रहित *rahit,* without, devoid of, destitute of.

301. Some of the prepositions, as सहित, रहित, समेत, सुधां, and a few more, are peculiar in not requiring the sign of the genitive before them, and they are sometimes written in composition with the words they govern; thus, जल सहित *jal sahit,* 'with water,' 'having water ;' ज्ञानरहित *gyánrahit,* 'without knowledge.' There are many also that may, in certain cases, dispense with the sign of the genitive ; thus, वह राजा समान बड़ी धूम धाम से निकला *wah rájá samán baṛí dhúm-dhám se nikalá,* 'he came forth like a king with great noise and parade ;' विद्या द्वारा उस ने जीत लिया *vidyá dwárá us ne jít liyá,* 'he gained the victory through knowledge.'

302. The personal and demonstrative pronouns are, with many prepositions used sometimes without the sign of the case as, इस पीछे *is píchhe,* 'after this ;' उस पास *us pás,* 'by or with him'; मुझ पास *mujh pás,* 'by or with me'; किस लिये *kis liye,* 'for whom or for what reason'; उस बिना *us biná,* 'without that.'

303. CONJUNCTIONS, यौगिक शब्द *yaugik śabd.*

1. COPULATIVE, मेलवाचक *melaváchak.*	2. DISJUNCTIVE, भिन्नवाचक *bhinnaváchak.*
और *aur,* and, also.	अथवा *athwá,* or, or else.
कि *ki,* that, for, because.	किन्तु *kintu,* but.

तो *to*, then.
फिर *phir*, again, moreover, then.
पुन *pun*, } again, on the other
पुनर *punar*, } hand.
भी *bhí*, also, even, too.
अथ *ath*, thus, then, so, now.*

क्या-क्या *kyá-kyá*, either-or, whether-or.
परन्तु *parantu*, but, however.
वा *wá*, whether, or.
चाहे-चाहे *cháhe-cháhe*, whether-or.
यदि *yadi*, } if.
जो *jo*, }

INTERJECTIONS.

304. विस्मयादिबोधक शब्द *bismayádibodhak śabd.*

हे *he !* the common respectful vocative.

ओ *O !* हो *Ho !* vocative interjections corresponding with the English O !, Ho ! They may be used as interjections of reminiscence also.

अजी *ají*, is less respectful than हे and is frequently used to express familiarity or friendship.

अरे *are*, अबे *abe*, रे *re*, are also vocative, but scarcely respectful, certainly less so then the preceding. They are frequently used to express contempt and change their terminations into ई *í* when the object is feminine; as, अरे लड़के *are larke*, 'O boy !' अरी लड़की *arí larkí*, 'O girl !'

धिक *dhik*, 'shame !' 'fie !' expresses aversion, contempt.
धन्य धन्य *dhanya dhanya*, 'how fortunate !' 'admirable !' 'well done !'
बाप रे *báp re*, (literally, 'O father.') 'dreadful !' 'Oh me !'
जय जय *jay jay*, 'huzza !' 'bravo !' 'victory !'
त्राह त्राह *tráh tráh*, or त्राहि त्राहि *tráhi tráhi*, 'save ! save !'

---

* अथ is an inceptive particle used at the beginning of a book, chapter, or narrative ; it is opposed to इति *íti*, which is used at the end of a book, chapter, or quotation signifying that it is ended.'

याय याय *háe háe*, 'alas! alas!'

लो *lo*, 'lo!' 'behold!'

दूर *dúr*, 'avaunt!' 'begone!'

चुप *chup*, 'hush!' 'silence!'

फिश *phis*, 'pish!' 'pshaw!'

ऊः *úh*, 'oh!' expressive of sudden pain or distress.

हा हा *há há*, 'alas!' 'woe!' expressive of surprise or grief.

छी *chhí*, or छी छी *chhí chhí*, 'fie!' 'tush!' 'tut!' expressive of reproach, dislike, or contempt.

CHAPTER VIII.

NUMERALS, संख्या *sankhyá.*

1. CARDINALS.

305. The cardinal numbers from one to a hundred are somewhat irregular; they are, with their corresponding figures, exhibited in the following tables.

1	१	एक	*ek.*		15	१५	पन्द्रह	*pandrah.*
2	२	दो	*do.*		16	१६	सोलह	*solah.*
3	३	तीन	*tín.*		17	१७	सत्रह	*satrah.*
4	४	चार	*chár.*		18	१८	अठारह	*athárah.*
5	५	पांच	*pánch.*		19	१९	उनीस	*unís.*
6	६	छः	*chhah.*		20	२०	बीस	*bís.*
7	७	सात	*sát.*		21	२१	इकाईस	*ikaís.*
8	८	आठ	*áth*		22	२२	बाईस	*báís.*
9	९	नौ	*náu.*		23	२३	तेईस	*teís.*
10	१०	दस	*das.*		24	२४	चौबीस	*chaubís.*
11	११	ग्यारह	*egyárah.*		25	२५	पचीस	*pachís.*
12	१२	बारह	*bárah.*		26	२६	छब्बीस	*chhabbís.*
13	१३	तेरह	*terah.*		27	२७	सताईस	*satáís.*
14	१४	चौदह	*chaudah.*		28	२८	अठाईस	*atháís.*

29	२९	उन्तीस	untís.	61	६१	एकसठ	eksaṭh.
30	३०	तीस	tís.	62	६२	बासठ	básaṭh.
31	३१	इकतीस	iktís.	63	६३	तिरसठ	tirsaṭh.
32	३२	बतीस	batís.	64	६४	चौंसठ	chauṅsaṭh.
33	३३	तैंतीस	teṅtís.	65	६५	पैंसठ	paiṅsaṭh.
34	३४	चौंतीस	chauṅtís.	66	६६	छियासठ	chhiyásaṭh.
35	३५	पैंतीस	paiṅtís.	67	६७	सरसठ	sarsaṭh.
36	३६	छत्तीस	chhattís.	68	६८	अड़सठ	aṛsaṭh.
37	३७	सैंतीस	saiṅtís.	69	६९	उन्हत्तर	unhattar.
38	३८	अठतीस	aṭhtís.	70	७०	सत्तर	sattar.
39	३९	उंतालीस	uṅtális.	71	७१	एकहत्तर	ekhattar.
40	४०	चालीस	chális.	72	७२	बहत्तर	bahattar.
41	४१	इकतालीस	iktális.	73	७३	तिहत्तर	tihattar.
42	४२	बयालीस	bayális.	74	७४	चौहत्तर	chauhattar.
43	४३	तैंतालीस	teṅtális.	75	७५	पचहत्तर	pachhattar.
44	४४	चौआलीस	chauális.	76	७६	छिहत्तर	chhihattar.
45	४५	पैंतालीस	paiṅtális.	77	७७	सतहत्तर	sathattar.
46	४६	छियालीस	chhiyális.	78	७८	अठहत्तर	aṭhhattar.
47	४७	सैंतालीस	saiṅtális.	79	७९	उनासी	unásí.
48	४८	अठतालीस	aṭhtális.	80	८०	अस्सी	assí.
49	४९	उनचास	unchás.	81	८१	एक्यासी	ekyásí.
50	५०	पचास	pachás.	82	८२	बयासी	bayásí.
51	५१	एक्यावन	ekyáwan.	83	८३	तिरासी	tirásí.
52	५२	बावन	báwan.	84	८४	चौरासी	chaurásí.
53	५३	तिरपन	tirpan.	85	८५	पचासी	pachásí.
54	५४	चौवन	chauwan.	86	८६	छियासी	chhiyásí.
55	५५	पचपन	pachpan.	87	८७	सत्तासी	sattásí.
56	५६	छप्पन	chhappan.	88	८८	अट्ठासी	aṭhásí.
57	५७	सत्तावन	sattáwan.	89	८९	नवासी	nawásí.
58	५८	अट्ठावन	aṭhháwan.	90	९०	नब्बे	nawwe.
59	५९	उनसठ	unsaṭh.	91	९१	एक्यानवे	ekyánawe.
60	६०	साठ	sáṭh.	92	९२	बानवे	bánawe.

93	६३	तिरानवे	*tiránawe.*	97	६७	सत्तानवे	*sattánawe.*
94	६४	चौरानवे	*chauránawe*	98	६८	अट्टानवे	*atthánawe.*
95	६५	पचानवे	*pachánawe.*	99	६९	निन्यानवे	*ninyánawe.*
96	६६	छियानवे	*chhiyánawe.*	100	१००	सौ	*sau.*

306. Some slight variations in the way of spelling some of the cardinal numbers may occasionally be noticed ; the following differ somewhat from the corresponding numbers in the above list :—

छ six, नव nine, ग्यारह eleven, उनीस nineteen, एकईस twenty-one, पच्चीस twenty-five, एकतीस thirty-one, अड़तीस thirty-eight, चवालीस forty-four, अड़तालीस forty-eight, एकावन fifty-one, त्रेपन fifty-three, एकसठ sixty-one, तरेसठ sixty-three, पचहत्तर seventy-five, एक्यानवे ninety-one, पच्यानवे ninety-five, etc.

307. The series of cardinals above one hundred is continued as in English, except that the conjunction, और 'and,' is generally omitted ; as, एक सौ दो *ek sau do,* 'one hundred (and) two'; दो सौ बीस *do sau bís,* 'two hundred (and) twenty'; तीन सहस्र पांच सौ दस *tín sahasra páńch sau das,* 'three thousand five hundred (and) ten.'

308. The word एक used immediately after any other number may convey the meaning of 'about,' or 'one more or less than,' that number; as, पन्द्रह एक *pandrah ek,* 'about fifteen'; सौ एक *sau ek,* 'about a hundred.'

309. In many instances, especially where any emphasis on the number is intended, when एक is used with a number to imply 'near,' or 'about' that number, the noun is placed before the numerals; thus, जन दस एक *jan das ek,* 'about ten persons.'

310. Indefiniteness in number may be expressed by using two numerals together, without any conjunction between them, thus, पांच छः घर *páńch chhah ghar,* 'five (or) six houses';

दस पांच बरस में *das pánch baras men*, 'in five (or) ten years'; दस ग्यारह गाय *das gyárah gáe*, 'ten or eleven cows'; सौ दो सौ मनुष्य *sau do sau manushya*, 'one or two hundred men'; लाख सवा लाख भेड़ *lákh sawá lákh bher*, 'a lakh or a lakh and a quarter of sheep.'

311. 2. AGGREGATE OR COLLECTIVE NUMBERS.

गंडा *gandá*, a four.

गाही *gáhí*, a five.

कोड़ी *korí*, a score.

चालीसा *chálísá*, a forty.

सैकड़ा *saikrá*, a hundred.

सहस्र *sahasra*, a thousand.

लाख *lákh*, a hundred thousand.

नियुत *niyut*, a million.

कोटि *koti*, करोड़ *karor*, } ten millions.

312. 3. ORDINALS.

पहिला *pahilá*, first.

दूसरा *dúsrá*, second.

तीसरा *tísrá*, third.

चौथा *chauthá*, fourth.

पांचवां *pánchwán*, fifth.

छठवां *chhathwán*, sixth.

सातवां *sátwán*, seventh.

आठवां *áthwán*, eighth.

नवां *nawán*, ninth.

दसवां *daswán*, tenth.

ग्यारहवां *egyárahwán*, eleventh.

बारहवां *bárahwán*, twelfth.

313. After the fourth the ordinals are regularly formed by addding वां to the cardinals. Being in reality adjectives, they are declined like adjectives ending in आ *á*; thus, in the oblique cases of the masculine, आ *á* (of the first four) and वां *wán* become, respectively, ए *e* and वें *wen*, and when used to qualify feminine nouns, they change to ई *í* and वीं *wín*; as, पहिला लड़का *pahilá larká*, 'the first boy'; पहिले लड़के से *pahile larke se*, 'from the first boy'; दूसरी लड़की *dúsrí larkí*, 'the second girl'; तीसरी लड़की का *tísrí larkí ká*, 'of the third girl'; सातवां मास *sátwán más*, 'the seventh month'; सातवें मास में *sátwen más men*, 'in the seventh month'; सातवीं घोड़ी पर *sátwín ghorí par*, 'on the seventh mare.'

314. Distributives are formed by repeating the number, whether cardinal or ordinal; thus, दो दो *do do*, 'by twos,' 'two each'; पांच पांच *pánch pánch*, 'by fives,' 'five to each'; दसवां दसवां *daswán daswán*, 'every tenth'; बारहवां बारहवां *bárahwán bárahwán*, 'every twelfth.'

315. Proportional numbers are formed by the addition of गुणा *guṇá*, sometimes गुण *guṇ*, to the cardinals, which in some instances are altered in form; thus, दूगुणा *dúguṇá*, 'twofold,' 'double'; तिगुणा *tiguṇá*, 'three times as much,' 'threefold'; सातगुण *sátguṇ*, or सतगुणा *satguṇá*, 'sevenfold,' 'seven times as much'; सौगुणा *sauguṇá* or सौगुण *sauguṇ*, 'a hundred fold.'

316. To the cardinals, or, in some cases, to slightly altered forms of them, लड़ा *laṛá* (from लड़ 'a string,' as of pearls, 'a strand of rope or cord') is added to express fold or reduplication, but this is allowable only when the idea of a 'string' or 'strand' is, literally or metaphorically, required; as तिलड़ा *tilaṛá*, 'triple'; चौलड़ा *chaulaṛá*, ' of four strings,' 'fourfold.'

317. Time or turn is expressed by adding बार *bár* or बेर *ber* to the cardinals, when the number of times is to be indicated, and to the ordinals, when any special time or turn is referred to ; as, चार बेर *chár ber*, 'four times'; नौ बार *nau bár*, 'nine times'; अनेक बेर *anek ber*, 'many times'; दूसरी बार *dúsrí bár*, ' the second time'; तीसरी बेर *tísrí ber*, 'the third time.' (बेर is a feminine noun; Thompson erroneously gives it as masculine.)

4. Fractional Numbers.

318. पौने *paune*, signifying 'a quarter less'; सवा *sawá*, 'a quarter more'; and साढ़े *sáṛhe*, 'a half more,' are used with the cardinal numbers to express fractions. The following table exhibits the use of them alone or with whole numbers, and in the expression of fractional parts of a rupee.

¼	पाव, चौचाई, *páo,* or *chauthái.*	पाव आना *páo áná,* quarter of an anna,	ﻝ
⅓	तिहाई *tihái.*		
½	आधा *ádhá,* in compos: आध.	आध आना *ádh áná,* half an anna,	ﻝﻪ
¾	पौने, पौन, *paune,* or *paun.*	पौन आना *paun áná,* ¾ of an anna,	ﻝﻪﻪ
1¼	सवा *sawá.*	सवा आना *sawá áná,* 1¼ of an anna,	ﻝﻪ
1½	डेढ़ *derh.*	डेढ़ आना *derh áná,* an anna and a half,	ﻝﻪ
1¾	पौने दो *paune do.*	पौने दो आने *paune do áne,* one and ¾ of an anna,	ﻝﻪﻪ
2¼	सवा दो *sawá do.*	सवा दो आने *sawá do áne,* 2¼ annas,	ﻝﻪ
2½	अढ़ाई ठाई, *arhái* or *dhái.*	अढ़ाई आने *arhái áne,* 2½ annas,	ﻝﻪ
3½	साढ़े तीन *sárhe tín.*	साढ़े तीन आने *sárhe tín áne,* 3½ annas,	ﻝﻪ
75	पौने सौ *paune sau.*	पौने सौ रुपैये *paune sau rupaiye,* 75 rupees,	७५)
125	सवा सौ *sawá sau.*	सवा सौ रुपैये *sawá sau rupaiye,* 125 rupees,	१२५)
150	डेढ़ सौ *derh sau.*	डेढ़ सौ रुपैये *derh sau rupaiye,* 150 rupees,	१५०)
175	पौने दो सौ *paune do sau.*	पौने दो सौ रुपैये *paune do sau rupaiye,* 175 rupees,	१७५)
250	अढ़ाई सौ *arhái sau.*	अढ़ाई सौ रुपैये *arhái sau rupaiye,* 250 rupees,	२५०)

319. The following are the symbols for pice, annas, and rupees :—

ﾘ one pice, ﾘﾘ two pice, ﾘﾘﾘ three pice ; ﾗ) one anna, ﾗ) two annas, ﾗ) three annas, ﾘ) four annas, ﾘ) eight annas, ﾘﾘ) twelve annas ; ﾘﾗ)ﾘ five annas and one pice, ﾘﾗ)ﾘﾘ six annas and two pice, ﾘﾗ)ﾘﾘ fifteen annas and three pice ; ૧) one rupee, ૫૦ﾘﾘ) fifty rupees ond eight annas, ૬૩૪ﾘﾗ)ﾘﾘ six hundred and thirty four rupees ten annas and nine pies.

CHAPTER IX.

DIVISIONS OF TIME.

320.   1. *Days of the Week.*

Days.	Sanskrit Names.	Common Hindi forms.	Signification.
Sun.	रविवार *ravivár*	इतवार *itwár* *	day of the Sun.
Mon.	सोमवार *somavár*	सोमवार *somwár*	„ „ Moon.
Tues.	मङ्गलवार *mangalavár*	मनगल *mangal*	„ „ Mars.
Wedn.	बुधवार *budhavár.*	बुध *budh*	„ „ Mercury.
Thur.	बृहस्पतिवार *vrihas-pativár*	बिफै *biphai*	„ „ Jupiter.
Frid.	शुक्रवार *śukravár*	सुक *suk*	„ „ Venus.
Sat.	शनिवार *śanivár.*	सनीचर *sanichar.*	„ „ Saturn.

321. The day of twenty-four hours is divided into eight parts, each of which is termed a पहर *pahar*, or watch of three hours duration. There are thus four watches of the day and four of the night, the first of each four beginning, respectively, at six o'clock in the morning and at six in the evening ; they are known as the first, the second, the third, or the fourth watch.

---

* इतवार, contraction of आदित्यवार *ádityavár*.

322.   2. *Months of the Year.*

वैशाख *vaisákh*,	April—May.	कार्त्तिक *kárttik*,	October—Novr.
ज्येष्ठ *jyeshth*,	} May—June.	आयह्रायण *ágraháyan*,	} Novr.—Dec.
जेठ *jeth*,		अगहण *ajhan*,	
आषाढ *áshárh*,	June—July.	पौष *paush*,	} Dec.—Jan.
श्रावण *srávan*,	July—August.	पूस *pús*,	
भाद्र *bhádra*,	} Augt.—Sept.	माघ *mágh*,	Jan.—Feb.
भादों *bhádon*,		फाल्गुन *phálgun*,	} Feb.—Mar.
आश्विन *áswin*,	} Sept.—Oct.	फागुन *phágun*,	
आसिन *ásin*,		चैत्र *chaitra*,	} March—April.
कुँआर *kunár*,		चैत *chait*,	

323.   The solar year of the Hindús is divided into twelve equal parts or months; but as they reckon their dates, not according to this division, but from the moon which terminates in the month, they may be called lunar mouths.

324.   The month is reckoned from full moon to full moon, there being 15 days for the waxing half (सुदी *sudí*), and 15 for the waning half (बदी *badí*). The word पक्ष *paksh*, answering in part to our fortnight, is also given to the semi-lunations; the fortnight of the waxing moon being termed शुक्लपक्ष *suklpaksh*, or bright half, and the fortnight of the waning moon, कृष्णपक्ष *krishnpaksh*, or dark half of the month.

325.   For domestic, commercial, and civil purposes in general, the Hindús enumerate the days, or तिथि *tithi*, as they are called, from one to fifteen twice in the course of the lunar month, so that the date of any given day, according to this system, is never higher than fifteen. For instance, a letter, or any not very important document might be dated thus,—मिती वैशाख सुदी २ दुस्रज, which would signify, ' *Date, Vaisákh, the lighted half, second day*; ' or thus,—मिती श्रावण बदी चौदश बुधवार, ' *Date, Srávan, the 14th of the dark half, Wednesday.*'

326. In matters of great importance, dates are reckoned according to the solar siderial system.

3. *The Seasons of the Year.*

327. The Hindús divide the year into six seasons, though there are but three distinctly marked seasons on the plains of India, viz., the hot season, the rainy season, and the cold season. The following table exhibits these divisions in detail.

Name of Season.	Nature.	Comprising the months.	Coinciding with the time from.
बसन्त *basant,*	Mild, or spring season,	चेत and वैशाख	15th Mar.—15th May.
ग्रीष्म *gríshm,*	Hot, or summer season,	जेठ „ आषाढ़	15th May—15th July.
वर्षा *varshá,* बरसात *barsát,*	Rainy season,	सावन „ भाद	15th July—15th Sept.
शरद *sarad,*	Sultry, or autumn season,	आश्विन „ कार्तिक	15th Sept.—15th Nov.
हेमन्त *hemant,*	Cold, or winter season,	अगहन „ पूस	15th Nov.—15th Jan.
शिशिर *sisir,*	Season of hoar frost,	माघ „ फागुन	15th Jan.—15th Mar.

328. This division of the seasons is more artificial than natural, and the assigning of the months to them is, of course, only approximate, and applies more especially to the northern part of India.

329. There is another mode of reckoning according to which the spring season begins with the month *Phágun,* coinciding with the middle of February, which makes all the seasons a month earlier.

4. *Ages and Eras.*

330 The Hindús believe in four ages, viz., सत्ययुग *satyayug*, त्रेता *tretá*, द्वापर *dwápar*, कलियुग *kaliyug;* which may be regarded as corresponding with the golden age, or age of truth, the silver age, the brazen age, and the iron age, or age of sin, of other nations. The *kaliyug*, or age of sin, is that in which we live; it is conjectured to have begun 3102 years before the christian era, and it is supposed that the number of its years will be 432000, after which the world will be destroyed. The *kaliyug* is never employed to indicate the year in the affairs of common life.

331. The era called संवत् *sanvat* is commonly used in northern India ; it is said to have begun with either the accession or the death of a hero, Vikramáditya, who reigned sovereign of Ougein, the ancient capital of northern India, and is supposed to have died about 57 B. C.

332. Another era called शाका *sáká* is in use, and is said to have been established by a sovereign whose name or whose capital was शालवाहन *Sálaváhan.* This era is supposed to have begun 78 years after the birth of Christ.

CHAPTER X.

ON THE DERIVATION OF WORDS.

शब्दोत्पत्ति *sabdotpatti.*

333. Derivative words are divided by native grammarians into two classes ; those of the first class are termed कृदन्त *kridant,* or words derived from verbal roots, and those of the second class तद्धित *taddhit,* or words derived from nouns, or from any other part of speech but the verb. This classification is borrowed from the Sanskrit and a thorough comprehension of it would imply

considerable acquaintance with that language.   It will better suit
our purpose to consider in order first the prefixes and then the
affixes that are added to words to form new words.

1. PREFIXES, उपसर्ग upasarg.

334.   The following Sanskrit prefixes are not in Hindí us-
able, like prepositions, at the speaker's discretion with any word
he may please, but are used with certain defined words whose
meaning they modify, and make them into new words, derived
words, in fact.   In this they quite differ from the corresponding
Greek prefixes, which are also prepositions.

अ a, 'in,' 'un;' a negative particle implying privation, negation;
as, ज्ञान gyán, knowledge, अज्ञान ignorance; धर्म dharm, virtue,
religion, अधर्म injustice, irreligion.   As a negative prefixed to
words beginning with a vowel, अ is changed to अन; as, आदि
ádi, first, prior, अनादि without a beginning; अन्त ant, end,
limit, अनन्त endless, illimitable.

अति ati, 'beyond,' 'over'; implies general excess; as काल kál,
time, अतिकाल delay; गुप्त gupt, secret, अतिगुप्त very secret.

अधि adhi, 'over,' 'above,' 'upon'; implies superiority in time,
quality, or quantity; as, मास más, a month, अधिमास an inter-
calary month; राज ráj (in compos :) 'a king,' अधिराज a great
king.

अनु anu, 'after,' 'like'; implies sequence or resemblance in time,
place, or degree; as रूप rúp, form, shape, अनुरूप like, resembling; दिन din, a day, अनुदिन day after day, every day.

अन्तर् antar, 'within'; implies centricity or concealment; as द्वार
a door, अन्तर्द्वार a private door; यामिन yámin, who stops or
restrains, अन्तर्यामी heart-searching, an epithet of God.

अप apa, 'away,' 'from'; implies privation, separation, detraction,
contrariety; as, यश yaś, fame, renown, अपयश infamy, dishonor;

लक्षण *lakshaṇ*, a mark, sign, अपलक्षण a bad sign, a bad omen; शब्द *śabd*, a sound, a word, अपशब्द ungrammatical language.

अभि *abhi*, 'towards'; implies tendency to, motion towards, superiority in; as, मत *mat*, thought, opinion, अभिमत approved, accepted; लष *lash*, to like, अभिलाष wish, desire.

अव *ava*, 'from,' 'down from,' 'away'; implying deprivation, disparagement, diffusion; as, गीत *gít*, a song, अवगीत reproach, blame, satire; गुण *guṇ*, a quality, attribute, अवगुण a defect, blemish.

आ *á*, 'to,' 'unto'; implies limit, extent, as, भोग *bhog*, pleasure, enjoyment, आभोग repletion, satiety; ज्ञा *jñá* (in Hindí, *gyá*) to know, आज्ञा an order, a command. When prefixed to words connected with गमन *gaman*, the act of going, दान *dán*, a gift, it has the effect of reversing their meaning; as, आगमन coming, arriving; आदान taking, acceptance.

उत् *ut*, or उद् *ud*, 'up,' 'above'; implies superiority in place, power, degree; पद् *pad*, to go, उत्पत्ति birth, creation; आहरण *áharaṇa*, taking, inducing, उदाहरण an example, an illustration.

उप *upa*, 'near'; implies, vicinity, resemblance, etc., in an inferior degree; as, पति *pati*, a husband, उपपति a paramour, वन *van*, a wood, उपवन a grove.

कु *ku*, 'bad,' 'evil'; implies depreciation, disparagement; as, डौल *ḍaul*, form, shape, कुडौल deformed, ill-shaped; पुत्र *putra*, a son, कुपुत्र, a bad or disobedient son.

दुर् *dur*, 'hard,' 'difficult'; a depreciative particle implying what is painful, laborious, inferior; as, अन्त *ant*, end, दुरन्त ending ill; गति *gati*, state, condition, दुर्गति poverty, indigence.

नि *ni*, 'down,' 'under'; implies failure, hindrance, etc.; as, पात *pát*, a falling, निपात death, dying; वारण *váraṇ*, obstacle, opposition, निवारण prohibition, hindering.

निर् *nir*, ' out'; implying freedom from, privation; as, आकार *ákár*, form, shape, निराकार having no form, incorporeal; दोष *dosh*, a fault, a crime, निर्दोष faultless, innocent.

परा *pará*, ' back '; implies reaction, return, retreat; as, जय *jay*, victory, triumph, पराजय defeat, overthrow; मर्ष *marsh*, counsel, परामर्ष discrimination, judgment, advice.

परि *pari*, ' around'; implies completeness, or intensifies the idea; as, पूर्ण *púrṇ*, full, परिपूर्ण completely full; जन *jan*, a man, a person, परिजन family, dependants. The influence of परि as a prefix is, in most cases, hardly perceptible.

प्र *pra*, ' forth,' ' forward'; implies advance in time, place, or degree; as, स्थान *sthán*, a place, प्रस्थान going forth, march; यत्न *yatn*, endeavour, effort, प्रयत्न persevering endeavour, continued effort. The influence of this prefix on the sense of the word is often scarcely perceptible.

प्रति *prati*, ' against,' ' back again'; implies reiteration, reaction, opposition; as, कर्म *karmma*, act, action, प्रतिकर्म retaliation, requital; शब्द *śabd*, sound, voice, प्रतिशब्द echo.

वि *vi*, ' away,' ' apart'; implies separation, change, dispersion; as, देशी *deśí*, belonging to a country, indigenous, विदेशी foreign, a foreigner; योग *yog*, union, junction, वियोग disunion, separation. In some cases वि seems not to affect the sense of the word to which it is prefixed.

स *sa*, ' with,' contraction of सह *saha*; implies possessed of, endowed with; as, देह *deh*, the body, सदेह with a body, bodily; गुण *guṇ*, a quality, property, सगुण endowed with qualities.

सं *saṅ*, or सम् *sam*, ' with'; implies connection, unity, participation; as, योग *yog* junction, meeting, संयोग intimate union, आगत *ágat*, come, arrived, समागत met, encountered, united. This prefix must not be confounded with सम (without the mark of *hal*) which is an adjective meaning 'like,' whence समदुःख *samaduhkh*, having like pain, sympathizing; समदर्शी *samadarśí*, viewing all alike, impartial.

सु *su*, 'well,' 'good'; implies goodness, excellence; as, जाति *játi*, caste, tribe, class, सुजाति of a good caste or tribe; पुत्र *putra*, a son, सुपुत्र a good or dutiful son. ✦

2. AFFIXES, अनुबन्ध *anubandh*.

335. We shall notice first the principal affixes used in forming nouns; secondly, those that are used in forming adjectives; and in the third place describe generally the formation of verbs from Sanskrit roots.

DERIVATIVE NOUNS.

336. *a.* NOUNS EXPRESSIVE OF AGENCY IN GENERAL, कर्त्तृवाचक *kartriváchak*.

हारा *hárá*, (or its modifications, आरा *árá*, हार *hár*, आर *ár*, and, probably, र *r*) added to the inflected form of the infinitive of verbs, and to the nominative singular of substantives, which must be inflected if it terminates in आ *á*; thus, मारना *márná*, 'to strike,' मारनेहारा *márnehárá*, 'one who strikes'; लिखन *likhan*, 'any writing,' लिखनहारा *likhanhárá*, 'a writer'; बनज *banaj*, 'trade,' 'traffic,' बनजारा *banjárá*, 'a trader' (in grain); चूरी *chúri*, or चुरी *churí*, 'a kind of bracelet,' चुरीहार *churíhár*, 'a seller of bracelets'; चाम *chám*, leather,' चमार *chamár*, 'a worker in leather'; लोहा *lohá*, 'iron,' लोहार *lohár*, 'a blacksmith.'

---

* The resemblance between some of the foregoing prefixes and some of the Greek and Latin prepositions is obvious:—अ, *a*; अन्तर, *inter.*; अप, ἀπό; अभि, ἐπί; आ, *ad*; उप, ὑπό; दुर, δυσ; परा, παρά; परि, περί, *per*; प्र, πρό, *pro*; सम, σύν, *cum*; सु, εὖ.

वाला *wálá*, (or its modifications, वाला *álá*, वाल *wál*, वार *wár*, वा *wá*,) corresponds in meaning and use and in almost all respects with the preceding affix; thus, दूध *dúdh*, 'milk,' दूधवाला *dúdhwálá*, 'a milkman'; बेचना *bechná*, 'to sell,' बेचनेवाला *bechnewálá*, 'a seller'; गौ *gau*, 'a cow,' ग्वाला *gwálá*, 'a cowherd'; रखना *rakhná*, 'to place,' 'to keep,' रखवाल *rakhwál*, 'a keeper'; गांव *gánw*, 'a village,' गंवार *ganwár*, 'a villager,' 'churl'; मछ *machchh*, 'a fish,' मछवा *machchhwá*, 'a fisherman.' हारा and वाला are among the most useful and extensively applied particles in Hindí; they correspond in great measure with the English terminations *man*, *er*, as in *ploughman*, *dairyman*, *thinker*, *speaker*, etc. When used with nouns they frequently indicate ownership, or occupation; as, बैलवाला *bailwálá*, 'the owner of the bullock'; तेलवाला *telwálá*, 'an oilman'; कपड़ावाला *kapṛáwálá*, 'a draper.' These affixes may also be used with the inflected infinitive of a verb to form idiomatically a sort of future participle; thus, वह जानेहारा है *wah jánehárá hai*, 'he is about to go'; वह मरनेवाली है *wah marnewálí hai*, 'she is about to die.'

बक *ak*, added generally to the root of a verb; as, पालना *pálná*, 'to cherish,' 'to protect,' पालक *pálak*, 'a cherisher,' 'a protector'; पूजना *pújná*, 'to worship,' पूजक *pújak*, 'a worshipper'; सेवना *sevná*, 'to serve,' 'to attend on,' सेवक *sevak*, 'a servant'; रक्षा *rakshá*, 'care,' 'defence,' रक्षक *rakshak*, 'a guardian,' 'a protector.'

इया *iya*, added to nouns and verbal roots; as आढ़त *áṛhat*, 'agency' 'brokerage,' अढ़तिया *aṛhatiyá*, 'an agent,' 'a broker'; जड़ना *jaṛná*, 'to bestud, set jewels,' जड़िया *jaṛiya*, 'a jeweller'; लखना *lakhná*, 'to see, behold,' लखिया *lakhiyá*, 'a beholder, spectator'; मक्खन *makkhan*, 'butter,' मक्खनिया *makkhaniyá*, 'a butterman.'

कर्त्ता *karttá*, affixed to nouns ; as, पालन *pálan*, 'rearing,' 'guarding.' पालनकर्त्ता *pálankarttá*, 'a provider,' 'a protector'; त्राण *trán*, 'safety,' 'deliverance,' त्राणकर्त्ता *tránkarttá*, 'a saviour,' 'a deliverer'; सृष्टि *srishṭi*, 'creation,' सृष्टिकर्त्ता *srishṭikarttá*, 'the creator,' 'God.'

दाता *dátá*, affixed to nouns ; as, जन्म *janm*, 'birth,' 'life,' जन्मदाता *janmdátá*, 'giver of life,' 'God'; मुक्ति *mukti*, 'deliverance,' 'release,' मुक्तिदाता *muktidátá*,' 'a deliverer,' 'a saviour.'

पाल *pál* and पालक *pálak*, added to substantives ; as, द्वार *dwár*, 'a door,' 'a gate,' द्वारपाल *dwárpál*, 'a porter,' 'a warder'; अश्वा *aśwá*, 'a horse,' अश्वापाल *aśwápál*, 'a groom,' 'a hostler'; पृथिवी *prithiví*, 'the earth,' पृथिवीपाल *prithivípál*, 'a ruler,' 'a king'; गो *go*, 'a cow,' गोपाल *gopál*, 'a cowherd.'

वैया *waiyá*, added to verbal roots ; as, उठना *uṭhná*, 'to rise up' उठवैया *uṭhwaiyá*, 'one who rises'; जलना *jalná*, to burn, जलवैया *jalwaiyá*, 'a burner'; जीतना *jítná*, 'to win, conquer,' जीतवैया *jítwaiyá*, 'a winner'; देखना *dekhná*, 'to see,' देखवैया *dekhwaiyá* 'a beholder, an observer.'

337 .*b*. INSTRUMENTAL NOUNS, करणवाचक *karaṇaváchak*.

These denote the means or instrument by which an action may be performed, and are formed as follows :—

नी *ní*, added to verbal roots ; thus, ओढ़ना *orhná*, 'to put on,' 'to wear,' ओढ़नी *orhní*, 'a kind of veil or mantle'; कतरना *katarná*, 'to clip,' 'to cut,' कतरनी *katarní*, 'scissors'; कुरेलना *kurelná*, 'to poke,' कुरेलनी *kurelní*, 'a poker'; घोटना *ghoṭná*, 'to rub,' 'to polish,' घोटनी *ghoṭní*, 'a rubber,' 'a polisher'; खोदना *khodná*, 'to dig,' 'to delve,' खोदनी *khodní*, 'a spade.'

आ *á*, added to verbal roots ; as, घेरना *gherná*, 'to surround,' घेरा *gherá*, 'a fence,' 'a circle'; झूलना *jhúlná*, 'to swing,' झूला

jhúlá, 'a rope to swing on'; फेरना, *phcrná*, 'to turn,' फेरा *phcrá*, 'a roll,' 'a wooden frame for measuring lime, sand, etc.'

Some instrumental nouns are the same in form as the infinitive; as, बेलना *bclná*, 'to roll or spread out,' and बेलना 'a rolling pin'; रमना *ramná*, 'to roam,' 'to range,' and रमना 'a park or enclosure for game.'

338. *c.* ABSTRACT NOUNS, भाववाचक *bhávaváchak.*

These are very numerous and the modes of their formation varied, as will be seen from the following affixes.

आव *áw*, added to verbal roots; as, चढ़ना *charhná*, to ascend, चढ़ाव *charháw*, ascent, rise; बिकना *biná*, to sell, बिकाव *bikáw*, sale, vent; मिलना *milná*, to mix, blend, मिलाव *miláw*, union, accord.

आई *áí*, added to adjectives and verbal roots; as, अधिक *adhik*, exceeding, excessive, अधिकाई *adhikáí*, increase, excess; चतुर *chatur*, cunning, clever, चतुराई *chaturáí*, cleverness, slyness; बोना *bóná*, to sow, बोआई *boáí*, the act of sowing; ठगना *thagná*, to cheat, ठगाई *thagáí*, cheating.

ई *í* added to nouns and to adjectives, is the most extensively used of all the affixes in forming abstract substantives; the following are examples,—लड़का *larká*, a boy, लड़काई *larkáí*, boyhood, childhood; भला *bhalá*, good, भलाई *bhaláí*, goodness, welfare; ऊंचा *únchá*, high, ऊंचाई *únchái*, height; लम्बा *lambá* long, tall, लम्बाई *lambáí*, length.

त्व *twa*, added to nouns and adjectives; as, मनुष्य *manushya*, a man, मनुष्यत्व *manushyatwa*, manhood; स्त्री *strí*, a woman, स्त्रीत्व *strítwa*, womanhood; पुरुष *purush*, a man, male, पुरुषत्व *purushtwa*, manliness; प्रमुख *pramukh*, best, chief, प्रमुखत्व *pramukhtwa* superiority, predominance.

ता *tá*, added to nouns and adjectives ; as, उत्तम *uttam*, good, उत्तमता *uttamtá*, goodness ; कोमल *komal*, soft, mild, कोमलता *komaltá*, softness, mildness ; मित्र *mitra*, a friend, मित्रता *mitratá*, friendship ; प्रधान *pradhán*, a chief, a leader, a noble, प्रधानता *pradhánatá*, supremacy, chieftainship.

पन *pan*, (or its modifications पना *paná*, पा *pá*) added to nouns and adjectives ; as, कुमारा *kúárá*, or कुमारा *kuárá*, an unmarried person, a bachelor, कुमारापन *kuárápan*, or कुमारपन *kuárpan*, celibacy ; रडा *ran̓lá*, a widow, रडापन *randápan*, widowhood ; मोटा *motá*, fat, मोटापा *motápá*, fatness, corpulency.

वट *wat*, added to verbal roots ; as, बनाना *banáná*, to make, बनावट *banáwat*, make, invention ; रंगाना *rangáná*, to color, रंगावट *rangáwat*, color, coloring ; सुखाना *sukháná*, to dry, सुखावट *sukháwat*, dryness.

हट *hat*, added to nouns, adjectives, and the roots of verbs ; as, कड़वा *karwá*, bitter, कड़वाहट *karwáhat*, bitterness ; चिकना *chikná*, oil, grease, चिकनाहट *chiknáhat*, greasiness, sleekness ; चिल्लाना *chilláná*, to cry out, scream, चिल्लाहट *chilláhat*, a scream, a shriek ; झनझनाना *jhanjhanáná*, to gingle, tinkle, झनझनाहट *jhanjhanáhat*, a gingling, tinkling.

Many abstract nouns are the same in form as the root of the verb ; as, दौड़ *daur*, a race, career, from दौड़ना *daurná*, to run ; खेल *khel*, a game, play, from खेलना *khelná*, to play ; बिचार *bichár*, thought, reflection, from बिचारना *bichárná*, to think, consider ; निकाल *nikál*, outlet, exclusion, from निकालना *nikálná*, to exclude.

339.　　　*d.* Diminutive Nouns,
ऊनवाचक *únaváchak.*

A large number of diminutives is formed by simply changing a final आ *á* into ई *í* ; as, रस्सा *rassá*, rope, रस्सी *rassí*, string, cord ; गोला *golá*, a globe, a large ball, गोली *golí*, a bullet, a marble ;

लकड़ा *lakṛá*, timber, लकड़ी, *lakṛí*, wood ; टोकरा *ṭokrá*, a large basket, टोकरी *ṭokrí*, a small basket ; डाला *ḍálá*, a bough, a branch, डाली *ḍálí*, a small branch, a twig.

The following affixes are also used in forming diminutives ;— अक *ak* ; as, मानव *mánav*, a man, मानवक *mánavak*, a little man, a dwarf ; वृक्ष *vriksh*, a tree, वृक्षक *vrikshak*, a small tree.

इया *iyá* ; as, खाट *khát*, a bedstead, खटिया *khaṭiyá*, a little bedstead.

DERIVATIVE ADJECTIVES.

340. Derivative adjectives are, for the most part, formed from nouns by means of affixes ; the most common and useful are subjoined.

ई *í* ; as, ऊन *ún*, wool, ऊनी *úní*, woollen ; धन *dhan*, wealth, धनी *dhaní*, wealthy ; बल *bal*, strength, बली *balí*, strong ; भार *bhár* a weight, burthen, भारी *bhárí*, weighty, heavy ; धर्म *dharm*, virtue, धर्मी *dharmmí*, virtuous.

Hindí abounds with adjectives of the above form: it may here be observed that the termination ई may be added to, perhaps, the greater number of nouns to form adjectives signifying *of* or *formed from* what is indicated by the noun ; it may in like manner be added to most adjectives to form abstract nouns.

इक *ik*, अक *ak* उक *uk* : as, परमार्थ *paramárth*, the best sense, best object, best pursuit. पारमार्थिक *paramárthik*, preferable, most desirable ; प्रमाण *bramán*, proof, प्रामाणिक *prámánik*, creditable ; शरीर *sarír*, the body, शारीरिक *sárírik*, having a body, carnal ; संसार *sansár*, the world. सांसारिक *sánsárik*, worldly ; धर्म *dharm*, virtue, धार्मिक *dhármmik*, virtuous. (Notice that in such formatives as the preceding the first syllable ought to be lengthened ; this may not always be observed, but the Sanskrit rule requires that it should. Some Pandits use both forms, प्रामा-

शिक् and प्रमाशिक. etc.) क्रम *kram*, order, क्रमक *kramak*, orderly; प्रवेश *praveś*, entrance, प्रवेशक *praveśak*, penetrating. Instances in उक are not numerous; the following is formed by substituting it for the final vowel, इच्छा *ichchhá* wish, desire, इच्छुक *ichchhuk*, desirous.

इत *it*; as. क्रोध *krodh*, anger, क्रोधित *krodhit*, angry; आनन्द *ánand* joy, आनन्दित *ánandit*, joyous; दुःख *duhkh*, pain, दुःखित *duhkhit* pained, afflicted.

इय *iya*, इया *iyá*, ईया *íyá*; as, समुद्र *samudra*, the ocean, समुद्रिय *samudriya*, oceanic; झांझ *jhánjh*, passion, झांझिया *jhánjhiyá*, passionate; खटपट *khaṭpaṭ*, contention, खटपटिया *khaṭpaṭiyá*, contentious; बालक *bálak*, a child, बालकीय *bálakíya*, childish.

ईला *ílá*, एला *elá*, ऐला *ailá*; as, सज *saj*, shape, सजीला *sajílá*, graceful; रङ *rang*, color, रङीला *rangílá*, gaudy; घर *ghar*, a house, घरेला *gharelá*, domestic; बन *ban*, a wood, बनैला *banailá*, woody, wild.

आ *á*; as, भूख *bhúkh*, hunger, भूखा *bhúkhá*, hungry; प्यास *pyás*, thirst, प्यासा *pyásá*, thirsty; मैल *mail*, dirt, मैला *mailá*, dirty.

ल *l*, लु *lu*, लू *lú*; as, दया *dayá*, kindness, दयाल *dayál*, kind, gracious; कृपा *kripá*, compassion, कृपालु *kripálu*, compassionate, merciful; झगड़ा *jhagrá*, quarrel, झगड़ालू *jhagrálú*, quarrelsome.

वन्त *want*; as, कुल *kul*, family, pedigree, कुलवन्त *kulwant*, of noble descent; बल *bal*, strength, बलवन्त *balwant*, strong; दया *dayá*, mercy, kindness, दयावन्त *dayáwant*, merciful, kind.

वान *wán*; as, आशा *ásá*, hope, आशावान *ásáwán*, hopeful; क्षमा *kshamá* forgiveness, क्षमावान *kshamáwán*, forgiving; ज्ञान *gyán*, knowledge, ज्ञानवान *gyánwán*, learned; रूप *rúp*, form, figure, रूपवान *rúpwán*, well-shaped, beautiful.

DERIVATION OF VERBS.

341. The different kinds of verbs and the rules by which they
are formed, when derived from simple or neuter verbs, have already been explained; it remains but to say that what are regarded as primitive verbs in Hindí are almost entirely derived from
Sanskrit roots. As those roots are, without exception, monosyllabic, and as the change they undergo in passing into Hindí never
lengthens them by more than one syllable, it may be taken· for
granted, that any Hindí verb of more than two syllables that may
be met with is not primitive, that is, is not derived immediately
from the Sanskrit root, but from a simpler verb already · existing
in Hindí.

342. The process by which Sanskrit roots are transformed
into Hindí infinitives is simple ; in many cases the root is affected
by either lengthening or shortening its vowel, in other instances
by changing or omitting altogether one of the consonants, when
the root has more than one, and, in every instance, ना, the sign
of the Hindí infinitive, is added to the modified root. The following examples exhibit some of these changes.

SANSKRIT ROOT.	HINDÍ INFINITIVE.
सह् *sah*, bearing,	सहना *sahná*, to bear.
हस् *has*, laughing,	हंसना *hansná*, to laugh.
वस् *vas*, dwelling,	बसना *basná*, to dwell.
दा *dá*, giving,	देना *dená*, to give.
म्र *mri*, dying,	मरना *marná*, to die.
पा *pá*, drinking,	पीना *píná*, to drink.
चर् *char*, moving,	चलना *chalná*, to move.
जीव् *jív*, living,	जीना *jíná*, to live.
क्र *kri*, doing,	करना *karná*, to do.
कथ् *kath*, saying,	कहना *kahná*, to say.
आप् *áp*, obtaining,	पाना *páná*, to obtain.

रक्ष् *raksh*, keeping,	रखना *rakhná*, to keep.
क्वल् *jwal*, burning,	जलना *jalná*, to burn.
गण् *gan*, counting,	गिनना *ginná*, to count.
प्रच्छ् *prachchh*, asking,	पूछना *púchhná*, to ask.
गम् *gam*, </br> या *yá*, going,	जाना *jáná*, to go.
जन् *jan*, producing,	जनना *janná*, to produce.
जि *ji*, conquering,	जीतना *jítná*, to conquer.
धा *dhá*, placing,	धरना *dharná*, to place.
पच् *pach*, cooking,	पकना *pakná*, to be cooked.
त्यज् *tyaj*, leaving,	त्यागना *tyágná*, to leave.
रच् *rach*, making,	रचना *rachná*, to make.

343. From the preceding examples it may be observed that the changes which Sanskrit roots undergo in passing into Hindí are mainly euphonic. Generally, when the root ends in a consonant, ना is simply added with, in some cases, a lengthening of the vowel, to form the Hindí infinitive. When a root ends in ऋ *ri* or ॠ *rí* the termination is generally changed to अर *ar*, before the addition of ना; as, तृ *trí*, crossing over, तरना *tarná*, to cross over.

CHAPTER XI.

SYNTAX,

वाक्यविन्यास *vákyavinyás.*

344. Syntax treats of the structure of sentences or the correct expression of thoughts in words.

345. In Hindí, as in every language, a sentence consists necessarily of two parts, viz., a Subject, or that of which something is said, and a Predicate, or that which is said of the Subject.

| SUBJECT, उद्देश्य | PREDICATE, विधेय |
| घास grass | उगती springs up. |

346. The Subject must be a noun or substantive-pronoun, an adjective or an infinitive verb used substantively, or a sentence.

347. The Predicate must be a verb, or a noun, pronoun, adjective, or numeral in connection with a verb, generally the substantive verb होना.

348. If the Predicate include other words besides a verb, those other words form a complement or attribute, and the verb is considered a copula, or link connecting the complement with the subject. In grammatical analysis the copula is regarded as included in the predicate, so that every sentence, however complex, may be divided into a subject and a predicate ; the connection between the two ideas which they present to the mind is the essence of the sentence.

349. The general rule for the arrangement of a Hindí sentence is to begin with the subject, after which the complement or attribute comes, and last of all the verb or copula.

Subject.	Predicate.	
	Complement or *attribute.*	*Verb* or *copula.*
आत्मा spirit	अमर immortal	है is.
वह he	नाटा short	है is.
हम we	शीघ्र quickly.	जावेंगे will go.
पीला yellow	एक रंग a color	है is.
पैरना to swim	कठिन difficult	है is.
किसी कारण से झूठ बोलना from any cause to speak falsely	उचित right	नहीं है. is not.

350. When the verb is transitive the predicate is not complete without the addition of an object to which the action refers : generally, the object of a transitive verb occupies the same position as the attribute in a sentence with an intransitive verb.

351. Most transitive verbs take a single object, but with many a double object is necessary to complete the sense. When the object is single, it may be a noun, a substantive-pronoun, or an adjective or infinitive used substantively.

Subject.	Predicate.	
	Object.	*Verb.*
किसान the husbandman	बीज seed	बोता है is sowing.
उन लोगों ने those people	शब्द the voice	सुना heard.
सांप the snake	तुम को you	डसेगा will sting.
वे they	भूखों को the hungry	खिलाते हैं are feeding.
लड़की the girl	सीना to sew	सीखती है is learning.

352. The preceding is the general, but by no means the invariable order of the words in a Hindí sentence. For the sake of emphasis or contrast in prose, or to secure euphony or suit the metre in poetry, the general order is occasionally departed from, the complement or the object taking the place of the subject or the verb; thus, मैं नहीं जानता तुम को 'I do not know you'; उस को तुम पहचानते हो 'do you recognise him?' लड़के को मैं ने सिखाया तुम ने सिखाया लड़की को 'I taught the boy, you taught the girl.'

353. With regard to the collocation of words observe further, that a noun in the genitive case usually precedes its governing noun, and an adjective the substantive that it qualifies. With a governing noun qualified by an adjective the order is,—

Gen. Noun.	*Adjective.*	*Gov. Noun.*
माली की the gardener's	छोटी little	टोकरी basket.
राजा की the king's	साहसी brave	सेना army.

354. With a genitive noun qualified by an adjective the general order is,—

Adjective.	*Gen. Noun.*	*Gov. Noun.*
बूढ़े the old	माली की gardener's	कुदाली spade.
धार्मिक the virtuous	राजा का king's	सेनापति general.

355. The order of an interrogative, does not, as a rule, differ from that of an affirmative sentence; thus, वे दौड़ सकते हैं, may mean, 'they are able to run,' or, 'are they able to run?'

356. The question then arises, how may an interrogative be distinguished from an affirmative sentence? In reading native books there are no notes of interrogation, nor, indeed, anything answering to our system of punctuation, by which to be guided. The presence, however, of any of the interrogative pronouns or adverbs, as, कौन 'who?' कब 'when?' कहाँ 'where?' कितना 'how many?' etc., always indicates a question, for they are never used except in interrogative sentences.

357. The word क्या 'what?' is frequently used to introduce a question, especially for the expression of surprise or reproof; thus, क्या यह वही जन है 'what, is this the same person?' क्या अब लौं ठहर गये हो 'what, have ye stayed till now?' क्या तुम मेरे संग एक घड़ी न जाग सको. 'what, could ye not watch with me one hour?'

358. In the absence of the interrogative pronouns the student must be guided by the scope of the context, and, in oral discourse, by the tone and manner of the speaker. This is a matter that is attended by but little or nothing of the difficulty that a learner might anticipate, for it is seldom that even a learner need hesitate as to whether a simple statement or a question be intended.

SUBSTITUTES FOR THE ARTICLE.

359. It has already been said that there is no article in Hindi answering to *a, an, the,* in English; thus, फल may mean 'a fruit,' 'the fruit,' or simply 'fruit.'

360. The place of the indefinite, *a, an*, is sometimes supplied by एक 'one,' or by कोई 'any'; thus, एक स्त्री रोती थी 'a woman was weeping'; कोई मनुष्य वहां था 'a man was there.'

361. When definiteness is necessary, the English definite article may be represented by the demonstrative वह, and very rarely by वह; thus, वह हल जो मैं ने आप के लिये बनाया सो कहां है 'where is the plough that I made for you, Sir?' वह पुस्तक जिस का चर्चा में करता था देखो 'behold the book I was speaking about.'

362. To avoid an unpleasant repetition of either of them, एक and कोई may be used alternately; as, एक विद्यार्थी किसी अन्य को पढ़ता था 'a student was reading a book'; किसी गाम में एक कवि रहता था 'in a village a poet was living.'

363. In translating from English into Hindi, unless great precision be requisite, the article, whether definite or indefinite, may generally be overlooked.

CONCORD OF THE VERB WITH ITS NOMINATIVE.

उद्देश्य और विधेय का मिलान ।

364. The subject of the sentence always stands in the nominative case; and, as a rule, the Hindí verb agrees in gender, number, and person with its subject or nominative case; as, गुरु सिखाता है 'the master is teaching'; चेले सीखते हैं 'the disciples are learning'; नदी बहती है 'the river is flowing'; मेघ गरजते हैं 'the clouds are thundering'; मैं किस उपाय से बचूंगा 'by what means shall I escape'; तुम इस औषधि के गुण जानते हो 'do you know the properties of this drug?'

365. The most common and important exceptions to the preceding rule are those occasioned by the peculiar construction that must be adopted in the past tenses of all transitive verbs.

They cause the nominative to be changed into the case of the agent with ने, and the verb to agree, not with the agent, but with the object, when it is in the nominative form, but when the object is in the accusative form with को, the verb must be used as it were impersonally, and always in the third person singular masculine; as, मैं ने लड़की देखी 'I saw the girl'; but, मैं ने लड़की को देखा; उस ने पोथियां लिखीं 'he wrote books'; but, उस ने पोथि, यों को लिखा.* See 216, 217.

366. Two or more nominatives, regarded collectively or as forming one idea, may take a verb in the singular number; as धरम धन जन स्त्री चौर राज मेरा चँगा न गया 'why did not my caste, wealth,

---

* That this peculiar construction has been transferred from Sanskrit into Hindí and other modern Indian dialects, will be apparent from the following quotations.

In Sanskrit "the past passive participle is constantly used to supply the place of a perfect tense passive ;.................the participle is made to agree adjectively with the object in gender, number and case, as in Latin ; and the agent, which in English would probably be in the nominative, and in Latin in the ablative, becomes in Sanskrit instrumental. Thus, in Sanskrit, the phrase, 'I wrote a letter,' would not be so idiomatically expressed by अहं पत्रं लि- खेय, as by मया पत्रं लिखितं or यया पत्रं लिखितं आसीत् 'by me a letter was written,' '*a me epistola scripta.*' So again, तेन बन्धनानि छिन्नानि 'by him the bonds were cut':.............तेन उक्तं 'by him it was said." "This instrumental or passive construction, which is so prevalent in Sanskrit, has been transferred from it to Hindí, Maráthí, Guzerátí, and other dialects of India. The particle ने *ne* in Hindí corresponds most clearly to the Sanskrit न *na*, the final letter of the commonest termination for the instrumental case ; and this particle can never occasion any difficulty if so regarded." *Monier Williams.*

family, wife, and kingdom go!' तीन बरस और चार मास बीत गया 'three years and four months have past.'

367. To denote respect or deference of any kind, a plural verb may be used with a singular noun; as, राजा फिर नगर में आये और धर्म राज करने लगे 'the king returned to the city and began to reign in righteousness'; सेवक ने कहा कि यह भेद स्वामी नहीं जानते हैं 'the servant said, the master does not know this secret.'

368. A peculiar idiom of Hindí grammar may here be noticed, viz., that the number of the subject affects that of the attribute, even though it be a noun; thus in the sentence, तुम इस नगर के निवासी हो 'are you an inhabitant of this city!' one person may be addressed, and so निवासी be singular, yet के, and not का, must be used before it; thus also in वे सब मिलके बड़े समाज बने ' they all together (or unitedly) became a large assembly,' बड़ा could not be correctly substituted for बड़े, although समाज is used in the singular number.

369. The masculine gender is regarded as superior to the feminine; when, therefore, there are two or more nominatives of different genders, the verb will generally agree with the masculine rather than with the feminine; as, नर नारी राजा प्रजा सब नगर से बाहर निकले 'man (and) woman, king (and) subject, all came out of the city'; पृथिवी चांद और सब यह सूर्य के आसपास घूमते हैं 'the earth, moon, and all the planets move round the sun.'

370. But if the last named nominative be feminine, and not far removed from the verb by intervening words, the verb may agree with it in gender; as, लड़के और लड़कियां उधर दौड़तीं हैं 'the boys and girls are running hither'; बैल और बकरी वहां चरती थीं 'bullocks and goats were grazing there.'

371. In Hindí grammar the first person is prior to the second, and the second to the third; if, therefore, there be two or

more nominatives of different persons in the same sentence, the verb will agree with the first rather than with the second, and with the second rather than with the third; as, हम और तुम वहां चलेंगे 'you and I will go there'; तुम और वे उस काम को करो 'you and they do that work.'

372. The nominative plural being frequently the same in form as the nominative singular, the verb is often the only guide as to the number intended.

CONCORD OF THE ADJECTIVE WITH THE SUBSTANTIVE,

विशेष्य और विशेषण का मिलान ।

373. Every adjective, or term used adjectively, must refer to and qualify some noun or pronoun expressed or understood. Adjectives that end in आ are alone capable of inflection; they must agree in gender and number with the nouns to which they are in attribution; thus, ऊंचा वृक्ष 'a tall tree'; उस की हरी पत्तियां 'its green leaves'; ऊंचे वृक्ष की लम्बी डाली 'the long branch of the tall tree'; अच्छा खेत 'a good field'; अच्छे खेत 'good fields'; अच्छे खेत से अच्छी खेती होती 'from a good field there is a good crop'; उधर के खेत में एक सूखा हुआ घोड़ा पड़ा है 'in the field yonder there lies a dead horse.'

374. Pronouns, ordinal numbers, and participles, used adjectively, change their terminations to agree in gender and number with the nouns to which they refer; as, मेरे फलवारे में बहते पानी का नाला है 'in my flower-garden there is a rivulet of running water'; तुम्हारे गहरे सरोवर में 'in your deep pond'; सातवें मास का नवां दिन 'the ninth day of the seventh month'; दसवीं स्त्री से 'from the tenth woman'; निकाला हुआ घोड़ा 'a broken-in horse'; निकाले हुए घोड़ों पर 'on broken-in horses'; ब्याही हुई पुत्री 'a married daughter.'

375. Adjectives not ending in आ undergo no change, what-

ever the gender, number, or case of the nouns they qualify; as, सुन्दर लड़का 'a beautiful boy'; उस की सुन्दर बहिन 'his beautiful sister'; सुन्दर बन 'a beautiful wood'; निर्मल मन 'a pure mind'; उस के निर्मल मन में 'in his pure mind'; धनवान मनुष्य 'a rich man'; धनवान लोगों में 'among wealthy people'; ज्ञानी लोगों की समझ में 'in the opinion of learned people.'

376. No adjective nor any term used adjectively can have a case ending of its own or take any of the plural terminations आं, एं, एं, ओं; it suffices that they accompany the noun. But if the adjective or other qualifying word be declinable, the inflected form of it must be used with nouns in the oblique cases; thus, नीले वस्त्र पर 'on a blue garment'; अनजाने ईश्वर को 'to the unknown God'; खोई हुई भेड़ें 'lost sheep'; भले लोगों की सङ्गति 'the society of good people'; लिखी हुई बातें 'written words.'

377. When the noun is not expressed, the adjective takes the case endings and plural terminations; as, कंगाल मनुष्य को मत सताओ 'do not teaze the poor man'; or, omitting the noun, कंगाल को मत सताओ; धनी पुरुष का आदर बहुत होता है 'a wealthy man has much respect'; or धनी का आदर बहुत होता है.

378. An adjective ending in आ, if separated from its noun and united with the verb, may often remain uninflected; as, तुम ने लोहे को क्यों टेढ़ा किया 'why have you made the iron crooked?' काठ के रंग को और गहरा कर दो 'make the color of the wood deeper.'

379. Observe that the preceding rule is not of universal application, for if the noun be feminine, the adjective, though connected with the verb, must be in the feminine form likewise; thus, it would not be correct to say मैं ने यह लाठी सीधा की 'I made this stick straight,' but rather सीधी की; thus also, चौड़ी निकालके खम्भ के सामने खड़ी करो 'bring out the mare and make her stand in front of the post'; here खड़ा करो would not be said. The adjective therefore must agree in gender with the noun, but

need not be inflected with a masculine noun in an oblique case; thus, घोड़ों को निकालके खड़ा करो 'bring out the horses and make them stand.' It is difficult to treat this point satisfactorily, for the usage of educated natives in regard to it is not uniform.

380. An adjective qualifying two or more nouns of different genders will, as a rule, agree with the masculine rather than with the feminine; but if the last named noun be feminine and not far removed from the adjective by intervening words, the adjective may agree with it; thus, उस घर के पत्थर ईंट और चुना अच्छे हैं 'the stone, brick, and lime of that house are good'; मेरे पिता माता और दोनों भाई जीते हैं 'my father, mother, and two brothers are alive'; सांवला लड़का और उस की गोरी बहिनें घास पर बैठी हैं 'the dark-complexioned boy and his fair sisters are seated on the grass.'

381. When one adjective is used with several nouns that are names of inanimate objects, it will agree in gender with the one nearest in position to it; as, कल की हाट में अनाज फल और तरकारी महंगी थीं 'in yesterday's market grain, fruit, and vegetables were dear'; घर और आसपास की भूमि अच्छी है 'the house and the ground around it are good.'

382. Two or more adjectives may be used with one noun, the first qualifying the second as an adverb, but all that are capable of inflection, will agree with the noun; thus, बड़ी लम्बी कड़ी 'a very long beam'; बड़े ऊंचे पेड़ पर 'on a very high tree'; स्वप्न में बड़ी ऊंची डरावनी सूरत मेरे सन्मुख आ गई 'in a dream a very tall frightful form came before me'; बड़ी निर्मल ज्योति 'a very pure light.'

CONCORD OF THE RELATIVE WITH ITS ANTECEDENT.

सर्वनामों का मिलान ।

383. The relative जो, sometimes written जौन, and the correlative सो, sometimes written तौन, answer respectively to the

English relative 'who,' 'which,' or 'what,' and correlative 'that'; but, unlike the order of English sentences, the correlative usually follows the relative instead of being antecedent to it.

384. As a rule, the relative जो and the correlative सो are placed at the beginning of their respective clauses, the relative clause being generally the first, the correlative immediately following. In the latter clause the correlative or demonstrative pronoun, answering to the relative in the former clause, is almost invariably expressed;* thus, जो मैं ने कहा सो उस ने किया 'what I said that he did'; जो मांगेगा सो पावेगा 'he who will ask shall obtain'; जो लड़कपन में नहीं सीखेगा वह बुढ़ापे में पछतावेगा 'he that will not learn in youth shall repent in old age.'

385. The preceding rule applies to the pronouns derived from the relative, correlative, or demonstrative; as, जैसा, तैसा, or वैसा; जितना, तितना, or उतना; thus, जैसा मैं चाहता था वैसा घर बन गया 'as I desired so the house was made'; जितने भागे थे उतने अब नहीं हैं 'as many as were formerly so many there are not now.'

386. Observe that when the relative refers to a first or second personal pronoun it follows it; as, तू जो लड़के को मारता है कौन है 'who art thou that art beating the boy?' हमें जो बलवन्त हैं उचित है 'for us who are strong it is right.'

387. The foregoing rules explain the order of relative and correlative clauses in a Hindí sentence; it is of importance to observe that only in rare instances is this order departed from in good idiomatic Hindí; as, वह निर्मल नदी जो वहां बहती थी सूख गई है 'that clear stream that used to flow there has dried up.'

388. The relative and correlative pronouns agree in number with the nouns to which they refer, whether expressed or under-

---

* It is well to notice this usage of Hindí as contradistinguished from Urdú.

stood : their form is the same in both genders ; as, जो थोड़े में अधर्मी है सो बहुत में भी अधर्मी है 'he who is unjust in a little is unjust also in much'; जो स्त्री रोगी थी सो चंगी हुई 'the woman that was sick has recovered'; जिन देव देवियों की सेवा वे करते हैं सो उन की सहायता नहीं कर सकते हैं 'the gods and goddesses whom they serve are not able to help them.'

389. The demonstrative वह is not unfrequently used, as in some of the foregoing examples, for the correlative, and generally with the effect of increasing the emphasis; thus, जो औरों को ठट्टे में उड़ाता है वह आपही ठट्टे में उड़ाया जायेगा 'he that holds others up to ridicule will himself be held up to ridicule'; जो अपने घर की सुध नहीं लेता है वह क्या औरों की रक्षा करेगा ' he who does not take care of his own house, what, will he protect others ?'

390. In complex sentences to avoid ambiguity the relative should be placed as near as possible to its own antecedent ; thus, in the sentence, राम दशरथ का पुत्र था जिसने रावण को मारा 'Rám was the son of Daśarath who killed Ráwan,' it is grammatically implied that Daśarath was the slayer of Ráwan, and it would be so understood by one unacquainted with Hindú mythology ; the ambiguity is avoided by changing the position of the relative, thus, राम जिस ने रावण को मारा दशरथ का पुत्र था.

391. जो, as a conjunction, signifying 'if', or 'that,' may be easily distinguished from the relative pronoun by the context; thus, जो आप आज्ञा दें तो मैं जाऊं ' if you, Sir, would give the order, then I would go'; मैं ने सुना है जो वह परदेश को जावेगा ' I have heard that he will go to a foreign country.'

CONCORD OF ONE SUBSTANTIVE WITH ANOTHER.

392. When one substantive is placed in juxtaposition with another, or with a personal pronoun, for the purpose of explaining or describing it, it is put, by apposition, in the same case, but not

necessarily in the same number; as. राजा परीक्षित आखेट को गये 'the king Paríkshit went to the chase'; तब पराशर मुनि बोले राजा जितने हम बड़े बड़े ऋषि हैं 'then Parásar the sage said, King! as many of us as are very great saints'; हम लड़के वहां खेलते थे 'we boys were playing there.'

393. A noun or pronoun may be in apposition with a part of a sentence; हम इस देश के निवासी उस रीति पर नहीं चलते हैं 'we inhabitants of this country do not follow that custom.'

394. Titles and most terms expressive of the higher professions where in apposition with nouns may be optionally placed before or after them; as, पण्डित जगत नारायण 'Pandit Jagat Náráyan'; राम जसन पण्डित 'Rám Jasan, Pandit'; रघुनाथ कवि कृत 'made or written by the poet Raghunáth.'

395. Names of trades and all inferior occupations follow the name of the person; as गंगा दास ठठेरा 'Gangá Dás the brazier'; राम गोपाल बनिया 'Ram Gopál the shop-keeper'; राम लाल बोटिया 'Rám Lál the porter.'

396. When the noun to which another noun is placed in apposition is the name of a city, town, village, island, or river, the adjective or verb will agree with the noun in apposition and not with the principal noun; thus, काशी नगर बहुत बड़ा है 'the city of Benares is very large'; here बड़ा agrees with नगर which is masculine, and not with काशी which is a feminine noun; तिरहुत देश गण्डक पर बसा है 'Tirhut is situated on the Gandak.'

397. Observe that the English idiom in using 'of' before the names of cities, seas, islands, etc., by way of distinction, is not admissable in Hindi; the name is simply put in apposition with the word which describes it; thus, कामरूप गांव, 'the village of Kámrúp'; लङ्का टापू, 'the island of Ceylon'; ब्रह्मपुत्र नद 'the river Brahmaputra.'

Syntax of the Noun.

1. Nominative Case.*

398. The subject of every sentence whether a noun, a substantive-pronoun, or an adjective or infinitive used substantively, must be in the nominative case; as, बसन्त बीत गया† 'spring has past'; हम नदी पार उतरेंगे 'we will go across the river'; धनी दरिद्र को दबाता है 'the rich (man) oppresses the poor (man)'; सुना देखने के समान नहीं है 'hearing is not like seeing.'

399. When a clause or entire sentence forms the subject it must be regarded as the nominative of the verb, and will influence it as a single term in the masculine gender singular number; as, बैरी के साथ भलाई करनी बुराई का पलटा है 'to do good to an enemy is revenge for evil.'

---

* It is well to observe that native grammarians represent the nominative as having two forms, termed प्रधान कर्ता and अप्रधान कर्ता; the former is the simple uninflected state of the substantive, and is never followed by a case ending, being, strictly speaking, in no case; the latter is what is known as the case of the agent and is invariably followed by its sign ने. The प्रधान कर्ता or principal nominative can not be correctly used with the past tenses of transitive verbs, except in the few anomalous cases noted in para. 252; the अप्रधान कर्ता or subordinate nominative is never correctly used except with the past tenses of transitive verbs; the inflected form of the personal pronouns, but never of nouns, may be followed by ने to form it.

† बसन्त is erroneously given by Thompson, Forbes, and others, as feminine; it is invariably used by educated natives as masculine, and वसन्त *vasanta*, the Sanskrit form of it, is also masculine.

400. Several neuter and passive verbs signifying to become, to appear, to be called, etc., take a noun in the nominative case, to complete the predicate; as, जो बीज में बोता हूं बड़ा पेड़ हो जावेगा 'the seed that I am sowing will become a large tree'; कोई मनुष्य पण्डित उत्पन्न नहीं होता है 'no man is born a pandit'; जो यह चार बरस लों मन लगाके सीखे तो बड़ा ज्ञानी निकलेगा 'if he applies his mind to study for four years he will turn out a very learned man'; दयावन्त राजा धर्मावतार समझा जाता है 'a merciful king is considered an incarnation of justice'; यह खरहरा कहलाता है 'this is called a curry-comb.'

401. When one nominative is common to two or more verbs, it is expressed before the first only and is understood with the others; as, वे न बोते हैं न लवते हैं न खत्तों में बटोरते हैं 'they neither sow nor reap nor gather into barns'; if emphasis be requisite, the nominative may be repeated with each verb; thus, वही करता है और वही कराता है 'he acts and he actuates.'

2. The Genitive Case.

402. The genitive is probably the most extensively used and the most varied in application of all the cases.

403. From the etymology of the word it seems to denote primarily, not so much possession, as connection or origin, a signification that belongs not less to the Sanskrit than to the Latin name of this case.

404. The three modes of expressing the genitive with का, के, की, and the rules which enable us to determine which of them must be adopted in any particular case, have been fully explained. See 78—85. There remains but to state under what conditions, and to express what relations, the genitive case is used.

1. When two nouns are so related to one another as to present one idea to the mind, they are connected by the genitive case;

thus, माली की कुदाली 'the gardener's spade'; कूंय का जल 'well water'; मनुष्य का स्वभाव 'man's disposition'; मेरे पिता का घर 'my father's house.'

2. Origin and authorship are indicated by the genitive; as, मेरे हाथ का बनाया हुआ 'made by my hand'; तुलसी दास का (or की) रामायण* 'the Rámáyan by Tulsí Dás'; लल्लु लाल का प्रेमसागर 'the Premságar by Lallu Lál'; बिहारी की सतसई 'the Satsaí by Bihárí.'

3. Possession of every kind may be expressed by the genitive; as, जिस का मन सन्तुष्ट होता उस का सब धन है 'he whose mind is contented is possessed of all wealth'; यह सब भूमि मेरी है 'all this land is mine'; मेरी मा के गहने का मोल तम्हारे पिता की सेना के सब हथियारों के मोल से अधिक है 'the price of my mother's jewels, is more than the price of all the weapons of your father's army.'

405. The preceding are the most general uses to which the genitive is applied; there are other and varied instances of its application the most common and important of which are as follows :—

a. Material of which a thing is made; as, लोहे का खम्भा 'an iron pillar'; सोने की अंगूठी 'a golden ring'; मिट्टी का बर्त्तन 'an earthen vessel'; हीरे का बना हुआ 'made of diamonds'; हाथीदांत का सिंहासन 'an ivory throne.'

b. Use or purpose; मुझे कहीं रहने की ठौर बताइये 'be pleased to shew me somewhere a place to remain in'; कुछ पीने का जल हम को दो 'give me some water to drink'; लिखनेकी पटरी मुझको चाहिये 'I am in need of a board to write on.'

c. Price or value; as, दस रुपये का थान 'a piece of cloth of

---

* रामायण is properly a masculine noun, but it is constantly used as feminine by the people of Benares.

ten rupees value'; यह साढ़े तीन सौ का है 'this is worth or valued at three hundred and fifty'; दो पैसे की मिठाई 'two pice worth of sweetmeats.'

d. Difference between two objects; as, स्वामी और सेवक का अन्तर 'the difference between master and servant'; आकाश और पृथिवी का भेद 'the difference between the heavens and the earth.'

e. Size or measurement; as, दो हाथ की लाठी 'a stick two cubits long'; बड़े पाट की नदी 'a very broad river'; कोस भर की सड़क 'a road two miles long.'

f. Age, period of life; as, बारह एक बरस की लड़की 'a girl of about twelve years'; जब वह चौदह बरस का हुआ तब परदेश को चला गया 'when he became fourteen years old then he went away to a foreign country'; अब वह पचीस बरस का होगा 'he may now be about twenty-five years of age.'

g. Totality; as खेत का खेत 'the whole field'; सब का सब 'all, the whole'; सब के सब 'the whole of them'; सखी सहेली सब की सब 'the whole of the female friends and companions.'

h. Object of some feeling or sentiment; as, स्त्रियों का कुछ विश्वास नहीं करते हैं 'they have no confidence in women'; किस का भरोसा करते हो 'on whom are you relying?' मैं उस के लौटने की आशा रखता हूं 'I am hoping for his return'; मैं तुम्हें देखने की लालसा करता हूं 'I am longing to see you'; किसी बात की चिन्ता मत करो 'do not be anxious about anything.'

i. Fitness or ability may also be sometimes indicated by the genitive; as, यह राज्य अब ठहरने का नहीं है 'this government cannot now continue, or it is not fit to continue'; वह चौकी रखने की नहीं है 'that chair is not worth keeping.'

j. In definitions and explanations; as, यह एक भांति का फूल है 'this is a kind of flower'; सांगर एक जाति की बड़ी मछली है 'the shark is a kind of large fish'; मन एक प्रकार का सोता है जिस से भलाई बुराई दोनों निकलती हैं 'the mind is a kind of fountain out of which both good and evil flow.' धन का लोभ सब बुराइयों का मूल है 'the love of wealth is the root of all evil.'

406. The genitive is frequently used to express relations that belong more to other cases, especially the dative and locative; observe the following,—उठने का (or की) सामर्थ्य मुझ को नहीं है* 'I have not strength to get up'; आने की आज्ञा मैं ने पाई ' I have received an order to go'; मेरे प्रश्न के उत्तर में ' in reply to my question'; परमेश्वर का धन्य मानना सभों को उचित है ' it is right for all to give thanks to God'; मैं ने आप का क्या अपराध किया है 'what offence have I committed against you'; किसीके हाथ की घूस लेना न चाहिये 'it is not right to take a bribe from the hand of any one'; उस रोग की कोई औषध नहीं है 'is there no remedy for that disease ?'

407. It may be occasionally used where even the accusative might have been expected; as, तुम जाकर सब यदुवंसियों का ऐसा नास करो कि एक भी जीता न बचे 'do you go and so destroy all the descendants of Yadu that not even one may escape alive.'

408. The sign of the genitive is frequently and idiomatically omitted, especially before some of the adverbial prepositions; thus, उस पास जाके कहो 'go to him and say'; सब तुम्हारी छाया तले बसते हैं 'all are living under your shadow'; तुम्हारी सहायता बिना मैं कुछ कर नहीं सकूंगा 'without your assistance I shall not be able to do anything.' When the word governed by the preposition is capable of inflection, the inflected form must be used, as if the sign of the genitive were expressed; as, अपने बेटे पास रहूंगा 'I will

---

* सामर्थ्य is given in the Dictionaries as masculine, and, according to the analogy of other nouns, which being neuter in Sanskrit become masculine when used in Hindí, it ought to be masculine; some of the pandits of Benares, however, use it as a feminine noun.

stay with my son'; मैं ने उस को लड़के पास छोड़ दिया 'I have left him with the boy'; रात को वह मुझ पास आया 'he came to me at night.'

409.   Observe that के is frequently omitted before लिये when used in connection with pronouns; as, वह लिये, उस लिये, किस लिये, etc.; it can not, however, be thus omitted when लिये governs a substantive.

410.   In the following and similar instances, the sign of the genitive being omitted, the governing and genitive nouns must be regarded as forming a compound noun; गंगा तीर पर 'on the bank of the Ganges'; नदी पार जाऊंगा 'I will go across the river.'

411.   The genitive is sometimes found governed by a noun or preposition understood; as, कृपा करके मेरी भी सुन लीजिये 'be pleased to listen to my (statement) also'; उन के कोई लड़का न था 'they had no son'; here लड़का, being masculine and in the nominative singular, can not govern उन के; some such word as पास or यहां must, then, be understood; जब पहिला पुत्र देवकी के हुआ 'when the first son of Devakí was born'; in this instance also some word or phrase, as यहां, गर्भ से, must be implied.

412.   The use of का or के must in some cases depend upon the view that may be taken of the governing noun, as plural or collectively singular; thus, उस ने दस मनुष्यों के सिर काट डाले, or दस मनुष्यों का सिर काट डाला 'he cut off the heads of ten men.'

413.   The adverb यहां governs the genitive with के like a preposition, to indicate, idiomatically, the house or family of the person referred to; as, पंडित बंसीधर के यहां जाके मेरा प्रणाम उन से कहो 'go to Pandit Bansídhar's and pay him my respects'; बसुदेव के यहां अवतार लो 'become incarnate in the family of Basudev.' With reference to the first of these two sentences, observe that

T

प्रणाम कहो, नमस्कार कहो, are correct, and not प्रणाम दो, etc. The Urdú phrase so commonly heard, *salám do*, is of this latter form and is incorrect; it should be, *salám kaho*.

414. There are a few adjectives also, signifying 'like,' 'near,' 'worthy,' that are used like prepositions and govern the genitive in के; thus, पृथिवी गोलाकार है नारङ्गी के समान 'the earth is round like an orange'; गांव के निकट पहुंचके वह बैठ गया 'having arrived near the village, he sat down'; आप का पुत्र कहलावने के योग्य नहीं हूं 'I am not worthy to be called your son.' नाईं is peculiar in governing the genitive with की; as, कपोत की नाईं 'like a dove.'

415. The verb होना, when it signifies possession governs the genitive case; as, आप को छोड़के मेरा कोई सहायक नहीं है 'besides you, I have no helper'; उस के कई एक सेवक हैं 'he has several servants'; उस मनुष्य का अधिक धन था परन्तु अब उस का कुछ नहीं है 'that man had great wealth, but now he has nothing.'

416. The genitive is frequently used in Hindí to connect a member of a species with the genus to which it belongs, where in English a compound would be formed; as, पीपल का पेड़ 'the pípal-tree'; साल की लकड़ी 'sál-wood.'

417. The use of the genitive is sometimes equivalent to a comparative or superlative degree; as, मैं अपने लोगों में बड़ों का बड़ा हुआ 'I became the greatest among my own people'; वह छोटों का छोटा है 'he is the least of all'; दरिद्री का दरिद्री 'the poorest of the poor.'

418. When anything is represented as belonging to two or more persons conjointly, the sign of the genitive is appended to the last named only; as, यह मोहन लाल बेनी लाल और जानकी का है 'this belongs to Mohan Lál, Bení Lál, and Jánkí.'

3. THE DATIVE CASE.

419. The dative is the case of the recipient and denotes that in which the object of an action rests ; its functions, therefore, apart from the influence of verbs, are but few.

420. The use or end to which anything is applied is frequently expressed by the dative; thus, कुछ जल लाओ नहाने को 'bring some water for bathing'; यह घास घोड़ों को रखी गई है 'this grass has been placed for the horses'; मैं यहां आया हूं मरने को 'I have come here to die'; वह मिलने को आया था 'he had come for an interview'; सारे नगर के लोग उस से भेंट करने को निकले 'all the people of the city came out to meet him.'

421. The intention or motive with which any thing is done may be denoted by this case; thus, वे गये हैं देखने को 'they have gone to see'; वह सब कुछ करता है दिखाने को 'he does every thing for display'; हम बुलाये गये हैं साची देने को 'we have been summoned to give evidence'; क्या मैं अपना भाई बचाने को भी झूठी किरिया खाऊंगा 'what, shall I take a false oath to save my own brother even !'

422. The dative case used before a verb in the infinitive mood followed by the verb होना expresses the necessity of the action; as, मुझ को बोलना है 'I have to speak,' or 'I must speak'; तुम को जाना होवेगा 'you will have to go'; उन को बैठना था 'they had to sit down.'

423. Many adjectives signifying 'fitness,' 'worthiness,' 'agreeableness,' etc., with their opposites, govern the dative ; as, लड़कों को उचित है कि मा बाप की आज्ञा को मानें 'it is right for children to obey their parents'; यह तुम को योग्य नहीं है 'this is not worthy of you'; दास ने कहा मैं यह करता हूं क्योंकि मेरे स्वामी को भावता 'the servant said, I do this because it is pleasing to my master.'

424. The dative is used in expressions of salutation ; as, कुशल आप को 'health or welfare to you.'

425. Observe that in native grammars के लिये as well as को is regarded as a sign of the dative case ; thus, यात्री यह दक्षिणा पुरोहित के लिये लाया है 'the pilgrim has brought this gift for the priest.' The same idea may be expressed in most cases by को or के लिये; but, strictly speaking, लिये is a preposition governing the genitive with के, and not a sign of the dative case.

4. THE ACCUSATIVE.

426. The accusative like the dative is of limited application in Hindí apart from verbs.

427. Motion to a place is frequently expressed by this case ; as, तब सब कोई अपने अपने घर को गये 'then each one went to his own house'; तीन मास हुए कि वे मथुरा को गये 'three months ago they went to Mathura'; वे अपने देश को लौट गये हैं 'they have returned to their country.'

428. The time when anything is done may also be expressed by a noun in the accusative; thus, वे भोर को आते और सांझ को फिर जाते 'they come in the morning and return in the evening'; मैं सोमवार को उन से भेंट करने को जाऊंगा 'I will go to visit them on Monday'; हम आधी रात को वहां पर पहुंचेंगे 'we shall arrive there at midnight.' Time and place are, however, frequently expressed by the locative or nominative form as well as by the accusative.

429. The accusative in Hindí being commonly the same in form as the nominative, just as in English there is no inflexional distinction in nouns denoting either the subject or the object in a sentence, the question arises when is the nominative form to be used and when the regular accusative form with the postposition को ?

430. The question has to do with one of the niceties of
Hindí grammar, and an answer to it propounding a rule applicable to every case can not be given, for extensive reading and
careful observation of the style of educated natives can alone enable a foreigner to use the nominative or accusative form freely
and correctly.

431. In the absence of a definite and invariable rule the
following may be taken as a guide :—

a. As a rule the accusative case in Hindí, as in English, is
the same in form as the nominative.

b. The accusative form with को is generally employed when
it is intended to make the object of the sentence definite.

c. Words signifying reasonable beings, or descriptive of their
occupations, usually take the accusative with को when they
stand in the objective relation to verbs.

d. Names of inanimate objects do not generally take the
accusative with को.

432. When the object of a sentence appears without the
postposition को, the word must not be regarded as in the regular
accusative case with the postposition simply omitted, for the inflected form of the word (when capable of inflection) would then
be used, as it invariably is in other cases when their postpositions
are left out ; but the inflected form of a word can not be used for
the accusative unless it be followed by को; thus; we may say,
मैं यह घोड़ा रखता हूं, or मैं इस घोड़े को रखता हूं 'I keep this horse,'
but not, मैं इस घोड़ा रखता हूं. Similarly, it is correct to say, तुम
ने अपने बेटे को अन्यदेश को भेज दिया 'you sent your son to a foreign
country'; but if, omitting the को, we say, तुमने अपने बेटे अन्यदेश
को भेज दिया, the sense becomes ambiguous and the construction
ungrammatical, for अपने बेटे would imply more than one son, and

दिया does not agree with it. The accusative must, then, be regarded as having two distinct forms, one of them identical with the nominative, as in English, the other indicated by its sign को.

5. THE ABLATIVE CASE.

433. The Sanskrit (अपादान) accords with the Latin (*ab* from, *latus* carried) name of this case in signifying, primarily, that from which anything is separated, or by or according to which anything is done; hence it is mainly employed to denote,—

a. The means or instrument of an action; as, अहेरी ने बान से भालुक को घायल किया 'the sportsman wounded the bear with an arrow'; उस लड़ाई में मेरा दहिना हाथ खड्ग से काटा गया 'in that battle my right hand was cut off with a sword'; राजा ने सभा में खड़ा होके हाथ से सेन किया 'the king standing up in the assembly beckoned with his hand.'

b. The manner or mode of an action; as, उस ने उन्हों पर क्रोध से चारों ओर दृष्टि किई 'he looked round upon them with anger'; यह सारी शक्ति से यत्न करता है 'he is endeavouring with all his might'; जो कुछ तुम करो सो अन्तःकरण से करो 'do heartily whatever you may do'; इस प्रकार से 'in this manner'; कपट से 'deceitfully.'

434. The ablative is by no means confined in its application to the means or the manner of an action; from these it passes to the expression of the most varied and diverse relations, as will appear from what follows.

435. The agent by whom anything is done may be expressed by this case when the verb is neuter, causal, or passive, but never with a transitive verb; thus, उस ने बेर बेर कहा कि यह अपराध मुझ से नहीं हुआ 'he said repeatedly, this offence was not committed by me'; रात को मुझ से कुछ हो नहीं सकता 'nothing can be done by me at night'; मुझ से बनता नहीं 'it can not be done by

me'; रावण राम से मारा गया 'Ráwan was killed by Rám'; मुझे निश्चय है कि यह कर्म उन से किया नहीं गया 'I am certain that this deed was not done by them'; चोरों से अपना सब काम कराता है 'he gets all his work done by others'; मुझ से चिट्ठियां लिखाती पढ़ाती है 'she causes letters to be written and read by me.'

436. The ablative often expresses cause or origin; as, आप से आप कुछ नहीं होता 'nothing is from itself,' i. e. has not its cause or origin in itself; कुंवारी से उत्पन्न हुआ 'born of a virgin'; ज्ञान से सामर्थ्य प्राप्त होता है 'strength is derived from knowledge'; मित्र के मिलने से सुख होता है 'there is pleasure from (in) meeting a friend.'

437. The price for which a thing is bought or sold may be put in the ablative; as, कल्याण कञ्चन से कौन नहीं सकते हो 'you can not buy happiness with gold'; आज कल अनाज किस भाव से बेचते हैं 'now-a-days at what rate are they selling grain?' हाथी को एक सहस्र दो सौ रुपये से मोल लिया 'he bought the elephant for one thousand two hundred rupees.'

438. This case is constantly used with words denoting length of past time; as, वह कहता है कि मैंने तीन दिन से कुछ नहीं खाया 'he says, I have eaten nothing for three days'; कई एक मास से बाहर कहीं नहीं गया 'for several months past I have not gone out anywhere'; उस समय से अब लों 'from that time to this'; आदि से लेके अन्त लों 'from the beginning to the end'; यह रीति हमारे पितरों के काल से चली आई है 'this custom has come down from the time of our fathers'; सनातन से 'from eternity.'

439. The ablative is frequently employed to express the idea of 'with,' 'through,' 'by,' 'in consequence of,' 'on,' or 'against'; as, जो वह एकही आंख से देखता है सो तुम दोनों आंख से देख नहीं सकते 'what he sees with but one eye you can not see with both eyes'; आप निश्चय करके उस बात को कहते हैं कि चटकल से

'do you say this certainly or by guess ?' उन्हों ने उस को हाथ से पकड़वाया 'they betrayed him through envy'; भय से लड़की भाग गई 'the girl has fled through fear'; ऋषि के शाप से मरने को गंगा तीर पर आ बैठा है 'in consequence of the Rishi's curse, having come to the bank of the Ganges to die, he has sat down there'; जो भया सो तुम्हारे आने से भया 'what has happened has happened through your coming'; मनुष्य केवल रोटी से नहीं जीता 'man does not live by bread alone'; पत्थर से ठोकर खाके वह गिर पड़ा 'having stumbled against a stone he fell down.'

440. The ablative may be used with most expressions of removal, separation, departure, etc.; as, कहते हैं कि पांच बरस हुए यहां से वह चला गया 'they say that three years ago h e went away from this'; मैं उस से अलग रहता हूं 'I live apart from him'; मुझ को भीड़ में से एकान्त ले जाके मेरे कान में कुछ फुसफुसाया 'taking me aside from the crowd he whispered something in my ear'; सब के सब हम से फिर गये हैं 'all of them have turned away from us'; उस से न्यारा रहूंगा 'I will keep aloof from him'; पहाड़ से नदी निकलती है 'the river issues from the mountain.'

The ablative is used in all instances of comparison. See 119—121.

441. The sign of this case is sometimes idiomatically left out; as, न आंखों देखा न कानों सुना 'neither seen with the eyes, nor heard with the ears'; आप का राज्य बिगाड़ निदान हरि के हाथ मरेगा 'having destroyed your kingdom, at last he will die by the hand of Hari.' मेरे हाथ चिट्ठी भेजता है 'he sends letters by me.'

6. The Locative.

442. The locative case denotes, primarily, the place at or in which something is, or is done. The sign commonly used with it is में 'in,' 'among,' 'at'; but पर and पे, 'on,' 'upon,' 'over,' तक and लों, 'till,' 'to,' 'up to,' are also regarded as signs of the lo-

cative; as, संन्यासी उपवन में बास करता है 'the hermit lives in a wood'; वृक्ष पर पक्षी बोल रहे हैं 'birds continued singing on the tree'; सीढ़ी पे चढ़के उस को उतार लाया 'having ascended a ladder he brought it down'; उस ने हमें नगर के बाहर लों पहुंचाया 'he conveyed us to the outside of the city'; नदी तक मेरे संग चलिये ' be pleased to come with me as far as the river.'

443. The ideas expressed by 'between,' 'among,' 'according to,' 'about,' 'concerning,' 'regarding,' etc., may be denoted by the locative; thus, उन दोनों में कुछ मेल नहीं है 'between those two there is no union'; इन लोगों में यह रीति होती है 'among these people this is a custom'; वह नित्य अपनी समझ पर चलता है 'he always goes according to his own opinion'; वे अपने पुर्खों की चाल पर चलते हैं 'they go according to the custom of their forefathers'; इस विषय में तुम क्या कहते हो 'what do you say about this matter?' इस विवाद में आप क्या विचार करते हैं 'what do you think regarding this dispute ?'

444. The locative is used with words denoting distance, time when, how long, etc.; as, तीन कोश पर 'at six miles distance'; एक कोश तक दौड़ा 'he ran two miles'; उस देश के सिवाने लों 'as far as the boundary of that country'; जब तक मैं न आऊं तब तक पढ़ने में मन लगा 'till I come apply your mind to study'; कब लों ठहर सकते हो 'how long can you stay?'

445. The sign of the locative may sometimes be omitted; but, if the word be capable of inflection, the oblique form of it must be retained; thus, घोड़े चढ़े आया पर गधे चढ़े जावेगा 'he came on a horse but he will go on a donkey'; यमुना के तीर 'on the bank of the Jumna'; अब के मास वहां आऊंगा 'I will go there this month.'

446. The following must be regarded as instances of the locative with the sign of the case omitted; they are peculiar as examples of the locative expressing indirect comparison; एमुखों के

बीच घोड़ा शीघ्रगामी होता है 'among animals the horse is fleet'; जीवों के मध्य सिंह और हाथी बलवन्त होते हैं 'among living creatures the lion and the elephant are strong.'

447. Sometimes a word in the locative case has the sign of the ablative joined to it; as, पेड़ की डाली पर से गिरा है 'he has fallen from (on) a branch of a tree'; जल में से निकाला गया 'taken (from) out of the water'; इस में से दो 'give it out of this.'

7. THE VOCATIVE.

448. The vocative is the case of one addressed, or that form of the noun which is used in calling attention, and can present no difficulty as regards its use. The particles that are prefixed to words in the vocative have been given, and the feelings of the speaker as indicated by them noted. See 74. 304.

449. With the vocative some one or other of the particles referred to is generally used, but there are numerous instances in which they are altogether dispensed with. Sometimes the nominative form of a word is used for the vocative, although the word be capable of inflection; as, बेटा ' O son !'

GOVERNMENT OF ADJECTIVES.

450. The change of termination to which adjectives ending in आ are subject when in attribution to nouns, and their position in the sentence having been considered, there remains but to explain their government with reference to the cases of nouns. See 353,354; 373—382.

451. Adjectives are simple in their government; the cases commonly taken by them are the genitive, ablative, and locative, sometimes the dative, but never the accusative.

452. Adjectives expressive of 'likeness,' 'equality,' 'nearness,' 'submission,' 'conformity,' require the genitive, and are used

after the manner of prepositions. Some of these have been referred to; the following are other instances:—समुद्र की लहर के तुल्य
'like a wave of the sea'; लड़की का वस्त्र पाले की नाईं उजला था
'the girl's garment was white like snow'; धर्महीन मनुष्य पशु के
समान है 'a man destitute of virtue is like a brute'; उस का मुंह
चांद के सदृश था 'his face was like the moon'; स्त्रियों को चाहिये कि
प्रत्येक बात में अपने अपने स्वामी के अधीन रहें 'it is right for wives to
be obedient to their own husbands in everything'; मैं आप की
आज्ञा के अनुसार सब कुछ करूंगा 'I will do everything according to
your command.'

453. Such words as प्रिया, प्यारा, 'dear,' 'beloved,' with their
opposites take the genitive, but they are then used like substantives; thus, वह लड़का अपने पिता का प्यारा है 'that boy is beloved of his father'; राजा को प्रिया थी 'she was dear to the king.'

454. Numeral adjectives used separatively take the ablative,
or the locative followed by the sign of the ablative; as,
उस से पांच लो 'take five from him'; पन्द्रह में से तीन रह गये 'of
the fifteen three remained'; उन में से चार बिक गये हैं 'four of them
are sold.'

455. The ablative is used with adjectives which signify
'full of,' 'satiated,' and their opposites; as, घर तेल के सुगन्ध से
भरा हुआ 'a house filled with the odour of oil'; वह धूंए से भर गया
'it became full of smoke'; वह मनुष्य बुद्धि से परिपूर्ण था 'that man
was full of wisdom'; भोजन से अतितृप्त 'sated with food'; कूआं
जल से सूना 'a well empty of water.'

456. Adjectives signifying 'wearied,' 'tired,' 'cautious,'
'attentive,' 'careful,' take the ablative; as, दौड़ने से थकित 'tired
of running'; बैरियों से चौकस है 'he is watchful against enemies.'

457. The word भर is frequently used with nouns without
any government to signify the whole or entirety of that which

is denoted by the word; thus, दिन भर 'the whole day'; तीन कोस भर 'full six miles'; मन भर 'a full maund' or 80lbs. weight; सेर भर 'two pounds in weight.'

458. Adjectives that denote properties or qualities in persons or things take the locative; as, मन में दीन 'humble in mind'; काम करने में आलसी 'slothful in doing work'; आत्मा में अनुरागी 'fervent in spirit'; सब बातों में बिश्वासयोग्य 'trustworthy in everything'; चलने में ढीला 'slow in walking'; वेद में निपुण 'acquainted with the Vedes'; लम्बाई में छोटा 'small in the length.'

459. It has already been said that there is no regular system of comparison by means of inflections in Hindí; the comparative is expressed by construing the adjective with the noun in the ablative case; the superlative is denoted by extending the comparison to all of the class by means of सब से; see examples, 118—121.

Syntax of the Pronouns.

460. Observations have already been made on the nature and use of pronouns, and the concord of the relative with the antecedent has also been fully explained. See 123—186, 383—391.

461. The plural forms of the first, second, and third personal pronouns are frequently used for the singular, not only to denote respect but also in common *parlance* between friends; thus, भला हम परसों तुम्हारे संग चलेंगे 'well, I will go with you the day after to-morrow'; तुम घोड़े के लिये बिछाली कब भेजोगे 'when will you send the bedding for the horse ?'; क्या दृष्टान्त देके तुम बोलते हो 'what, do you speak parabolically ?'

462. A speaker, unless of high rank, should always use a singular pronoun when speaking of himself, not only in addressing an equal or superior, but even in speaking to an inferior.

463. The second person singular is appropriately and exclusively used in addresses to the Divine Being to indicate reverence; used of other beings it generally implies contempt or disrespect; as, स्वर्ग तेरा पृथिवी भी तेरी सृष्टि और उस की भरपूरी तू ने बनाई 'heaven is thine, the earth also is thine; creation and its fullness thou hast made'; तू कौन है और क्या करता है अपना बयान कर 'who are you, and what are you doing? Give an account of yourself'; अरे अधर्मी पापी चंडाल तू ने यह क्या अंधेर किया जो मेरा सत खो दिया 'O unjust sinful wretch, what outrage you have committed in despoiling me of my purity!'

464. The second person singular can be used without indicating disrespect, only when great familiarity is allowed, or in a fond and caressing manner, as between a mother and her child.

465. The third personal pronoun may be used in the singular number of a person in his absence without implying any disrespect, but in his hearing the plural should be used; as, वह बड़ा ज्योतिषी और उस का पुरोहित है 'he is a great astrologer and his family-priest.'

466. In addressing superiors, the word आप, or some other term expressive of respect or honor, should be used with plural verbs in the third person, and in speaking of them the third person plural of both verb and pronoun should be employed; as आप सब कुछ कर सकते हैं 'Your Highness can do everything'; कृपानिधान मुझ पर बड़ी दया की जो इस समय आप ने मेरी सुध ली 'Mansion of mercy! you have shewn me great favor, that you have at this time remembered me'; दीन दयाल अब दया कर कृष्णावतार की कथा कहिये 'Kind to the poor! now be pleased to relate to me the account of the incarnation of Krishn.'

467. The general use of the plural forms of the personal pronouns when in reality but one person is spoken of, has led to the necessity of denoting the real plural either by some auxiliary

term, as, लोग, सब, or by appropriating the plural forms with ओं for the numerical plural as distinguished from that of mere respect ; thus हम is frequently, but in bad taste, used when the speaker refers to none but himself, and to indicate that others are also intended हम लोग or हम सब is said. Similarly तुम ने, इन ने, उन ने, are applied to an individual, and the real plural is denoted by हम लोगों ने, तुम्हों ने, इन लोगों ने, उन्हों ने, etc.

468.   The plural forms with ओं, though generally used for the real plural, are occasionally found when the singular is meant ; it were well, however, to avoid such usage, for if some distinction be not observed in the application of the plural forms, ambiguity can not always be avoided in a language in which the plural is so constantly used for the singular.

469.   The nominative form of nouns is frequently used, as we have seen, for the accusative with active verbs ; but when a personal pronoun is governed by an active verb, the accusative form with को must always be employed ; thus, मैं तुम को (not तुम) सिखाता हूं 'I am teaching you'; उस ने हम को or हमें (not हम) दूर से देखा 'he saw us from a distance.' But when the third personal pronoun is used as an adjective or demonstrative the nominative form of it may be used as the object of a verb ; as मैं यह कहता हूं 'this is what I say'; क्या आप अपनी चोर से यह कहते हैं 'what, do you say this of yourself?'

470.   With the conjunctive·participles the nominative of the demonstrative pronoun is idiomatically used ; thus, यह सुनके वह बोल उठा 'having heard this he exclaimed'; यह कहकर वह चला गया 'having said this he went away.'

471.   The genitives of the personal pronouns are constantly used as possessives in the sense of 'my,' 'thy,' 'his'; 'our,' 'your,' 'their,' but they are also used as genitives strictly in the

sense of 'of me,' 'of you,' 'of him,' etc. : thus, मेरी आज्ञाओं का पालन करो 'keep my commandments'; मैं तुम्हारा विश्वास करूंगा किन्तु अपने प्रेम के रखने का प्रमाण तुम से चाहता हूं 'I will confide in you, but I desire a proof from you that you entertain love of me.'

472. When one verb occurs in a sentence with two pronouns of different persons separated by a disjunctive conjunction, the verb is usually repeated with each pronoun; thus, मैं उसे कहूंगा चाहे वह कहेगा 'I will say it, or he will'; तुम करो अथवा वे करें 'you can do it, or let them do it.'

473. In English it is considered polite to put the second person before the first, in the order of the sentence, but the Hindí idiom is in the reverse order; as, हम तुम वहां क्या करें 'what could I and you do there?' मुझे से तुम से क्या कहेंगे 'what will they say to me and to you?'

474. When यह and वह are used as demonstratives with a noun expressed, the noun alone can take the case endings, but the inflected form of the pronoun is placed before the noun; as, उस देश के निवासी 'the inhabitants of that country,' but not उस के देश के निवासी, which would be, 'the inhabitants of his country'; उस प्रधान के सन्तानों में 'among the descendants of that chief'; उन स्त्रियों का डर देख मुसकुराके बोला 'seeing the fear of those women, smiling he said.'

475. The word आप is constantly used as a possessive and common reflexive pronoun; its genitive form, अपना, ने, नी, is conveniently used as a substitute for any of the possessives, when they are found in the complement of the sentence and refer to the subject of it; as, लड़की अपनी पोथी पढ़ती है 'the girl is reading her book'; तुम अपने काम में न रहोगे 'will you not continue in your work?' उस ने अपना चोसर आनके खड्ग उठाके उस को मारा 'he, perceiving his oportunity, having raised his sword, struck him.' Observe

that अपना can only be used in the manner just explained when it refers to the subject of the sentence ; in all other cases the genitive of the personal pronouns must be employed ; thus, मैं अपने घर में आता था 'I was going into my own house,' but, मैं उस के घर में आता था 'I was going into his house.'

476. As simply reflexive आप may be used for the three persons and in both numbers ; as, मैं ने आप उसे देखा 'I saw him myself'; तुम आप क्यों नहीं गये 'why did you not go yourself ?' वह आप अपने को बचा नहीं सकता है 'he can not save himself'; हम आप अपनी अज्ञानता से सब कुछ बिगाड़ देते हैं 'we ourselves through our ignorance are marring everthing.'

477. अपना is sometimes found where the genitive of a personal pronoun might have been expected ; as, अपना धन भी खोया जाता है 'my own property also is being lost'; यदि अपना निज बेटा ऐसा करता मैं उस को न बचाता 'if my own son had done so I would not have saved him'; this usage is not idiomatic, and ought not to be copied.

478. To denote distribution or division अपना is repeated ; as, वे अपने अपने घर को गये 'they went each to his own house'; सब अपनेही अपनेही लिये यत्न करते हैं 'they are striving each one for himself.'

479. Care must be taken not to confound the word आप as a reflexive, with the same form of word used as an honorific pronoun ; though alike in the nominative they differ in the oblique cases ; the आ is shortened to अ in the oblique forms when the word is possessive or reflexive, but remains unchanged when it is an honorific pronoun.

480 The honorific आप is generally used of the second person, but it may also be used of the third person in the presence of the individual intended, the motion of the hand or the direction in which the speaker looks indicating that a third person is referred

to. To denote the real honorific plural, लोग must be used with
आप ; as, क्या आप लोगों में कोई उस के समान ज्ञानी नहीं हैं ‘what,
among you, Sirs, are there none learned like him ?’

481. When the relative pronoun precedes its noun it agrees
with it in number, and may be said to agree with it in case,
though it can not have a postposition of its own ; (See 128.) but
when the relative follows in the sentence, it agrees with the noun
in number, but not necessarily in case. In its own member of
the sentence it may be governed in the genitive by another noun,
or be the object of a verb, or be in any case ; as, जो उतावली
करता है सो चूक करता है और जो धीरज रखता है सो मनोरथ को पाता है
‘ he that hastens misses, and he that has patience obtains his end’ ;
जिन अक्षरों को मैं ने बताया उन का रूप स्मरण करो ‘remember the form of
the letters I explained’ ; मेरे यहां दो बेटियां थीं जिन को मैं ने ब्याह दिया
‘in my family there were two daughters whom I gave in marriage’ ; दो अनाथ लड़के थे जिन की रक्षा मैं ने की ‘there were two
orphan children of whom I took care’ ; तुम्हारे देवता झूठे हुए जिन्हों
ने कहा था कि देवकी के आठवें गर्भ में लड़का होगा ‘your gods were false
who had said that Devakí’s eighth child would be a boy.’

482. The particle कि is sometimes used redundantly with
the relative ; as, अब राजा की कथा सुनाता हूं कि जिस की चार रानी
थीं ‘now I tell the story of the king who had four queens’ ; जो
लाभ कि हम को पहुंचा है उसे न खो देवें ‘let us not lose the gain
that has come to us’ ; ज्ञानी वह है कि जिस ने अपने आत्मा की पह-
चान की है ‘he is wise who has formed acquaintance with himself.’

483. Sometimes the relative pronoun is idiomatically substituted for an indefinite pronoun ; as, जो जिस पर बीत गया ‘what
has happened to any one’ ; जो जिस के पास था सो दिया ‘whatever
any one had he gave.’

484. A similar construction is sometimes found with adver-

bial terms; as, जहां जिस का धन तहां उस का मन 'wherever any one's wealth is there his heart is'; जैसी जिस की करनी वैसी उस की भरनी 'as is the conduct of any one so is his reward.'

485. The interrogatives कौन and क्या are used for the relative in sentences of doubt or negation, or in which a question is implied; as, मैं जानता हूं कि ये कौन हैं 'I know who these are'; हम तो कह नहीं सकते कि कौन कौन गये और कौन कौन ठहरे 'we can not say who went and who remained'; वह जानता है तुम्हें क्या क्या आवश्यक है 'he knows what things are necessary for you.'

486. The indefinites, कोई and कुछ, are similar to the interrogatives, कौन and क्या, in the relation they bear the one to the other; like कौन, कोई is generally applied to persons; and कुछ, like क्या, to things. This distinction in the application of कोई to persons and कुछ to things holds only when they are used as simple indefinites, it is not observed when they are employed as adjective pronouns. The following are instances of the use of the indefinite pronouns;—कोई है उस घर में 'there is some one in that house'; कुछ है उस थैली में 'there is something in that bag'; उन फूलों में कोई कोई लाल हैं और कोई कोई पीले हैं 'among those flowers there are some red and there are some yellow'; एक मनुष्य किसी पहाड़ के तले रहा करता 'a man used to live under a certain mountain'; वह आया तो है पर उस के साथ कुछ लोग नहीं हैं 'he has come but there are no people with him.'

487. Observe that कोई and कुछ are not declinable in the plural; (the forms किनी, किन्, are very doubtful, native grammarians reject them.) their nominative forms may be used for the accusative, when they do not refer to a person, and none of the cases but the nominative, and the accusative in the nominative form, can be used in the plural.

Syntax of Verbs.

I. Government of Verbs.

488. The government of verbs can present but little difficulty, as, in this respect, they correspond in a great measure with verbs in English.

489. It has already been said that neuter and passive verbs signifying 'to become,' 'to be called,' 'to be thought,' etc., take a noun in the nominative case after them (i. e. in the order of the sense) to complete the predicate ; this nominative is rather in apposition to the nominative of the verb than governed by the verb ; the following are additional examples of this rule :—वह अनाथ लड़का उस धनी का लेपालक हो गया है 'that orphan boy has become the adopted son of that rich man'; जो स्त्री अपने पति की आज्ञा मानती है पतिव्रता कहलाती है 'the woman that observes her husband's command is called a virtuous wife.'

490. The genitive case is from its nature more connected with and dependent upon nouns than upon verbs ; it is doubtful whether in Hindí it is ever governed by a verb, except as usurping what are properly the functions of other cases.

491. It is scarcely an exception to the foregoing statement that many nouns compounded with करना, लेना, etc., to form nominals, are often preceded by a noun in the genitive instead of the accusative case, for in these cases the governing word is obviously the noun ; as, मैं उस की बिनती करता हूं 'I am entreating him'; वह किसी बात को चिन्ता करता है 'he is thinking of some matter'; मेरी सुध लीजिये 'be pleased to remember me'; ऋषि आसन मारे नैन मूंदे हरि का ध्यान लागाये 'the Rishi, seated and having his eyes closed, was in deep meditation on Hari.'

492. Verbs of 'giving,' 'communicating,' etc., take an accusative of the object and a dative of the recipient, the nominative form

of the accusative being generally used to avoid the repetition of को; thus, मैं ने काठ बढ़ई को दिया हल बनाने को 'I gave wood to the carpenter to make a plough'; भोजन विष से मिलाया हुआ उस को खिला दिया 'he fed him with food mingled with poison'; उस ने इस भांति राजा को साप दिया 'in this way he cursed the king'; ब्याह के समय ब्राह्मणों को अधिक धन बांट दिया 'at the time of the marriage he divided great wealth among the bráhmans.'

493.   Verbs signifying to 'to show,' 'to tell,' 'to inform,' 'to clothe,' etc., take a dative of the person; as, मैं पेड़ तुम को दिखाऊंगा जिस से उस ने यह फूल तोड़ा 'I will shew you the tree from which he plucked this flower'; वह तुम्हें बतावेगा कि क्या करना चाहिये 'he will explain to you what ought to be done'; ज्यों मैं ने कथा सुनी है त्यों तुम को सुनाई है 'as I heard the story so I have related it to you'; लड़के को कपड़ा पहिनाके चलो 'having dressed the child go'; उसे बैजनी वस्त्र पहिराया 'they put on him a purple robe.'

494,   The verb बोलना 'to speak' generally takes a dative of the person addressed, as कहना 'to say,' takes the ablative; this rule is, however, not unfrequently reversed, बोलना taking the ablative of the person, and कहना the dative; as, जब वह उन के संमुख आया तब उन्हों से एक बात बोल न सका 'when he came before them then he could not speak one word to them'; जो मैं तुम को कहता हूं सो मत भूलियो 'do not forget what I am saying to you.'

495.   The dative of the person is generally used to whom any feeling, quality, or state is ascribed; as, मुझे अभिलाष है उन के पास आने का 'I have a desire to go to them'; हम को आशा है कि उस के आने से हमारी भलाई होय 'we have hope that through his coming we may be benefited'; मुझ को निश्चय होता इस विषय में 'I am certain of this matter'; मृत्यु सभों को होती 'death comes to all.'

496. A few neuter verbs that are used impersonally govern
the dative ; as, ऐसी करनी हम को सोहती नहीं 'such conduct is not
becoming in us'; तुम को नहीं सूझता 'is it not visible to you?'
मुझे देख पड़ता है 'to me it appears'; राजाओं को चाहिये प्रजा की रक्षा
करना 'it is right for kings to protect their subjects'; उस का
समाचार हम को पहुंचा है 'news of him has reached us.'

497. The ablative in connection with verbs usually conveys
the idea of 'from'; hence all verbs signifying 'departure,' 'removal,' 'differing from,' 'freeing from,' etc., require the ablative ;
as, वे उस ग्राम से चले गये हैं 'they have gone away from that village';
ये उन से भिन्न हैं 'these differ from those'; इन बन्धनों से मुझ को
कौन छुड़ावेगा 'who will rescue me from these bonds?'

498. Verbs of 'fearing,' 'hiding,' 'being ashamed,' etc.,
take the ablative also ; as, मैं उस से डरता हूं 'I am afraid of him,'
मार तो डालूं पर अपजस से डरता हूं 'I would kill (her) but I fear
the infamy'; झाड़ में अपनी तरैं मुझ से छिपाते हैं 'they are hiding
themselves from me among the bushes'; मैं अपनी दशा से लजाता
हूं 'I am ashamed of my condition.'

499. The following are additional instances of verbs in connection with the ablative ;—पड़ोसी से डाह मत रख 'envy not your
neighbour'; आप के अनुग्रह से हम कल्याण से रहते हैं 'through your
favor we live in happiness'; मैं आप से बिन्ती करता हूं मुझे क्षमा
कीजिये 'I implore you, be pleased to forgive me'; इतनी बात
कहने से क्या प्रयोजन है 'what need is there of saying so much?'
बुद्धिहीन सदा अपने कर्मों से प्रसन्न रहते हैं 'the ignorant are always
pleased with their own doings'; बुराई से घिन करता है 'he abhors
evil'; उन से बिदा होके मैं चला गया 'having taken leave of them
I went away'; वहां बैठके ब्राह्मण से बिबाद करने लगा 'having sat
down there, he began to dispute with the bráhman'; उस ने चढ़ने
से मुझ को रोक लिया 'he prevented me from ascending'; नदी पार
आने से उस को बरजा 'he forbad him to cross the river'; इस विषय

वे हाथ धोऊँगा 'I will wash my hands of this matter'; थकित होके लड़ने से विश्राम किया 'being wearied he ceased from fighting'; उन लोगों से सुचेत रहो 'beware of those people'; उस ने लड़का को डूब जाने से बचाया 'he saved the young man from being drowned'; वह प्रतिमा से प्रार्थना करता है 'he is praying to an idol'; मैं भूख से मरता हूँ 'I am dying of hunger'; तुम ने मुझ से कपट न किया 'you have not deceived me'; उन से पूछिये जो जानें 'enquire of those who may know'; माता अपने बालक से प्रेम रखती है 'a mother loves her child'; एक दूसरे से बैर रखते हैं 'they bear enmity one against another'; दूल्हे से मिलने को सब निकल गये हैं 'they have all gone out to meet the bridegroom.'

500. The locative in connection with verbs ordinarily expresses the place, time, or condition in which the subject or object of the sentence is, acts, or suffers; as, मैं नाव पर था 'I was on a boat'; वह नाले में नहाता था 'he was bathing in a stream'; तीन मास में पूरा कर सकता हूँ 'in three months I can complete it'; झील पर आंधी उठी और वे जोखिम में थे 'a storm arose on the lake and they were in danger'; कब लों उस दशा में रही 'how long did she remain in that condition?'

501. The locative is as frequently used with verbs of motion as the dative or accusative; thus, हम बन में चलें 'let us go to the wood'; अचानक वह प्रधानों की सभा में लौटा 'suddenly he returned to the assembly of the chiefs'; उस के घराने में फूट पड़ी 'dissension has arisen in his family'; वह समय पर आया 'he came in time'; नगर में पहुंचके अचंभे में हुए 'having arrived in the city they were astonished.'

502. Verbs that in English take the prepositions 'in,' 'into'; 'on,' 'upon'; 'among,' 'between,' generally require the locative case in Hindí; as, विक्रमादित्य के राज्य के पांचवें बरस में वह मर गया 'in the fifth year of the reign of Vikramáditya he died'; वे एक साथ मन्दिर में जाते थे 'they were going together into the

temple'; श्वेत घोड़े पर चढ़के आता है 'he is coming mounted on a white horse'; मेरी निश्चिन्तता के कारण तुम पर यह बिपत पड़ी है 'through my carelessness this calamity has fallen on you'; उस के सन्तानों में उस के समान ज्ञान में कोई न भया 'among his descendants there has been no one equal to him in knowledge'; उन में मत जाओ 'do not go among them.'

503. Sometimes 'regarding,' 'concerning,' etc., may be expressed by the locative case of the word to which reference is made; but more frequently बात, or बिषय, is used in the locative governing the word in the genitive to express the same idea; as, उस के आने के अभिप्राय में 'concerning the design of his coming'; लेनदेन के बिषय में 'regarding buying and selling.'

II. Use and application of the Tenses.

1. *Tenses from the Root.*

504. *a.* THE PROSPECTIVE CONDITIONAL :—It has already been said that this tense is not indicative, for it is never correctly used in a simple assertion; it always supposes a conjunction preceding, though not always expressed, and it invariably implies a relation to some other action. As, moreover, it is generally, though not always, followed by a verb in the future tense, or in the same tense denoting futurity, the name, 'Prospective Conditional,' accords more with its nature than that by which it is commonly known.

505. 'This tense is used for the expression of 'possibility,' 'liberty,' 'obligation,' 'inclination,' etc., in reference, especially, to future time; as, आशा रखता हूं कि वह आवे 'I am hoping that he may come'; आज जो बने तो भला 'if it can be done to-day, then, well'; समय में जो इस पेड़ पर फल लगे तो रखने दूं नहीं तो काट डालूं 'in the season, should there be fruit on this tree, I will let it remain; otherwise, I will cut it down'; यदि वहां पहुंचूं तो उस से मिलूंगा 'if I arrive there I will meet him'; उन को आने दो कि

वे भी देखें 'let them come that they also may see'; प्रत्येक से कहो कि कल मेरे पास आवे 'tell each one that he must come to me to-morrow'; चाहिये कि प्रतिज्ञा करें जो अपने बचन से न हटें 'they ought to promise that they will not swerve from their word.'

506. The conjunctions यदि, जो, कि, etc., are generally accompanied by this tense unless there be a reference to a past action; as, जो मैं चलूं तो मुझे क्या देंगे 'if I go what will you give me!' यदि चाहो पैदल चलो 'if you wish go on foot'; यह सब करते कि औरों से देखे जावें 'they do all this that they may be seen by others.'

507. This tense is also used to express present time conditionally, especially in requesting, wishing, praying, and often in proverbial expressions; as, जो कुछ हो सके वही करो 'whatever may be done, that do'; ईश्वर करे कि ऐसा न होवे 'may God grant that it may not be so'; जो आप चाहें तो मुझे संग ले चलिये 'if you wish take me with you'; ऊंट चढ़े कुत्ता काटे 'mounted on a camel the dog bites him.'

508. *b.* The Future :—This tense is used to denote future time, definitely or indefinitely; as, मैं उसे तुम को दूंगा 'I will give it to you'; वह कल आवेगा 'he will come to-morrow'; वे पांच बरस में लौटेंगे 'they will return in five years.'

509. The future perfect is expressed by using the verb चुकना as an auxiliary with the root of the principal verb; as, मैं पार उतर चुकूंगा आंधी के आने के आगे 'I shall have crossed over before the storm comes'; उस समय के पहिले हम सब मर चुकेंगे 'before that time we shall all have died.'

510. A future event that is about to take place is sometimes expressed by means of चाहना with the past participle of the principal verb; as, वह चला चाहता है 'he is about to go, or will go just now.'

511. Occasionally the future is used to denote uncertainty or probability; as, जिस ने ऐसा काम किया वह बड़ा ज्ञानी होगा ' he who did such a work must be a very wise man'; वे आते होंगे 'they may be coming, or probably are coming'; वह घर गया होगा 'he may have gone home.'

512. The present indefinite and the perfect are sometimes used idiomatically for the future; as, मैं अभी आता 'I will go just now'; a servant may often be heard to say मैं लाया his meaning being, 'I will bring it quickly'; अभी उस के यहां आता हूं और उस को लाके आप के संमुख उपस्थित कर देता हूं 'I will go just now to his house and having brought him will present him before you.'

513. The distinction between 'will' and 'shall' can not be expressed by the Hindí verb.

514. *c.* THE IMPERATIVE :—The imperative being in form the same as the prospective conditional (except the second person singular) is likely to be confounded with it. The second person singular is used in general prohibitions, as laws, enactments, etc., and in addresses to God it is considered reverential. It is never used, even in speaking to the humblest person, except in contemptuous or abusive language.

515. Observe that the form ending in इयो is a mild form of the imperative, but differs from the form ending in इये which is used to indicate respect and may be singular or plural. See 215.

516. The following are instances of the use of these forms ;—उस बात को मत भूलियो 'do not forget that matter'; कल मेरे पास उसे लाइयो 'bring him to me to-morrow'; लड़के को मारियो मत 'do not strike the boy'; मेरी बेटी की सुध लीजिये 'be pleased to take care of my daughter'; जो इन में से आप को चाहिये सो लीजिये 'whichever from among these you require be pleased to take'; जो आप चलिये तो मैं भी चलूंगा 'if you will be pleased to go then I will also go.'

517   The forms चाहे, चाहो, of the verb चाहना are in use as disjunctive conjunctions; thus, चाहे यह चाहे वह 'either this or that'; चाहो इस को लीजिये चाहो उस को 'take either this or that as you please.' The form चाहिये from the same verb, is frequently used impersonally in the sense of 'it is right,' 'it is fitting,' etc., and then governs the dative case; as, मुझ को सीखना चाहिये 'I ought to learn'; अब तुम को जाना चाहिये 'now you ought to go.'

518. The negatives मत, न, नहीं, are used with all verbs and may generally either precede or follow them; मत is used with the imperative only; न may be used with the imperative but is not restricted to it; नहीं is never used with the imperative, but it may precede the infinitive used imperatively. नहीं is a more emphatic negative than न, and in connection with the past tenses of transitive verbs is to be preferred to it in order to avoid confusion with ने, the sign of the case of the agent.

519. At the end of a sentence नहीं often occurs without a verb; in such cases the substantive verb होना must be understood, and generally its present tense; as, वह आप के संमुख खड़े होने के योग्य नहीं 'he is not worthy to stand before you'; यहां बैठने को स्थान नहीं 'there is no place to sit down here'; इन के पास कुछ नहीं 'they have nothing'; कुछ भी डर नहीं 'there is not any danger.'

520. The particle तो used immediately after नहीं gives to it the sense of 'otherwise,' 'else,' 'if not'; as, उसे त्यागो नहीं तो वह तुम को नाश करेगा 'abandon it, otherwise it will ruin you'; शीघ्र आओ नहीं तो मैं आऊंगा 'come quickly, if not I will go.'

2. Tenses from the present Participle.

521.   a. The Present Indefinite and Retrospective Conditional :—The name indicates that the main functions of this tense are, first, to denote continuous or habitual action having no definite reference to past or present time; and, secondly, it is used as a re-

trospective conditional, in which case it is very commonly preceded by a conjunction and followed by a verb in some past tense, or in the same tense pointing to the past. The following are instances ;—इस देश के लोग मांस नहीं खाते 'the people of this country do not eat flesh'; अपने लड़कों को जीने नहीं देते 'they do not allow their children to live'; जहां जहां वे जाते तहां तहां यह भी जाता ' wherever they used to go, there he also used to go'; इस गांव के लोग उस गांव के लोगों के संग व्यवहार नहीं करते 'the people of this village have no dealings with the people of that village'; राजा से लेके प्रजा तक सब भकोर लेते 'from the king to the subject all take bribes'; यदि गाय न चरतीं तो मर जातीं 'if the cows had not grazed they would have died'; जो तू मुझ से मांगता तो मैं तुझ को देता 'if you had asked of me I would have given to you'; जैसा मैं चाहता वैसा हो गया 'as I wished so it happened'; जो मेंह न पड़ता तो घास न उगती 'if rain had not fallen then grass would not have sprung up.'

522.   The presence of a conjunction distinguishes the retrospective conditional from the present indefinite; but sometimes there is an omission of the conjunction in the former part of the sentence, or, in the latter part, of the particle तो, which is generally used to introduce the second part of a conditional proposition; thus, मेरे पास धन होता तो भीख क्यों मांगता 'if I had wealth why did I beg ?' यदि वह जानता मुझ को कह देता 'if he had known he would have told me.'

523.   The present indefinite is occasionally used for the present definite; as, वह क्या समझता 'what does he think ?' तुम क्या करते 'what are you doing?' Europeans are apt to use this tense as if it were generally equivalent to the present definite; it is well, however, to remember that indefiniteness as to time is the main feature of this tense, though generally it refers to the past.

524.   *b.* THE PRESENT DEFINITE :—The primary use of this tense is to denote an emphatic present; as, मैं लिखता हूं 'I am

writing'; मेंह बरसता है 'it is raining'; वे चूधर दौड़ते हैं 'they are running here.'

525.   It is also used for the expression of general statements or truths; as, कहते हैं जिस समय घर में कुपूत आता है तिसी समय जस और धर्म्म जाते हैं 'they say that when a bad son enters a house honor and virtue leave it'; मनुष्य जैसा आप होता है वैसा दूसरे को जानता है 'as a man himself is so he thinks another is.'

526.   'Habitual or continuous action' is frequently denoted by this tense; as, वह अच्छा बोलता है 'he speaks well'; रात दिन वह मन लगाके सीखता है 'night and day applying his mind he studies.'

527.   In animated narrative the present definite is used to describe past acts or events, and when a person describes what he saw or heard, this tense is used to depict the scene as if still present to view, or the very words as they were heard are quoted ; as, वहां पहुंचके क्या देखता हूं कि एक बसती है जिस में से अनेक लोग आते हैं 'arriving there what do I see? That there is a village out of which many people are coming'; उस ने उत्तर दिया कि मैं नहीं जानता हूं 'he replied, I do not know'; वे हंसके कहने लगे कि हम निश्चय आवेंगे 'they laughing said, we will certainly come.'

528.   This direct form of speech is a characteristic feature of Hindí idiom, and is far more forcible and impressive than the indirect form which is more usual in English. The indirect mode is occasionally noticed in Hindí, but natives, as a rule, seldom adopt it, and even an ordinary message is given in the words of the sender; thus, उस ने मुझ को कहला भेजा कि आप से भेंट करने को सांझ को आऊंगा 'he sent me to say, I will come in the evening to visit you'; स्वामी से कहो गुरु कहता है कि पाहुनशाला कहां है जिस में अपने शिष्यों के संग रहूं 'say to the master, the teacher says, where is the guest-chamber in which I may stay with my disciples?'

529. The present definite sometimes conveys the sense of a near future ; as, हम बेगहो जन्म ले तुम्हारी चिन्ता मेटते हैं 'we quickly taking birth will remove your anxiety'; जिस भांति देवी बलदेव को गोकुल ले गई तिसी रीति से कथा कहता हूं 'I will relate to you the very manner in which Devi took Baldev to Gokul.'

530. c. The Imperfect :—This tense denotes the progression of a past action during the time in which something else took place ; as, वे अपने दीपक जलाते थे सूर्य्य के अस्त होने पर 'they were lighting their lamps on the going down of the sun'; रात को सोते थे कि एक सांप ने नन्दराय का पांव पकड़ा 'they were sleeping at night when a snake laid hold of Nandaray's foot'; मैं अपना खाना पकाता था जब वह आया 'I was cooking my food when he came.'

3. Tenses from the Past Participle.

531. a. The Historical Past:—The peculiar construction that must be followed with all past tenses when the verb is transitive is explained at 216. The name, Historical Past, clearly defines the use of this tense as denoting an action or event as past and complete without any definite reference to time; thus, मैं ने एक चिट्ठी लिखी 'I wrote a letter'; तू ने पुकारा 'you called out'; उस ने उन से कहा 'he said to them'; वे बोले 'they spake.'

532. This tense is often repeated with the particle तो between to express idiomatically that the action can not be reversed ; as, हुआ तो हुआ, मारा तो मारा, गया तो गया, etc.; these expressions, not literally, but in corresponding idiomatic English might be thus rendered, 'what is done can not be undone'; 'if he has killed him, why he has killed him'; 'if he has gone, he has gone and there is an end of it.' Similarly, जो हमारे बड़ों ने जाने अनजाने इन्द्र की पूजा की तो की पर अब तुम ज्ञान बूझकर धर्म्म का पन्थ छोड़ उबट बाट क्यों चलते हो might be translated, 'if our forefathers, knowingly or unknowingly, worshipped Indra it can not be helped; but now,

why knowingly leaving the way of virtue are you walking in an impassable path?'

533. The historical past tense (or past participle as it may be regarded) of a few verbs is used as a noun; thus, कर्म का लिखा कोई मेट नहीं सकता 'the writing of fate no one can obliterate'; वह मेरा कहा नहीं मानेगा 'he will not regard what I have said.'

534. *b*. THE PERFECT DEFINITE :—This tense represents the action as past and complete at the time spoken of, but generally refers it to some recent period; as, वह आया है 'he has come'; मैं ने खाना खाया है 'I have eaten my food'; वे गये हैं 'they have gone'; किस देश से आये हो 'from what country have you come?'

535. *c*. THE PLUPERFECT :—This tense denotes that the action or event was past before some other action or event to which usually it has some reference; as, रथ से वे उतरी थीं जब वह दिखाई दिया 'they had descended from the chariot when he appeared'; तुम्हारे आने के आगे वह गया था 'before you came he had gone'; जब नाव पर चढ़ गये चांद उदय हुआ था 'when they embarked on the boat the moon had risen.'

536. Sometimes this tense is used when no other past action is specified, and it is frequently used where in English the simple past is employed; as, वह बोला था 'he spoke'; तुम को बुलाया था 'he called you'; वे आये थे 'they came.'

537. An anomaly may here be noticed in the usage of the past tenses of the transitive verb देना when compounded with दिखाई or सुनाई, viz., that it can not when thus compounded take the transitive construction with the case of the agent, but must be treated as a neuter verb; thus, वे (not उन ने) दिखाई दिये 'they appeared'; शब्द सुनाई दिया 'a voice was heard.'

III. The Infinitive.

538. The infinitive in Hindí is of extensive and varied application; strictly speaking, it is no part of the verb, but rather a noun signifying the action denoted by the verb; it has no direct reference to an agent or to time, and defines nothing but the bare act.

539. When used as a noun to express the act of the verb, the infinitive is subject to inflection like a masculine noun or an adjective en ding in का, and takes the postpositions in all the cases except the agent and vocative; thus, मारना सुगम है पर जिलाना कठिन है 'killing is easy, but bringing to life is difficult'; अब शिकार को जाने का समय है 'now is the time to go to the chase'; गुरु की शिक्षा सुनने को आते हैं 'they are coming to listen to . the instruction of the teacher'; हटने से मरना भला है 'death is better than yielding'; उच्चारण करने में वह अति शुद्ध है 'he is very correct in pronunciation.'

540. Used as a verbal noun, an infinitive may become the subject or the predicate of a sentence; as, मरना लाभ है 'death is gain'; बुरे को भला जानना बुरा करना है ' the regarding evil as good is doing evil'; अपने को जानना सब ज्ञान से उत्तम है 'to know oneself is the best of all knowledge.'

541. An infinitive may be used adjectively with a noun as part of the subject or the predicate of a sentence and must agree with it in gender and number; as, मिथ्यावादी की बात न. मानो यही उस का दंड है 'the not regarding the word of a liar is his punishment'; मैं ने इस देश की भाषा बोलनी नहीं सीखी है ' I have not learnt to speak the language of this country'; बहुत बातें बनानी अच्छा नहीं 'to make many excuses is not good'; पशु को बिन चारा रखना दयाहीन होने का लक्षय है 'to keep an animal without fodder is a sign of being cruel.'

542.   The object of an action is frequently denoted by the inflected infinitive with or without को; as, लकड़ी बटोरने को आई 'she came to gather wood'; गोरु चराने को खेत में गया है 'he has gone to the field to graze cattle'; मुझे आने को कहा 'he told me to come'; वह खोये हुए को ढूंढने और बचाने आया है 'he has come to seek and to save the lost.' The infinitive governed in the genitive by a noun may also indicate the object of an action; as, उस ने बैठने की आज्ञा दी 'he gave an order to sit down.'

543.   The infinitive is governed in the genitive by prepositions just like nouns; thus, रानी को ढूंढने के लिये बाहर निकले 'they went out to search for the queen'; बिन देखे आने के 'without being seen'; दौड़ने के आगे 'before running.'

544.   The infinitive is sometimes idiomatically used with the sense of the imperative, and may then take either मत or न before it; as, उन के यहां कभी न आना 'never go to their house'; मुझ को मत भूलना 'do not forget me.' This idiom is not considered elegant; it belongs more to Urdú than to Hindí.

545.   With the verb होना the infinitive is used to convey a sense of necessity or obligation; as, अब मुझे जाना है 'now I must go'; जो करना है सो शीघ्र कर 'what is to be done do quickly'; यूं होना था 'thus it was to be'; हम सभों को मरना है 'we must all die'; इन को पार भेजना है 'these must be sent across.'

IV. PARTICIPLES.

546. *a.* PRESENT AND PAST PARTICIPLES :—When used in a strictly participial or adjectival sense to qualify the nominative or the object in a sentence, and not to form a tense, these participles have the auxiliary हुआ (हुए, हुई) as a rule added to them; the cases in which the auxiliary is omitted are chiefly those in which the participle follows the noun; when thus used they agree, like adjectives, with the nouns that they qualify, but not unfrequently

the past participle of a transitive verb may happen not to agree with the noun it qualifies, as in the last of the following examples;—मेरी ब्याही हुई बेटी भी आती है ' my married daughter is also coming'; उस ने कहा बचे हुए टुकड़े बटोर लो 'he said, gather together the fragments that are left'; कितने एक लड़के खेलते हुए वहां आये 'several children engaged in play came there'; मैं ने लड़के को आते हुए देखा 'I saw a boy coming'; गांव की स्त्रियां रंगीला वस्त्र पहिने हुए नाचती थीं 'the women of the village wearing gaudy clothes were dancing.'

547. In the following instances the auxiliary is omitted :— ऋषि नैन मूंदे हरि का ध्यान लगाये तप कर रहे थे 'the Rishi, with closed eyes and meditating on Hari, was doing penance'; पोथी कांख में लिये राजा के संमुख आये 'taking their books under their arms they came before the king'; लड़कों को साथ लिये आती थीं 'they (women) were coming bringing their children with them'; उन के वहां रहते वह मर गया 'whilst they remained there he died.'

548. The past participle of a *transitive verb* may be used in the masculine plural form to qualify a singular or a feminine noun; but when the verb is *not transitive* its past participle must agree in gender and number with the noun qualified by it ; as, लड़की छाता लगाये बाप के पीछे दौड़ी जाती थी 'the girl holding an umbrella was running behind her father'; बाप बेटे को गोदी में लिये और खड़ा हुआ अपने भाई से बात चीत करता था ' the father holding the son in his arms and standing was conversing with his brother'; वह घोड़े पर चढ़ा हुआ आता था 'he was coming riding on a horse'; लड़की आभूषण पहिने हुए बाहर आई 'the girl wearing ornaments came out.'

549. The repetition of the present participle denotes the continuation of the action; as, राजा आखेट को गये और खेलते खेलते प्यासे भये 'the king went to the chase and continuing the sport he became thirsty'; मार्ग में जाते जाते वे किसी नगर के पास पहुंचे 'as

X

they journeyed on the way they came to a certain town'; दौड़ता दौड़ता वह थक गया 'continuing to run he became tired.'

550. The present participle is often used in the inflected form as a verbal noun; thus, मेरे रहते कोई तुम से कुछ नहीं कहेगा 'in my presence, or whilst I remain, no one will say anything to you'; अपने पिता के जीते वह चैन से रहा करता 'during the life of his father he used to live at ease'; मुझे देखते वह घबरा गया 'at the sight of me he was perplexed.'

551. In the following and all similar expressions the participles seem to be used adverbially;—भोर होते 'when it was morning'; सांझ हुए 'when it was evening'; जीते जी 'during the lifetime'; जाड़े के आते 'the coming on of the cold weather.'

552. *b.* Conjunctive Participle :—It will be remembered that there are five forms of this most useful participle, all of them indeclinable and all having the same signification. They are in constant use to connect the members of a sentence, without the use of conjunctions ; they refer generally to the nominative, but sometimes to the object of the verb, and are connected with the past more than with other tenses, to express the performance of an action prior to another action denoted by a subsequent verb; thus, यह कहकर उस को बन्धन से छुड़ाकर बिदा किया 'having said this (and) having released him from bondage he dismissed him'; वहां आकर सब कुछ समझाके जीघ आओ 'having gone there (and) having explained everything come quickly.'

553. Observe that the verb आना is peculiar in taking the forms आन, आनके, in addition to the regular forms आ, आके, etc. ; as, इतने में सब सखी सहेली आन मिलीं 'in the mean time, all the female attendants having come met (her).'

554. *c.* The Adverbial Participle :—The inflected form of the present participle with the emphatic particle ही added to it

forms what is termed the adverbial participle. It partakes more of the nature of a verbal noun than of a participle, and is an instance of what has been said before, that the inflected present participle generally expresses state or condition. Sometimes its signification differs from that of the conjunctive participle only in conveying the idea of greater promptness or speed; as, भोर होते ही वह उठके चला गया 'as soon as it was dawn he arose and went away'; उस के जाते ही वे आये 'immediately on his departure they came'; इस बात को सुनते ही उस ने उत्तर दिया 'on hearing this statement he replied'; from these examples it will be observed that the adverbial participle may take a noun in the nominative, the genitive, or the accusative case before it.

555. There remains but little to say regarding verbs : of the six uncommon tenses (See 255-261.) there are but two, the present dubious, and the past dubious, that are at all likely to be occasionally met with ; the others are, from their nature, of rare occurrence. The following are instances of the present and of the past dubious, in which be it observed that the second verb, though future in form, is not often so in sense, but rather expresses sometimes uncertainty, sometimes probability;—वह कहीं जाता होगा 'he is perhaps (or probably) going somewhere'; वे आते होंगे 'they may be coming'; तुम ने यह दृष्टान्त सुना होगा 'you may have heard this proverb'; मैं नहीं जानता हूं कि उसने क्या किया होगा 'I do not know what he may have done'; कौन कह सकता कि उस ने उन से क्या न किया होगा 'who can say what he may not have done with them ?'

556. The passive voice is not nearly so common in Hindí as in most other languages owing to the construction that is necessary with the past tenses of transitive verbs, which, in reality, is a passive construction. It is most frequently employed when the agent is not known or is not expressed; as, इन लोगों को भोजन दिया जावेगा 'food will be given to these people'; मैं

सुना है कि वह किसी के हाथ से मारा गया 'I have heard that he was killed by the hand of some one'; वह उन से पहचाना कभी नहीं आवेगा 'he will never be recognised by them.'

557. There are a few verbs that acquire from their connection with other words a meaning somewhat different from their ordinary signification; the most important are as follows :—

आना 'to come' when used with nouns often serves to supply the place of other verbs; as, उस को उन पर दया आई 'he had pity on them,' literally 'to him on them pity came'; मुझे निश्चय नहीं आता; 'I am not certain'; निदान उनको चेत आया 'at last they remembered'; तुम को शास्त्र नहीं आता 'you do not understand the Sasters.'

उठाना 'to lift,' 'to raise up,' often acquires the sense of 'to endure,' 'to enjoy,' 'to spend,' etc.; as, मैं इन दिनों में बहुत दुःख उठाता हूँ 'I suffer much pain in these days'; व्यर्थ तुम रुपये उठाते हो 'you are spending money uselessly'; वह सब कुछ उठा चुका है 'he has spent everything'; इधर से आओगे तो सुख उठाओगे और उधर से आओगे तो दुःख उठाओगे 'if you will go in this way you will obtain happiness, and if you will go in that way you will suffer.'

कहाना and कहलाना though causal forms from the verb कहना are peculiar in having a passive sense; as, यह फल आम कहाता है 'this fruit is called mango'; उधर का गांव रामपुर कहलाता है 'the village over there is called Rámpur.'

खाना 'to eat' when used with some nouns acquires a sense that seems but little connected with the ordinary meaning of the word; as, वह किरिया खाता है 'he is taking an oath'; वह उस को किरिया खिलाता है 'he is administering an oath to him'; उस के सेवक रिश्वत खाते 'his servants take bribes'; उस ने उसे बहुत से घूस खिलाये 'he gave him many bribes'; लड़के ने मार खाई 'the boy got a beating'; मैं तुझे मार खिलाऊंगा 'I will give you a beating';

वह घाम खाता है 'he is warming himself in the sunshine'; वे भय खाते हैं 'they are afraid.'

चुकना 'to finish' is in constant use as an auxiliary in forming compound verbs; (See 275) it is rarely used alone and never with the first or second person; as, गेहूं चुका है अथवा कुछ शेष रहा 'is the wheat finished or is there some left?'

बना 'to be made' is often idiomatically used as in the following instances;—हम से उन से कभी नहीं बनेगी 'there will never be agreement (or friendship) between us and them'; कुछ बनी कुछ बिगड़ी 'some answered (suited), some failed'; राजा का स्वरूप बनकर 'assuming the form of a king.'

मारना 'to smite,' 'to strike,' has the following among other peculiar uses;—उस ने हाय मारके कहा 'he having sighed said'; छान मारना 'to search for, rummage'; डुबकी मारना, 'to dive,' 'to plunge into'; बन्धक मारना 'to put in pledge'; भोला मारना 'to blight,' 'to blast.' When used with the name of an instrument or weapon it signifies to strike with it; as, गोली मारना 'to shoot a bullet at'; हाथ पांव मारना 'to shuffle,' 'to scuffle'; उस ने उसे खड्ग मारा 'he struck him with the sword; घोड़े ने उस को लात मारा 'the horse kicked him.'

THE REPETITION OF WORDS.

558. The repetition of words is very common in Hindí to denote distribution or division; as, एक एक को दो दो पंख हैं 'they have each two wings'; अपने अपने सामर्थ्य के अनुसार 'each one according to his ability.'

559. Two past participles are often used together, the second being in the feminine gender, to express 'reciprocity of action'; as, छाना छानी 'scrambling and scratching'; खेंचा खेंची 'pulling and hawling'; मारा मारी 'scuffling'; कहा कही 'altercation.'

560. Sometimes a word is repeated with the effect of giving force or intensity to the idea; as, इस मेले में दूर दूर के लोग आये हैं 'people from a very great distance have come to this fair'; जो उस के पास हैं सो छोटे छोटे हैं 'what he has are very small'; मेरी बारी में लम्बे लम्बे पेड़ हैं 'in my garden there are very tall trees'; वह धीमे धीमे चलता है 'he goes very slowly.'

561. To express the idea of *et caetera*, or *and so on*, a word having no meaning, but that will rhyme or jingle with the word used is added to it; as, पानी वानी लाओ 'bring the water, etc'; रोटी वोटी कहां रखी तुझ ने 'where have you put the bread and other things?' Sometimes words of similar meaning that resemble each other in sound are used together, the second having no effect on the sense; as, रगड़े झगड़े 'disputings'; भूंड़ार भेड़ें तितर बितर करता है 'the wolf is scattering the sheep.'

ADVERBS, PREPOSITIONS AND CONJUNCTIONS.

562. Adverbs have no definite position in the sentence, but, as a rule, they should be placed near the words qualified by them.

563. Many adverbs admit the signs of the cases after them like nouns; as, वहां का जल खारा है 'the water of that place is brackish'; तुम कहां से आये हो 'where have you come from?'

564. Many of the adverbs are used in pairs as relative and correlative, one being in the former part of the sentence and the other in the latter; as, जब तक मैं न आऊं तब तक तुम यहां से मत जाओ 'till I come do not go from here'; जहां मैं आता हूं तहां तुम आ नहीं सकते हो 'where I am going there you can not come'; ज्यों सूर्य उदय होता त्यों घास को सुखाता है 'as soon as the sun rises it withers the grass.'

565. On adverbs formed from nouns and adjectives (See 297, 298,) and add the following examples:—वह पैदल आवेगा 'he will come on foot'; वह गाड़ी करके आई 'she came riding in a carriage';

मैं ने उन को चुपके से बुलाके उन से गब्ब से पूछा 'having called them secretly I carefully enquired of them'; विशेष करके 'especially.'

566. The compound adverb अब तक, or अब लों 'until,' is used with the past or future tenses, preceded generally, though not invariably, by the negative न; as, अब लों दो मास पूरे न हुय तब लों वह ठहर गया 'he remained until two months were completed': अब तक तुम्हें न भेजूं तब तक वहां मत जाओ 'do not go there till I send you.'

567. The affix तः (from the Sanskrit तस्) is sometimes added to nouns and adjectives to form adverbs, and generally gives the sense of *with* or *from*; as, सामान्यतः ऐसा नहीं हो सकता 'it can not be generally so'; similarly, यथार्थतः 'certainly,' 'suitably'; विशेषतः 'especially'; वस्तुतः 'substantially,' 'réally'; etc.

568. पूर्वक (the Sanskrit पूर्वकं) signifying 'prior to,' 'preceded by,' is added to nouns and adjectives to form adverbs of manner; as, अन्यायपूर्वक 'unjustly'; यथार्थतापूर्वक 'correctly,' 'exactly'; सम्मतिपूर्वक 'concurrently,' 'unanimously'; साहसपूर्वक 'boldly,' 'courageously.' Adverbs of this form and those of the preceding rule are used in books and among Pandits, but not often in common conversation.

569. The ablative case of रूप is often used with nouns and adjectives to form adverbial phrases; as, प्रधान रूप से 'chiefly,' 'especially'; सम्पूर्ण रूप से 'entirely,' 'completely'; पृथक रूप से 'distinctly,' 'separately'; साधारण रूप से 'commonly,' 'generally.'

570. Prepositions as a rule govern the genitive case and follow the nouns they govern; the placing them before the noun is in imitation of the Urdú idiom; thus, घर के आगे 'before the house,' but not आगे घर के.

571. A few prepositions, as बिन, or बिना 'without,' सहित 'with,' रहित 'without,' govern their noun in the nominative form;

बिन or बिना is peculiar in being frequently placed before the noun; as, बिना कारण मुझ से क्रोध करता है 'without a cause he is angry with me'; उस की सहायता बिन में क्या करूँ 'without his assistance what can I do?' समाज सहित आता है 'he is coming with the assembly.'

572. बिन is often used with the inflected past participle of a verb; thus, बिन जाने 'without knowing'; बिन कहे सुने 'without speaking or hearing.'

573. जो and कि are used as conjunctions with the sense of 'that,' 'because,' 'since'; as, मैं चाहता हूँ कि वह इस से लाभ उठावे 'I desire that he may obtain benefit from this'; मैं नहीं जानता हूँ जो वह लिखेगा 'I do not know that he will write.'

574. जो as a conditional conjunction generally requires तो in the following part of the sentence; as, जो मैं आज जाऊँ तो कल लौटूँगा 'if I go to-day I will return to-morrow.' The conjunction is sometimes omitted; as, आप देंगे तो क्यों नहीं ले जाऊँगा '(if) you will give it then why shall I not take it away?'

CHAPTER XII.

Prosody, छन्द chhand.

___

The Prosody of Sanskrit and its dialects, प्राकृत *Prákrit*, will be found to be richer than that of any other known language, in variation of metre, whether regulated by quantity, मात्रा *mátrá,* or by syllables, वृत्त *vritta*, both with and without rhyme. Prákrit is a term applied by native authors to those dialects of the Sanskrit which are generally employed by dramatic writers ; but in a general sense it may be used for any regular provincial dialect corrupted, अपभ्रंश *apabhrans*, from the Sanskrit. The affinity of the Prákrit, and especially of the dialects used by dramatic writers, to the Sanskrit is so great that the laws of versification, permutation, alliteration, &c. may be considered as common to both.

There are several Prákrit dialects such as the शौरसेनी *Saurseni,* मागधी *Mágadhí,* पैशाची *Paisáchí,* &c. on the formation of which from the Sanskrit, several treatises have been written by native authors. Besides those cognate dialects, dramatic writers have introduced other dialects, an enumeration of which will be found in the साहित्यदर्पण *Sáhitya darpana* and also in other works on Rhetoric and Prosody. We shall in the following pages deal especially with the Prákrit in common use among the Hindoos, which has received the general term *Hindí*, in contradistinction to the dialect used mostly by Mahommedans and by many Hindus of the upper classes, which is called *Urdú* or *Hindústání*.

Accents and *emphasis* form no distinguishing part of Hindí versification. Rhyme, *tuk* तुक, is generally used. The construction of Hindí poetry is unique and ingenious. There being no doubtful vowels in the language, the rules to distinguish the quantity of

Y

syllables for scanning, or for constructing poetry, are necessarily few; the following will be found sufficient.

Rule 1.—अ इ उ ऋ ऌ are *short*, and आ ई ऊ ॠ ॡ ए ऐ ओ औ *long* by nature, whether used separately or joined to a consonant.

Rule 2.—A vowel short by nature becomes long by position, that is, when it comes before a double consonant. It is of no consequence whether the double consonant follow the vowel in the same word or in a consecutive word; thus, विद्या and धर्म्म ध्यान, the short इ of विद्या and the inherent अ of म्म are to be counted long.

Rule 3.—A short vowel before a double consonant the last of which is the liquid र may be optionally long or short.

Rule 4.—A short vowel followed by (.) *anuswár*, or by (:) *visarg*, is always long.

There are a few other modifications, but they belong more to Sanskrit than to Prákrit Prosody.

OF QUANTITY.

गुरु *guru*, long; लघु *laghu*, short.

In native prosody they are marked ॽ and ।, equivalent to our — and ᴗ, *longus* and *brevis*.

OF PAUSE, विराम *Virám*.

There are commonly two pauses, the *sentential* and the *harmonic;* the former is indicated by the sign ।, the latter has no distinctive sign in Prákrit poetry, the ear must guide.

CLASSES OF VERSIFICATION.

वृत्त छन्द and जाति छन्द

Versification, छन्द, is divided into two classes.

The 1st, called वृत्त छन्द *vritta chhand*, measured by the number of syllables (or letters) वरण *varana*.

The 2nd, called जाति छन्द *játi chhand*, measured by the *instants* or time occupied in the pronunciation, that is, by the मात्रा *mátrá* or कल *kala*, being long or short.

ON THE ORDERS.

The *first* Class, वृत्त छन्द *vritta chhand*, is divided into three *orders;* that is, 1. सम *sama*, 2. अर्ध सम *ardhasama*, and 3. विषम *vishama*.

1.—*Sama* has an equal number of syllables in all the four charaṇas (or pádas) of the verse.

2.—*Ardhasama* has an equal number of syllables in the first and third, or the *odd* charaṇas, and in the second and fourth, or the *even* charaṇas.

3.—*Vishama* has an unequal number of syllables in each of the four charaṇas.

EXAMPLES.

1. सम वृत्त ।

भुजंगप्रयात छन्द ।

महावीर श्री राम ज्योंहीं चढे हैं   कपी सैन के ठठ्ठ आगे बढे हैं ।
भिरे खग्ग सों खग्ग कीन्हें भतंका   चढी ही छवारी सर्व जीति लंका ॥

य × 4 i. e. 4Bs in each charaṇa.

---

2. अर्धसम वृत्त ।

द्रुतमध्या छन्द ।

कानन चौ सूय होत हरीरो   जहं तहं आनु सुखी तन धीरो ।
बोलत मोर सबे घन भीरो   भुदित चरावत गाव बधोरो ॥

1st and 3d charaṇas. अ × 3 + ग × 2 i.e. 3Ds 1 Sp.
2d. and 4th do. न + र × 2 + य. i.e. T+2C+B.

---

3. विषम वृत्त ।

सौरभ छन्द ।

हरिमाधवा चरतु शोक मधु मथन नन्द नन्दना ।
गोपिका रमय नाथ हरे   तुम्र पाद पत्कम युग वाख वाख सों ॥

1st. charaṇa	$\left\{ \begin{array}{l} \text{स + ज + स + ल} \\ \text{A + S + A + B} \end{array} \right.$	2d. charaṇa	$\left\{ \begin{array}{l} \text{न + स + ज + ग} \\ \text{T + A + S + L.} \end{array} \right.$
3d. do.	$\left\{ \begin{array}{l} \text{न + र + भ + ग} \\ \text{T + C + D + L} \end{array} \right.$	4th do.	$\left\{ \begin{array}{l} \text{स + ज + स + ज + ग} \\ \text{A + S + A + S + L.} \end{array} \right.$

NOTE :—The four charaṇas of every verse are divided by native authors, for brevity and convenience of reference, into two groups or pairs, or as we might call them the *odd* and *even* groups—1. विषमचरण *vishama charaṇa*, composed of the first and third, and 2. समचरण *samacharaṇa*, composed of the second and fourth charaṇas.

ON THE METHOD OF CONSTRUCTING OR SCANNING.

There are three kinds of feet, गण *gaṇa*, commonly used in Hindí poetry, monosyllabic, dissyllabic and trisyllabic, and sometimes polysyllabic, Ex :—

Monosyllabic, comprising two species.

Anglice.

गुरु, abbreviated ग, named *háru* ऽ, – Longus L.
लघु, " ल, " *meru* ।, ‿ Brevis B.

Dissyllabic, comprising four species or combinations.

गग named करण *karaṇa* marked ᵕᵕ spondee — — Sp.

गल   „   ताल *tála* „ ᵕ ∣ trochee — ⌣ Tr.

लग   „   ध्वज *dhwaja* „ ∣ ᵕ iambus ⌣ — I.

लल   „   सुपिय *supriya* „ ∣ ∣ periambus ⌣ ⌣ P.

Trisyllabic, comprising eight species or combinations, called emphatically गण *gaṇa.*

		Anglice	
गण	प्रस्तार		
मगण 1	ᵕ ᵕ ᵕ	Molussus	— — — M.
यगण 2	∣ ᵕ ᵕ	Bacchic	⌣ — — B.
रगण 3	ᵕ ∣ ᵕ	Cretic	— ⌣ — C.
सगण 4	∣ ∣ ᵕ	Anapæst	⌣ ⌣ — A.
तगण 5	ᵕ ᵕ ∣	Hypo.-or Anti-bacchic	— — ⌣ H.
जगण 6	∣ ᵕ ∣	Scolius or Amphibrach	⌣ — ⌣ S.
भगण 7	ᵕ ∣ ∣	Dactyl	— ⌣ ⌣ D.
नगण 8	∣ ∣ ∣	Tribrach	⌣ ⌣ ⌣ T.

Proceleusmatic or *Polysyllabic,*—is formed by a combination of the above three kinds.

Of Genera and Species.

The *first* class of poetry comprises 26 Genera or variety of metres, consisting of from one to twenty-six syllables in each *charaṇa ;* and each genus comprehends several species, according to the different modes in which long or short syllables may be combined, so that in a metre consisting of 26 syllables to the *charaṇa,* almost an infinite variety of metres can be formed. Thus in a verse in which the *charaṇa* consists of three syllables (as above tabulated) eight varieties can be formed, and in one of six syllables sixty-four varieties, and so on.

Rules are given by native authors for computing the number of species, भेद *bhed,* in each genus, and for finding the numerical places (उदिष्ट *udisht*) of any single variety in the प्रस्तार *prastár,* or conversely, for finding the metre (नष्ट *nasht*) of any species of which the numerical place is assigned in the *prastár.* But it should be borne in mind that it is not likely that all the species can ever be brought into use. The different sorts which have been used by poets must be very few in comparison with the vast multitude of possible metres. It will answer our purpose if we exemplify but a few of those that are most commonly used under each genus.

1st CLASS

वर्ण वृत्त

OR

Metres measured by the number of Syllables.

1st ORDER

सम वृत्त *Sama vritta,*

OR

Verses that have an equal number of syllables in each of the four charaṇas.

Note.—The number of the Genus indicates the number of syllables in a charaṇa of that genus.

Examples of the 1st and 2nd charaṇas only are given.—In this class the first and second and the third and fourth charaṇas rhyme together.

Species.	Feet in one charaṇa.	Genera.	Examples.
		उक्था I GENUS.	
श्री	ग		मा था ।
		अत्युक्था II GENUS.	
1 काम	गग		रामा कृष्णा ।

2	मक्ती	भग	हरे हरे ।
3	छघु	भल	हरि हरि ।
4	छार	गल	राम कृष्या ।

मध्या III Genus.

1	ताली or नारी	म	कन्वारें शोभारें ।
2	मृगी or प्रिया	र	प्रेमछीं पागिरो ।
3	शब्री	य	भवानी सुबानी ।
4	रमया	स	विधुकी रजनी ।
5	पश्चाल	त	शोछध्वे संसार ।
6	कमल	न	कमल कुमुद ।

प्रतिष्ठा IV Genus.

1	तीर्वा or कन्या	मग	छैगोविन्दा छैगोविन्दा ।
2	धारी	रल	नन्दलाल कंसकाल ।
3	नगानिका	जग	करोचितें नर्चचले ।
4	सती	नग	छलतर्वे सुखलछे ।

सुप्रतिष्ठा V Genus.

1	छम्मोछा	मगग	श्रीराधामाधो आराधोछाधो ।
2	चारित	तगग	गौरीभवानी छैजेमछानी ।
3	हंसी	भगग	मोछनमाधो गावछछाधो ।
4	जमक	नलल	भरखाजग धरखानग ।

गायत्री VI Genus.

	Name	
1	श्रेवराज or विधुरेखा	मम
2	हिल्ल or तिलक	छछ
3	मालती	जज
4	तनुमध्या	तय
5	श्रग्विवदना	नय
6	वसुमति	तछ
7	विभोद्धा &c.	रर

गोविन्दागोपाला केशीकंसाकाला ।
प्रभुषोंकांछिये दुखमोंहरिये ।
गुविन्द गुपाल रूपाल दयाल ।
मोहीयकलेश्रा टारोकरिवेश्रा ।
हरिहरिकेश्रो सुभग सुवेश्रो ।
गोपालकछिये श्रानन्दलछिये ।
देवकीनन्दनं भक्तभोभभञ्जनं ।

उष्णिक् VII Genus.

	Name	
1	भभानिका	रयग
2	वास	नज
3	करहञ्च	नछल
4	शीर्षरूप	भभग
5	भद्रलेखा	मसग
6	मधुर्मति &c.	ननगा

रामरामगाईये रामलोकपाईये ।
भजुमनमोछन परमसुछोछन ।
हरिचरणछेउ सुखपरमलेउ ।
छेछैकृष्णागोपाला राधामाधोषीपाला ।
गोविन्दार्कछिमाधो केश्रीछीछरिछाधो ।
भजुहरिचरणा असरणाचरणा ।

अनुष्टुप् VIII Genus.

	Name	
1	विद्युल्माला	भमगग
2	प्रभानिका or नाराच	अरलग
3	मल्लिका	रजगल
4	हुंगा	ननगग

छेंछैछेंयोराधाकृष्णा केश्रोकंछारातीविष्णा ।
भजोभजोगुपालको रूपालनन्दलालको ।
रामकृष्णारामकृष्णा वासुदेवविष्णाविष्णा ।
गगनजलदछाये मदनजगसुहाये ।

5	कमल	नसलग
6	कुमारललिता	जसोलग
7	चित्रपदा &c.	भभगग

हरिहरिकेठोकठो सबसुखलठोलठो
भजोजुसुखकन्दको हरोजुदुखदन्दको
दीनदयालुदेवा मीनकरीप्रभुसेवा

वृहती IX Genus.

राधिकावल्लभभेजार्ईले छोनिर्दन्द्राउनेपाईले
हरिहरिकोगोर्कहिये सबसुखसारालहिये
श्रायोश्रालीजलदसमी केकोकूर्जंजियभरमी
कमलसरसनयनी शशिमुखिप्रियकवयनी
तुलसिवनकेलिकारी सकलजनचित्तहारी
नवनीलनीरदंश्याम शुकदेवग्रोभननाम
श्रृंगावंगाकालिंगाकाश्री गंगासिन्धुसंगामाभासी

1	महालक्ष्मी	ररर
2	सारंगिका	नयस
3	पार्वता	मभस
4	कमला	ननस
5	बिम्ब	नसय
6	तोमर	सजज
7	रूपमाली &c.	ममम

पंक्ति X Genus.

हरिरूप्यकेशववामना वसुदेवमाधवपावना
कंसनिकन्दाकेशवरूप्या धामनमाधोमोहनविष्या
रामरमापतिरूप्याहरी दीननकेसुविपर्त्तिहरी
राधारमनावाधाहरना साधोग्ररनामाधोचरना
हरिहरिकेश्वरकर्कहिये सुरसरितीरंजुरंहिये

1	संयुत	सजजग
2	चंपकमला	भमसग
3	सारखती	भभभग
4	सुखमा	तयभग
5	अमृतगति &c.	नजनग

त्रिष्टुप् XI Genus.

वासुदेववसुदेवछहायी श्रीनिवासहरिजीयदुरायी
गोविनगोकुलगोपछहायी माधवमोहनश्रीयदुरायी

1	सुपथ	रनभगग
2	नीलस्वरूप or दोधक	भभभगग

No.	Name	Gaṇa	Example
3	सुमुखी	नजजलग	हरिहरिकेशयकृप्याकृष्टा — निश्यदिनसंगतिसाधुगच्छा
4	दमनक	नननलग	भ्रमलंकमलदलनयनं — जलनिधिजलकृततथयनं
5	श्येनिका	रजरलग	रूप्याकृप्याकेशिकंशकन्दना — देहुदेहुसुख्वनन्दनन्दना
6	मालती	मममगग	रामाकृप्यागायीयेकन्ता — केशोकाह्दोयेयोश्रानन्ता
7	इन्द्रवज्रा	ततजगग	गोविन्दगोपालरूपालकृप्या — माधोमुरारीव्रजनाथविष्णा
8	उपेन्द्रवज्रा	जतजगग	गुपालगोविन्दमुरारिमाधो — रमेशनारायणसाधसासाधो
9	गंगाधर	रनभगग	रामरामरघुनन्दनदेवा — वीरभद्रममममानहुसेवा
10	उपजाति &c.		

जगती XII Genus.

No.	Name	Gaṇa	Example
1	भुजंगप्रयात	यययय	धरेचन्दमाधेमहाजोतिराजे — चढ़ीचयिडकासिंहदंयामगाजे
2	तोटकं	ससस स	शिवशंकरशम्भुत्रिगूलधरं — शितिकयठगिरिशफणीन्द्रकरं
3	लक्ष्मीधर	ररर र	श्रीधरमाधवेरामचन्द्राभजो — ट्रेङकोमोछकोश्रोधकोतुतजो
4	सारंग	सततत	गोपालगोविन्दयोकृष्याकंसारी — केशोकृपाचिन्धुमोपापसंहारि
5	मौक्तिकदाम	जजजज	गुपालगुविन्दहरेननन्द — दयालरूपालसदासुखकन्द
6	मोदक	भभभभ	केशवकृप्याकृपालरूपाकर — मूरतिमेनमुकुन्दमनोहर
7	तरलनयनी	नननन	कलुखहरणहरिश्रघहर — कमलनयनकरोगिरिधर
8	सुन्दरी or हुतविलम्बित	नभभर	मदनमोछनमाधवकृप्याञ्जू — गरुडवाहनवामनविष्णाञ्जू
9	प्रमिताक्षरा &c.	सजसस	व्रजराजकृप्याकरपच्चधरं — रघुनाथरामपददेववरं

अतिजगती XIII Genus.

No.	Name	Gaṇa	Example
1	माया	मतयसग	नन्दानन्दागोकुलचन्दाजगयन्दा — केशोकृप्याकंसनिकन्दासुखकन्दा।

2 तारक	छछछछउग	हरिजूदहरियेसबपापहरमारे धरमसँखचकारिकितोकनतारे
3 कन्दुक	ययययल	हरेकष्यकेशोगोदृपीकेशगोपाल विद्यारोमुरारोसुरारीनकेकाल
4 यकावली	भनजजसं	मोहनमदनमुरारिमनोहर दानवदलनदयालदमोदर

शर्करी XIV Genus.

सुखदायक	तयछतलल	केशोहरिगोपालसुजैजैश्यामघन केशोवकचानूरनिपातोवीररन
चक्र or चक्रविरति	भनननलग	केशवकमलनयनहरिकिच्चिये रातिदिवससुरसरितटरच्चिये
वसन्ततिलक	लभजजगग	राजीवलोचनरमापतिरामभद्रा देवाधिदेवविजयीजितशत्रुभद्रा

अतिशर्करी XV Genus.

चामर	रजरजर	नन्दलालकंछकालभक्तिपालपालिये । कामक्रोधलोभमोहज्ञानखानिजानिये ॥
निश्रिपाल	भजसनछ	देवमनिराजमनिधीरमनगादृये । गोपगयसंगश्रनभयामघनध्यादृये ॥
मनहंस	छंजजभर	वसुदेवनन्दनकंछकन्दनध्यायिये । दिनरेनकेशवपाद्येंचितलायिये ॥
मालती	मनमयय	यदुवरगिरिधारीपूतनाप्राणहारी । तुलसिवनविहारीलोकञ्ञानन्दकारी ॥
शरभ	ननननछ	श्रमलकमलदलसुभगसुनयनी । सरसगरदश्रयिमुखिर्पिकवयनी
शार्ङ्गिक	ममममम	केशोकृष्णाकालिन्दीकूलातेजोकंठोकाली । बाजावेंवेनुचाराबेंधेनृगांवेंभूपाली ॥
भ्रमरावली or मनोहरण	छछछछछ	करुणानिधिकृष्णरूपालरूपाकरिये । मनमोहनमाधवमोदुखकोहरिये ॥

षष्टी XVI Genus.

नाराच	जरजरजम	रूपालपालदीनकोदयाललालगायिये । अनन्तगोपनायिकात्रिलोकनाथध्यायिये ॥
नील	भभभभभग	गोविनगोकुलचन्दगदाधरकृष्णहरी । देवदयालदयानिधिदीनबिपत्तिहरी ॥
चव्वला	रजरजरल	देवदेववासुदेवराधिकापतेगुपाल । कामरूपकामदानिकंछकालवृष्णिपाल ॥

अत्यष्टि XVII Genus.

पृथ्वी	जसजसयलग
मालाधर	नसजसयलग

हरेचरतृपापकोकरतराउरोराजापको । अनन्तगिरिधारिजूकरदुद्दूरिमोपापको ॥
मुकुटशिखिगोश्चेशुभगश्रीधरोशोहयो । अधरधरिवेणुयोजगतकोमनामोहयो ॥

धृति XVIII Genus.

महामोदकारी	यययययय
चर्चरी	रसजजभर

हरेकृष्ण्यकेगोरूपासिंधुमाधोमुकुन्दामुरारी ।
हृषीकेशकेगोरिपोनन्दनन्दागदाचक्रधारी ॥
कृष्ण्यकेशवकंसकालियकेशकेकुलखगइन ।
श्यामसुन्दरश्रीलसागरसेव्येननन्दना ॥

अतिधृति XIX Genus.

शार्दूलविक्रीडित	मसजसततग
चन्द्रमाला	मननजननल

केगोकृष्ण्याकृपालसिंधुश्ययनेकंसारिमाधोहरी ।
दीननाथदयालवेदनसेवंतेदीनकीहरी ॥
कमलनयनहर्हरिहरकेगयकलुयचरण ।
मधुमथनगतगुरुश्रीपतिधर्राणिधरण ॥

कृति XX Genus.

गीत	सजसभरसलग
दधिष्का	रजरजरजगल

वसुदेवनन्दनविश्ववन्दनकंसकन्दनगायिये ।
हरिकृष्णकेगयकेशिसूद नवासुदेवद्धियायिये ॥
रामकृष्णारामकृष्णावासुदेवविष्णाविष्णादेवदेव ।
दीनबंधुज्ञानसिंधुराधिकारमेघनाथरामदेव ॥

प्रकृति XXI Genus.

स्रग्धरा	मरमनययय

जेकेश्रीकंसहारीमधुमथनहरेराधिकानाथमाधो ।
गोविन्देश्रीमुकुन्देसुररिपुश्रघद्दासिंधुकृष्ण्यासुसाधो ॥

आकृति XXII Genus.

हंसी	ममसनननछग	गोपीनाथारामाकृप्याकमलनयनहरिमधुरिपुदेवा । दीजेबुद्धीकेगोकीजिंगिरिवरधराचरणतवसेवा ॥
मदिरा सवैया	भभभभभभभभग	गोविनगोकुलचन्दगदाधरगावतगेंवरगाढगयी । पञ्चनमेवरपञ्चकरीप्रभुपञ्चपतीपतिराखिलयी ॥
मोदकसवैया	भभभभभभमछल	कंसविदयडनजेंअघखयडनकेंयवज्जेंयोकरतार । **गोकुलनायकजेंसुखदायककनन्दनगोपीप्राणश्रधार** ॥

विकृति XXIII Genus.

मालतीसवैया चन्द्रगजेन्द्रगति } सुमुखीसवैया	भभभभभभभभगग जजजजजजजलग	सेंजसमेंसुखमन्दिरटम्पतिकेलिकरीश्रपनेमनमानी । सोंदगयोंमिलिमोहनराधिकज्ञानतनोंछिनरेंविह्वानी ॥ सुनेकविराजागरीबनेवाजुकरीजुकरीप्रभुजूसुकरी । बढेपरबीननवीनमहासुहरीजिनदीनविपत्तिहरी ॥

सक्कृति XXIV Genus.

वामसवैया	जजजजजजजय	धरेंसिरमोरपखामुरलीकरिकेसरिपीरगरेवनमाला । कदम्बसमीपकलिन्दसुतातटखेलतकान्हलियेवनमाला ॥
माधवीसवैया	सससससससछ	गुनआगरश्रीनटनागरजूभवसागरतंजनकोतारिये । कविराजगरीवनिवाजवडोवजराजककूदुतहठरिये ॥
गंगाजलसवैया	रररररररर	श्रीधरेकृप्याकेश्योरमानाथमाधोमुकुन्दागदाचक्रपाणीहरी । कंसकेश्रीरिपोकंठभारीरूपाज्ञानभारेभलेदयहलेभूधरी ॥
किरीटसवैया	भभभभभभभभभ	साहसिसिंघफतेसहिङुकविराजवढोगुनगावतसारद । वाजतडाढिगम्वरगाजतनाचतयोगिनियारसुनारद ॥

अतिकृति XXV Genus.

सुन्दरीसवैया   स द ग   रजनीकरतेश्रतिचारुमहासुकुहाकछियेधनघारतछीको ।
       घरछीरुहसन्तछिताछमञ्देछितरूपधरेधरईयजतीको ॥

उत्कृति XXVI Genus.

मुखसवैया   स द लल   रघुवंशविभूषयाटूपयाटूपयाटूपयासोंदुखदूरिसभैकरि ।
       वरदानिवहेतुमदीनदयालदरिद्रदयानलदेवदयाधरि ॥

All verses containing more than twenty-six syllables to the charaṇa come under the following genus (दयडक) which is supposed to comprehend 999 species.

दयडक XXVII Genus.

सुधासार   भ४ त३ भ२   पूरनब्रह्मसनातनयोपतितूंसातुर्हिदागुसाईदयालदयाकर ।
       कोनगुणीगुनगाइसकेप्रभुवदोनभेदोजुज्ञानेकछूखदमोदर ॥

महीधर   XXVIII   जरजरजरजरजग   खिखयडखयडमायदिसनालकञ्ज्ञहायहेगुपालयालसायरैसमैलिये ।
       गरेसरोजमालहिसुखेणयीविग्नानहेजुलालख्यारभालहिभलीदिये ॥

वसुधाधर   XXIX   सE लल   करुणाकरकैयवरूप्याकूपालसुरारिमुरारिमनोहरसूरतियीधर ।
       वरदानिदयानिधिदीनदयालदरिद्रदयानलदेवदमोजुदमोदर ॥

नीलवक्त XXX   =   गल × 15

मनहर or
घनाछरी   } XXXI   =   10+6+10+5

जलहरण XXXII   =   16+16
    &c.   &c.   &c.

2ND ORDER.

अर्धसमवृत्त *Ardhasama vritta*

OR

Verses that have an equal number of syllables in the *odd* and *even* charaṇas, i. e. the first and the third, and the second and the fourth charaṇas, are alike.

This order does not admit of genera and species as the first order. The following genera are mostly used. The rythmical syllables are *underlined.*

वेगवती छन्द

1st and 3rd charaṇas स × 3 + म -2nd and 4th charaṇas भ × 3 + गग

गिरिजापतिमौमनभायो   नारदशारदपारनपायो ।
धरणीतिलयधीनभभागे   ठाकुभयेवरदायकभागे ॥

अदिति छन्द

1st and 3rd charaṇas स + ज + गग 2nd and 4th charaṇas स × 2 + ज + ग

भवभाविनोऽनुमाया   ममपातकपुञ्जनाशिनी ।

चित्रा छन्द

1st and 3rd charaṇas न × 2 + र + य 2nd and 4th charaṇas न × 2 ज + र + ग

द्रुतबुरितराधिकोरमेया   ललितविचित्रविदारगोपवेश्या ।

रमणो or शिशुलीला

1st and 3rd charaṇas स × 2 × ज + गग 2nd and 4th charaṇas स + भ + र + य

जगतारकोऽजुगंगभ्रायो   सुरधारातिमुलोबसुछायो ।

द्रुतमध्यां छन्द

1st and 3rd charaṇas भ × 3 × गग 2nd and 4th charaṇas न + ज × 2 + य

केशवमाधवतुरधीरा   भतुलदयालसुभावसुधीरा ।

3RD ORDER.

विषम वृत्त *Vishama vritta,* or verses which have the four charaṇas *dissimilar.*

हंसवती छन्द

ज   त   ज   र   ज   त   ज   र
हरेषु | रारेज | गदीग्ब | माधवा   विम्रूट | मोज्ञानि | रूपाब | रोक्रो ।

ज   त   ज   र   ज   त   ज   गग
दयात्र | विष्णोव | नमालि | यादवा   नमोन | मोपाद | सरोज | तेरो ॥

सौरभ छन्द

स   ज   स   न   न   स   ज   भ
हरिमा | धवाह | रघुश्रो | क्र   मधुम | घनन | न्दनन्द | मा ।

र   न   भ   ग   स   ज   स   ज   ग
गोपिका | रमय | नाथह्न | रे   तुभ्रपा | दपक्र | युगदा | सदाह | हो ॥

ललिता छन्द

स   ज   स   ग   न   स   ज   ग
भज्रुरा | धिकार | मय्यमा | धो   सकल | मनका | मदार्नि | को ।

न   न   स   स   स   ज   स   ज   ग
मजुवि | बमवि | बयभा | बनक्का   अगज्ञा | नियेस | कलिह | न्द्वज्ञास | सें ॥

सुरभि छन्द

न   ज   र   न   ज   ज   र
वजप | तित्तूंक | छायक्वे   मधुन | गरीष्ठ | रिआय | कोरष्टो ।

न   ज   र   ग   न   ज   ज   र   ग
परम | कठोर | चित्तते | रो   म्दन | गुपाल | जुद्बीन | कोविद्या | रो ॥

गिरिकन्या छन्द

स स ज गग   स भ र य

गिरजा | पतिपा | दपक्म | तेरो   गहिहों | पातक | नाघको | छबेरो ।

स स ज य   स ज स स ग

मतिदे | छुखदा | महेष | गिरीषो   समिल | जङ्ख | अपरा | धहुमा | रो ॥

Note.—The student will recognise the letters placed above the lines as indicating the measure of the feet in the tables given at page 197 of this chapter.

2ND CLASS.

जाति छन्द *Játi chhand,* or metres principally regulated by instants, *mátrás* or *kalas.*

In this Class verses are not regularly composed of *four charaṇas* as in the first Class, but of two or more *parts:* when of *two,* they are called *dalas* (दस), and when of more than two parts, *charaṇas.*

This Class is generally divided into two orders.

1 *The first* called गण छन्द, *Gaṇachhand,* sometimes गण वृत्त *Gaṇa vritta,* in which the metres are regulated by feet, *gaṇa,* composed of a certain number of *instants,* mátrá or kala.

2 *The second* called मात्रा छन्द *mátrá chhand* in which the metres are chiefly regulated by the number of instants comprising a charaṇa or dala, without particular reference to any kind of feet employed.

The student should bear in mind that although this may be considered as the general nature of the metres in this *order,* there are *very few* metres indeed in which peculiarity of feet is entirely disregarded.

1st Order.

गण छन्द *Gaṇachhand*

Metres, measured by feet and quantity, i. e. by gaṇas and mátrás.

This order has but one genus, गाहा *gáhá* or गाथा *gáthá*, in Sanskrit चार्य्या *áryyá*, comprehending *twenty-seven* species.

The generic *measure* of the metre is *thirty* instants for the first *dala* (i. e. for the first and third charaṇas) and *twenty-seven* instants for the second dala (i. e. for the second and fourth charaṇas.) Each *dala* must have seven and a half feet ; each foot (the 6th of the second line excepted) must have four instants, a pause (or virám) in each *dala* after the 3rd foot or 12th instant.

The sixth foot of the 1st line must be a scolius *(Jagaṇa)* or a proceleusmatic, and the sixth foot of the 2nd line must be a short syllable, *laghu.* The first, third, fifth and seventh feet of the second line must *not* be scolia or *jagaṇas.*

The gaṇas in the rest of the feet are optional, provided they contain four instants each, as will be seen from the following examples :—

EXAMPLES.

गाहा छन्द

1	2	3	4	5	6	7	½
मधुरिपु	मोक्षन	माधौ	षोमुर	स्रीधर	मुरारि	षौरा	धौ ।

1	2	3	4	5	6	7	½
परिक्षरि	कैंभप	राधौ	माधौ	त्रिबम्स	नि	सेमा	धौ ॥

लछी छन्द

गौरी वायें भागे   खोयें भाछे सुराप गौमा यें   ।
देवा खोयमें काटे   माया आली नि ऊँछा यें   ॥

वुछी छन्द

तुँछे दीनद थानो   मोशें नाछीं मछीत लौछीना   ।
देख्यो नामे भौरे   न्यारो संछार तेंकी ना   ॥

It will be seen that the different species are formed by the combination of short and long syllables in the optional feet. This measure is much used in Sanskrit poetry.

2ND ORDER.

मात्रा छन्द *Mátrá chhand*, metres chiefly regulated by the number of instants composing a *charaṇa* or *dala*, without particular reference to any kind of feet employed.

There is a variety of metres in this order; we shall give a few examples of those most commonly in use.

स्वन्धक or स्वन्था छन्द

8 feet of four instants in each dala = 32 mátrás.

मखिमय चिंछा सनपें   खोमा साखें छिय सछि तराम खोछँ   ।
मानछु रतिपति कीम्रू   रति ओीनन खखेज गतमन मोछँ   ॥

वैरवा or नन्था छन्द

1st and 3rd charaṇas twelve instants, 2nd and 4th seven = 19 m.

भूलत पलना रघुवर   पुलखित माछ   ।
चिलखति सेति बलैया   नखखति आछ   ॥

तोमर or मदुगति

Twelve instants in each charaṇa or twenty-four in a dala = 48 m.

थैसी परे अव भाद्द   तीसी तवे कञ्चि याद्द ।

तव छिया लायो चोरि   ब्रब देहु वाको चोरि ॥

दोहा, दोछडा or द्विपथा

Thirteen mátrás in the 1st and 3rd charaṇas, eleven in the 2nd and 4th; each charaṇa of 3 feet, i. e. 6+4+3—6+4+1.

In the *odd* charaṇas the 3rd foot must *not* be a trochee, and the 3rd foot in the *even* charaṇas *must be* a brevis or *laghu*. The Doha has many varieties, as the syllables increase or decrease by combination of *guru* and *laghu* in the feet. This chhand is very commonly and familiarly used.

मेरीभववाधाहरो   राधानागरिसोय ।

यातनकीभ्रांञीपदे   भ्यामहरितद्दुतिद्योय ॥

This is the initiatory verse of the celebrated poem of Bihári, called *Satsaiyá*, consisting of seven hundred Dohas, of exquisite beauty and finish.

सोरठा छन्द

The Doha reversed with the same rules of feet and combination.

श्रेहिसुमिरतसिधिद्योय   गयानायककरिवरवदन ।

करोअनुपहद्योय   बुखिरागियुम्रगुयाछवन ॥

This is the initiatory verse of the celebrated poem, the *Rámáyan*, by Tulsí Dás.

रोला छन्द

Four charaṇas of 6 feet each—24 instants =

6+4 × 4+L—pause at the 11th instant of each charaṇa.

गोकुलचन्दगुविन्द	गरुडगामीगिरिधारी ।
नारायणनरसिंह	नीरनिधिनीरविद्धारी ॥
वासुदेवसुखदेव	कहतकरुणामयटेरे ।
हरहुसकलसंताप	घरघाभायोजनतेरे ॥

There are twelve varieties of this chhand.

दीपछन्न छन्द or चतुष्पदिका

Four charaṇas of 8 feet each—30 instants = 4 × 7+L; pauses
at the 10th and 18th instants of each charaṇa.

प्रगटेजगरायी ∙	स्वसुखदायी ∙	अनरंजनभगवन्ता ∙
अद्भुतअवतारा ∙	कृपाअपारा ∙	शुभयरणागतसन्ता ॥
ऐश्वर्य्यत्रिभुले ∙	दाउठकूले ∙	अन्मलीन्हजगभूपा ∙
महिमादरभावे ∙	प्रेमसुभावे ∙	यीसुछिवालकरूपा ॥(J.C.)

चौपाई, कुलपाई, or पादाकुलक छन्द

Four charaṇas of four feet each—16 instants = 6+4 × 2+L̇

बन्देप्रसुयीमूअगतारा ∙	जिनबिनुकोनकरेभवपारा ।
बन्देनाथयुगलकरजोरे ∙	सर्वविधपातकदेमतुमोरे ॥ (J.C.)

This chhand is very commonly used. Tulsí Dass' Rámáyan
is in this measure. The Rámáyan may be considered the standard of classical Hindí. Every student of the language and every
lover of the beauty of Hindí poetry should study it.

घसानन्द छन्द

Two charaṇas or dalas, nine feet each = 31 instants—4 × 2+3.
4+3. 4 × 3+1, pauses at the 11th and 18th in each dala.

अद्विकन्दियकुलकंस • बलिविध्यंस • केशियवकदानयदरन ।
सोहरिदीनदयाल • भक्तकृपाल • कविसुखदेवकृपाकरन ॥

भद्रिल्ल or भरिल्ल छन्द

Four charaṇas (rhyming with each other) of 16 instants each. Jagaṇas or scolia excluded.

केशवकृष्णमहादुखधारण • वारणारिकीकीककुवारण ।
याहगहोतारोष्भुवारण • हींभ्रतिदीनकरोज्जनिवारण ॥

काव्य छन्द

Four charaṇas of 5 feet each = 24 instants, $6 + 4 \times 3 + 6$, pause at the 11th instant of each charaṇa.

केशवकृष्णकृपाल • कंसकालियकुलकंजन •
गोकुलेयगोविन्द • सकलसज्जनमनरंजन ।
दामोदरदेवेश • दयानिधिदानवक्षयदन •
जयजययादवनाथ • जगतगुरुभसुरविक्षयदन ॥

कुयडलिभा

Eight charaṇas, that is a Dohá and a Kábya, the commencement of the 5th charaṇa must be a repetition of the 4th charaṇa, or it must be a singháblokan (सिंह अवलोकन,) and the commencement of the 7th charaṇa must be a repetition of the 6th charaṇa or a *jamak* (जमक alliteration) and the last two syllables of the metre must be a repetition of its two first syllables.

1 कीरतिकलिकोकल्पतरु • 2 फतेसाहसविचार ।
3 सोहतिसोहतिधरा • 4 सकलधामपरचार ॥
5 सकलधामपरचार • चारुघनसारसुलद्धी ।
6 सुवनसुदरयनरूप • सुमतिसुखदेवसुभद्धी ॥
7 सुवनसुदरयनरूप • सद्गयदियदियदयनीरति ।
8 भज्जुनसमसमरथ • गद्धीभज्जुनपरकीरति ॥

The celebrated poem of Girdhárí is written in this metre.

उल्लास छन्द

Four charaṇas, the 1st and 3rd of 4 feet and the 2nd and 4th of 3 feet each—4 × 3+3 6+4+3 = 15 and 13 instants; pause at the 15th instant.

कटिआतपापघटिआतदुख • सुखसम्पतिसउन्नतितिलछित ।
विनविनउवोतभतिघातहत • हरिचरणान्विचितकरतछित ॥

छप्पै छन्द

The काव्य *kábya* and उल्लास *ullál.*

वलितलनितमञ्जोर • मञ्जुगिअञ्जितअनुरञ्जित ।
व्यतिदमकातिनखचन्द • चमकजनमनतमगञ्जित ॥
भमलविमलजनुकमल • नवलकमलाकरपरगित ।
गरणगरणधरिपरम • धरमकरमनिकाद्विदरगित ॥
तुलसीभतुलदलफूलफल • मलयजपूजितसुरवरण ।
भुषणभुमकतारणतरण • गरणसुमिरिनरहरिचरण ॥

There are seventy-one varieties of this metre formed by the combination of long and short vowels in the feet. It is much used in laudatory and heroic poetry.

पद्मावती छन्द

Four charaṇas of 33 instants each. The last syllable must be a गुरु L; pauses at the 10th and eighteenth instants. No Jagaṇas (S.) admitted. Feet 4 × 8.

जयगोकुलनन्दा • आननकन्दा • मोहनमाधोकरुण्यहरी ।
वसगोपसुवेशो • गिरिधरकेशो • दीननधुकोविपत्तिहरी ॥
वारणदुखवारण • गणिकातारण • मनकोदाताकुछतिहरी ।
वृन्दावनचारी • रासविहारी • कविसुखदेवसुखानकरी ॥

त्रिभंगी

Four charaṇas of 32 instants each. Pauses at the 10th, 18th

and 26th instants. Each charaṇa must have a *guru*, L, at the end. No Jagaṇas (S.) admitted.

जयजयगरुडासन	•	दुष्टविनासन	•	कैटभसासन	•	त्रैलधरं	I
सज्जनसुखदायक	•	दुर्जनधायक	•	दासबलायक	•	देवधरं	II
मुरलीमनमयडन	•	कंसयिद्ददन	•	मघधुलखयडन	•	कुमतिहरी	I
सुखमासुखसागर	•	रूपडङ्गागर	•	सबगुणभागर	•	सुमतिकरौ	III

हरिगीता or महीधरी छन्द

Four charaṇas of 29 instants each, pause at the 16th instant of each charaṇa. The last syllable of each charaṇa must be a *guru*, L. Seven feet $= 4 \times 5 + 6 + L$.

हरिचरणसेवदुगरणभयरण	•	सकलकलिमलक्रन्दना	I
पच्छिरदुविभूयगयामिलसुभगवत	•	करतुछिर्नाछिनयन्दना	II
घनश्यामसुन्दरमदनमोहन	•	हरहुदुखसुखदानिहि	I
मनयचक्रमसंछेदयेसो	•	हरहसंकटभानिहि	II

जलहरणा छन्द

Four charaṇas of 8 feet each $= 32$ instants each charaṇa. $4 \times 7 + A$ (or ꢰ), pauses at the 10th, 18th and 24th instants.

जययदुपतिनरहरि	•	कमलनयनकाहि	•	कलिनिमलहर	•	करगिरिधरये	I
जगपतिविटजयजय	•	गुरुजगजयजय	•	मनसिजजय	•	जयमनहरये	II
जयपरमसुमतिकर	•	कुमतिनचयकर	•	जगततपति	•	हरनरखरये	I
जयजलदसद्ययकवि	•	सुजननलिनरवि	•	पठतसुकवि	•	असुखगपरये	II

दुर्मिला छन्द

Four charaṇas of 32 instants each, pauses at the 11th and 18th instants. The two last syllables of each charaṇa must be a spondee.

उनछितदलभूषया	•	निरखितकयया	•	स्वच्छफलफूलतेफूले	I
पछिन्दमिलिधावत	•	हसिफिरिभ्रावत	•	तरमकिभ्रमकियावनिभूल	II

यनकरतिकन्नोलनि ।   कोकिलबोलनि ।   ग्वालबालकठुकठुमने ।
कठेस्यरटेरत ।   हरिकोटेरत ।   कठ्तुटेरतुनेतुने ॥

The above examples will be sufficient to give the student an idea of Hindí versification, and stimulate him to further research. Hindí metres have an almost exhaustless range, but the space alloted to this chapter will not permit us to enlarge. The student if desirous of further information may with advantage consult some work on Sanskrit or Hindí Prosody by a native author.

It is of importance to know that the Hindús have a quaint and somewhat mystical mode of denoting numerals by symbolical names, which is often employed in all kinds of calculations.   This method which for some time puzzled the savans of Europe till the key to it was found, is not unfrequently used in the calculation of poetic metres.   The following is a list of the symbolic names indicating their equivalent numerals.

N. B.—All the *synonyms* also of these names indicate the same numerals as the names themselves.

0.   ख, अनन्त, आकाश &c. Space, heaven, zero, cypher, &c.
1.   पृथ्वी, भूमि &c. The earth.
   चन्द्र, इन्दु &c. The moon.
   रूप &c. Form, color.
2.   पक्ष &c. A wing, the half of a lunar month.
   नेत्र, नयन, चक्षु, &c. The eye.
   भुज बाहु &c. An arm.
   यम &c. Twin, also the deity of Narak or hell.
   अश्विन् The twin sons of Suryya.
   हद &c. The jaws.
3.   वह्नि, वह्नि &c. Fire.
   राम The three Ráms.

पिनाकनयन A name of Śiva, the three-eyed.

गुण The three qualities.

4. वेद The four veds.

अर्णव, सिन्धु &c. An ocean.

कृत The 1st of the 4 ages.

युग An age.

जल, वारि Water.

5. बाण &c. An arrow.

प्राण Inspiration, the 5 modes of inspiration.

6. अङ्ग The members of the body.

रस Taste, or savour.

राग Modes of Music.

ऋतु The six seasons.

तर्क Shantras.

अरि An enemy, or dangers.

7. मुनि, ऋषि The Sages.

स्वर A vowel, the notes of music.

नग, अचल, पर्वत &c. A mountain.

अश्व A horse, the seven-headed horse of Súryyá's cár

8. वसु The eight demigods.

गज The eight elephants of the 8 cardinal points.

नाग A serpent the 8 species.

मंगल Happiness, good fortune.

9. अङ्क A numeral, i. e. 1 to 9.

छिद्र An inlet, the nine orifices of the body.

ग्रह A planet, the planets.

10. दिश A side, quarter, point, the 8 cardinal points.

11. ईश, रुद्र A name of Shiv' and of his 11 inferior manifestations.

12. सूर्य्य The sun and his 12 monthly appellations.

चक्र A wheel, the zodiac with its 12 signs.

13. विश्व The universe.

काम Cupid, the lord of the tithi or lunar days.

14. भुवन The world, the 7 upper and 7 nether heavens.

इन्द्र The god Indra, renewed at 14 epochs.

मनु The 14 mans or saints.

15. तिथि A lunar day, 15th a semi-lunation.

16. कला A digit, one sixteenth of the moon's diameter.

अष्टि A metre of sixteen syllables.

नृप &c. A king, from the history of the 14 kings in the máhábhárat.

17. अत्याष्टि A metre of 17 syllables.

18. धृति A metre of 18 syllables.

19. अति धृति A metre of 19 syllables.

20. नख A nail, finger and toe nails.

21. स्वर्ग Heaven, the 21 heavens.

22. जाति Race, cast, reckoned to be 22.

24. जिन A Jaina, the 24 Jinas of the Buddhists.

25. तत्व An element, a principle.

26. उत्कृति A metre of 26 syllables.

27. ऋ, नक्षत्र A star, the 27 lunar mansions in the year.

32. दन्त The 24 human teeth.

33. देव One of the 33 crores of Hindú gods.

49. तान A tune, the 7 octaves of seven notes each.

वायु The air, wind.

To express any number greater than nine, place consecutively the terms representing the digits according to this system, beginning with the figure in the unit's place, or right-hand figure.

HINDI SELECTIONS.

यह कौन चिड़िया है?
तुम्हारे पास छोरी है?
उस का शब्द अच्छा है.
हाथ धोने का जल लाओ.
उस का रूप बुरा है.
तुम्हारा नाम क्या है?
हम भूखे पियासे हैं.
ये लड़के निर्भय हैं.
कौन चिल्लाता है?
आज खूब बवली है.
कहां से आये हो?
यहां कौन रहता है?
यहां आने की छैन करो.
कुछ फल और पानी लाओ.
उस के हाथ पांव बांधो.
द्वार पर एक भिखारी खड़ा है.
घास पर बहुत औस है.
उन के माता पिता मर गय हैं.
उस के दांत में पीड़ा है.
तुम्हारी घड़ी अच्छी चलती है?
एक दिन का भाड़ा क्या है?
क्या तुम क्रोध करते हो?
यह कपड़ा बहुत मोटा है.
उस का मन उदास है.

उस के बहुत मित्र हैं.
कितने मनुष्य उपस्थित हैं?
पालकी मेरे पास भेजो.
यह बहुत अच्छा है.
उतरो नहीं तो गिरोगे.
यह किस का घोड़ा है?
उस का मन दुःखी है.
ये सब चुप रहे.
जल ठंडा करो.
तुम क्या कहते हो?
यहां फिर मत आओ.
हम को बड़े भोर जगाओ.
सांझ हुई आगे चले जाओ.
उन को हमारे घर भेज दो.
यह बहुत अच्छा फल है.
यह बहुत अच्छी रोटी है.
तुम कौन काज करते हो?
उस का बड़ा घाटा हुआ है.
तुम्हारा क्या काम है?
नाव का कितना भाड़ा है?
यह फल बहुत खट्टा है.
यह बड़ा कठिन काम है.
तुम काज के योग्य हो.
यह कहानी सब झूठी है.

यह बहुत अच्छी वस्तु है।
यह वस्त्र कितना लम्बा है?
यह अदर कुरूप है।
तुम बहुत धीमे बोलते हो।
देखो आकाश कुछ सुना है?
ये बहुत कुछ जानते हैं।
ये सब किस लिये हंसते हैं?
यह फूल हम को सूंघने दो।
इतका गुड कैसे बेचें होंगे।
उस उपवन में फूल बहुत हैं।
इन वस्तुओं का क्या मोल है?
तुम दोनों में कैसा झगड़ा है?
यह कपड़ा किस भांति का है?
नदी के तीर पर बड़ी कीच है।
इस वृक्ष की छांह में बैठो।
विद्या में कुछ निपुण है।
मैं भी बाहर जाया चाहता हूं।
तुम कबतायें चल सकोगे?
इस ने बहुत धन बटोरा है।
हम बैरी के हाथ से निकल भागे।
इन दोनों में से कौन भला है।
वह पीपल के वृक्ष तले सोता है।
तुम ने यह समाचार कहां सुना है?
यह सेना चलने नहीं आगती है।
यह लड़का हमारा बहुत पियारा है।
इस लड़के का पालनेहारा कौन है?
वह बड़ा चतुर और बुद्धिमान है।
एक थोड़ा इतना बोझा खींच सकेगा?

उस का बहुत अच्छा घर है।
उस का मन निर्दय है।
यह सब से अच्छा होगा।
हमारे संग तुम्हें आना होगा।
हम सब कुछ जानते हैं।
उन से हम को बड़ा दुःख है।
यह घर हमारा नहीं है।
उस द्वार का ताला खोलो।
इस आलसी लड़के को मारो।
कल से आज जाड़ा अधिक है।
इन दोनों में क्या भेद है?
इस ताल में कुछ मछली है?
इस कोठरी में ताला नहीं है।
इस मास में बहुत वर्षा हुआ।
वे एक दूसरे पर गिर पड़े।
कहो तो तुम क्या कहता है?
वृक्ष पर काहे को चढ़ते हो?
जो भोजन बना हो तो लाओ।
तुम आगे आओ हम आते हैं।
दो दीवट हमारे लिये मोल लो।
वे कठिन से दिन काटते हैं।
हम नदी के तीर टहलें।
यह पाथर कितना भारी होगा?
इस पोथी में कितने अध्याय हैं?
हम ने बंसी से एक मछली पकड़ी।
हम को चाहिये कि दयावन्त होवें।
वह प्रति दिन टटका दूध पीता है।
पानी बरसता है हम को भीतर जाने दो।

आज की रात हम कहां रहेंगे?

आओ हम तुम कुछ बातचीत करें.

उस को हिन्दी भाषा में क्या कहते हो?

क्या आवश्यक इतनी सावधानी का है?

इस में हमारी प्रसन्नता अधिक होगी.

हमारा घर धुंओं से छायावान है.

आज उन के घर एक पाहुन है.

वे नाना प्रकार का अंधेर करते हैं.

हम क्यों भागें यहां कुछ भय नहीं.

कितने को मेरे स्वामी के हाथ बेचोगे?

यहीं रहो जब तांई हम फिर न आवें.

तुम जल की बाट आओगे या थल की बाट?

ये यह समाचार सुनके बहुत लज्जित हुए हैं.

यहां सब मनुष्य मारे भूख के मर गये.

उस ने गंगा के तीर पर एक घर बनाया है.

ये घोड़े पर से जो गिरे तो चोट बहुत आई.

ये माली इस फूल का बीज उपवन में बोओ.

उस ने कुल्हाड़ी से लकड़ी का कुंदा चीर डाला.

उस ने बड़े यत्न से हम को सिखलाया है.

ईश्वर की कृपा से हम भले चंगे हुए हैं.

कितने दिन भए कि तुम ने यह संदेसा पाया है?

वे अपने माता पिता के साथ रहते हैं.

जो तुम शीघ्र आते तो हमारी सहायता होती.

तुम क्यों अपना समय अचेतो में गंवाते हो?

उस के मरने से सारे नगर में शोक हुआ.

उत्तम है कि तुम उस का अपराध क्षमा करो.

वह बड़े भोर उठके अपनी बाट चला गया.

हमारे साथ आओ हम नदी के पार जावेंगे.

हम उन को सारे दिन ढूंढते हैं.

यहां चढ़के आओ और खड़े रहो.

धूप की आड़ के लिये कुछ खड़ा करो.

तुम्हारा आना वहां कुछ आवश्यक नहीं.

तुम ने अपनी चिट्ठी पर छाप की है?

हम तुम को एक सुन्दर चित्र दिखावेंगे.

बहुत अंधेर हुई हम को घर जाने दो.

हम इस समय दूर की यात्रा करते हैं.

इस भांति की बातें सुनके वे हंसने लगे.

तुम कुछ जानते हो कि वे कहां गये हैं?

हमारे हाथ से छड़ी नदी में गिर गई.

वह अपने सिर का बोझ फेंक के चला गया।

वह अपने पति के मरने से बहुत रोई।

किस लिये ऐसा करते हो तुम को कुछ दया नहीं आती?

हम इस काम से कुछ सम्बन्ध नहीं रखते हैं।

हम को कुछ काम था इस लिये नेवता न लिया।

वे बन्दीगृह में थे परंतु अब छूट गये।

हम को उचित है कि विपत में धीरज धरें।

तुम जानते हो कि उन की औषध कौन बैठा करता है?

तुम बहुत शीघ्र बोलते हो मैं नहीं समझता हूँ।

जो तुम जानते हो तो क्यों नहीं उत्तर देते हो?

उस ने अपने माता पिता को बड़ा दुःख दिया है।

वे अपना समय नाचने गाने में गंवाते हैं।

हम ने इय वस्तुओं के बनाने की आज्ञा दी है।

यह घोड़ा हम ने दो सौ रुपयों को मोल लिया है।

जब लों मैं वहां रहा तब लों वे अप्रसन्न रहे।

जो हम कहते हैं सो सुनो तिस के पीछे उत्तर दो।

वह अपने सब रुपये उधार देके निर्धन हो गया।

वह इतनी दूर पालकी पर चढ़के थक गया।

ईश्वर की कृपा से यह औषध खाके हम बचे।

वह यह काज केवल हमारे दुःख देने के लिये करता है।

इस काम में तुम हमारी कुछ सहायता कर सकते हो?

वह अपने घोड़े से गिर पड़ा, और पांव टूट गया।

वह सब रुपये व्यय करके अब भिक्षा मांगता है।

बढ़ई से कह इस पाटी को भारी से दो कर देवे।

अपना काज जो भली रीति से न करोगे तो मैं तुम्हें छुड़ा दूंगा।

रह रह के बोल तो हम तेरी बात समझेंगे।

हमारा यह परामर्ष है तुम थोड़े दिन धीरज धरो।

तुम घोड़े पर बैत से बैठो ऐसा न होवे कि गिर पड़ो।

कल एक ऊख की भरी गुई नाव गड्ढा में डूब गई।

इतनी बात कहने से क्या प्रयोजन? उस का आधा भी में नहीं डूबता हूँ।

॥ उड़ाऊ पुत्र का दृष्टान्त ॥

फिर उसने कहा किसी मनुष्यके दो पुत्र थे। उनमेंसे छुटकेने पितासे कहा हे पिता सम्पत्तिमेंसे जो मेरा भाग होय सो मुझे दीजिये. तब उसने उनको अपनी सम्पत्ति बांट दिई। बहुत दिन नहीं बीते कि छुटका पुत्र सब कुछ इकट्ठा करके दूर देश चला गया और वहां लुचपनमें दिन बिताते हुए अपनी सम्पत्ति उड़ा दिई। अब वह सब कुछ उठा चुका तब उस देशमें बड़ा अकाल पड़ा और वह कंगाल हो गया। और वह जाके उस देशके निवासियों-मेंसे एकके यहां रहने लगा जिसने उसे अपने खेतोंमें सूअर चरानेको भेजा। और वह उन छीमियोंसे जिन्हें सूअर खाते थे अपना पेट भरने चाहता था और कोई नहीं उसको कुछ देता था। तब उसे चेत हुआ और उसने कहा मेरे पिताके कितने मजूरोंको भोजनसे अधिक रोटी होती है और में भूखसे मरता हूँ। में उठके अपने पिता पास जाऊँगा और उससे कहूँगा हे पिता मैंने स्वर्गके विरुद्ध और आपके सामने पाप किया है। में फिर आपका पुत्र कहावनेके योग्य नहीं हूँ मुझे अपने मजूरोंमेंसे एकके समान कीजिये। तब वह उठके अपने पिता पास चला पर वह दूरही था कि उसके पिताने उसे देखके दया किई और दौड़के उसके गलेमें लिपटके उसे चूमा। पुत्रने उससे कहा हे पिता मैंने स्वर्गके विरुद्ध और आपके सामने पाप किया है और फिर आपका पुत्र कहावनेके योग्य नहीं हूँ। परन्तु पिताने अपने दासोंसे कहा सबसे उत्तम बस्त्र निकालके उसे पहिनाओ और उसके हाथमें अंगूठी और पांवोंमें जूते पहिनाओ। और मोटा बछड़ू लाके मारो और हम खावें और आनन्द करें। क्योंकि यह मेरा पुत्र मूआ था फिर जीया है खो गया था फिर मिला है. तब वे आनन्द करने लगे। उसका जेठा पुत्र खेतमें था और जब वह आते हुए घरके निकट पहुंचा तब बाजा और नाचका शब्द सुना। और उसने अपने सेवकोंमेंसे एकको अपने पास बुलाके पूछा यह क्या है। उसने उससे कहा आपका भाई आया है और आपके पिताने मोटा बछड़ू मारा है इसलिये कि उसे भला चंगा

पाया है। परन्तु उसने क्रोध किया और भीतर जाने न चाहा इसलिये उसका पिता बाहर आ उसे मनाने लगा। उसने पिताको उत्तर दिया कि देखिये मैं इतने बरसोंसे आपकी सेवा करता हूं और कभी आपकी आज्ञाको उल्लंघन न किया और आपने मुझे कभी एक मेम्हा भी न दिया कि मैं अपने मित्रोंके संग आनन्द करता। परन्तु आपका यह पुत्र जो बेश्याओंके संग आपकी सम्पत्ति खा गया है ज्योंही आया त्योंही आपने उसके लिये मोटा बछड़ू मारा है। पिताने उससे कहा हे पुत्र तू सदा मेरे संग है और जो कुछ मेरा है सो सब तेरा है। परन्तु आनन्द करना और हर्षित होना उचित था क्योंकि यह तेरा भाई मुझा था फिर जीआ है खो गया था फिर मिला है।

॥ प्रेमसागर ॥

॥ ५९ अध्याय ॥

श्री शुकदेव जी बोले, कि महाराज! जों ही कृष्णचंद दल समेत जरासंध को जीत, कालयवन को मार, ब्रज को तज, द्वारका में आय बसे, तों मैं सब कथा कहता हूं, तुम सचेत हो चित्त लगाय सुनो; कि राजा उग्रसेन तो राजनीति लिये मथुरापुरी का राज करते थे, और श्री कृष्ण बलराम सेवक की भांति उनकी आज्ञाकारी; इस से राजा राज प्रजा सुखी थी, पर एक कंस की रानियां हीं अपने पति के शोक से महादुखी थीं, न उन्हें नींद आती थी, न भूख प्यास लगती थी, आठ पहर उदास रहती थीं.

एक दिन वे दोनों बहन अति चिंता कर आपस में कहने लगीं, कि जैसे नृप बिन प्रजा, चंद बिन यामिनी शोभा नहीं पाती, तैसे कंत बिन कामिनी भी शोभा नहीं पाती; अब अनाथ हो यहां रहना भला नहीं, इस से अपने पिता के घर चल रहिये सो अच्छा. महाराज! वे दोनों रानियां ऐसे आपस में शोच विचार कर, रथ मंगवाय. उस पर चढ़ मथुरा से चली चली मगध देश में अपने पिताके यहां भाईं, और जैसे श्री कृष्ण बलराम जी ने सब असुरों समेत कंस को मारा, तैसे उन दोनों ने रो रो समाचार अपने पिता से सब कह सुनाया.

सुनते ही जरासंध अति क्रोधकर सभा में आया, और लगा कहने कि ऐसे बली कौन यदुकुल में उपजे, जिन्होंने सब असुरों समेत महाबली कंस को

मार मेरी बेटियों को रांड किया ; मैं अभी अपना सब कटक ले चढ़ धाऊं, और सब यदुर्वंशियों समेत मथुरापुरी को खलाय राम कृष्ण को छाती बांध लाऊं तो मेरा नाम जरासंध, नहीं तो नहीं.

इतना कह उसने तुरंत ही चारों ओर के राजाओं को पत्र लिखे, कि तुम अपना दल ले ले हमारे पास आओ, हम कंस का पलटा ले यदुर्वंशियों को निर्वंश करेंगे. जरासंध का पत्र पाते ही सब देश देश के नरेश, अपना अपना दल साथ ले, भूट चले आये ; और यहां जरासंध ने भी अपनी सब सेना ठीक ठाक बनाय रक्खी ; निदान सब असुरदल साथ ले जरासंध ने जिस समें मगध देश से मथुरापुरी को प्रस्थान किया, तिस समें उसके संग तेईस अक्षौहिणी थीं. इक्कीस सहस्र आठ सौ सत्तर रथी, और इतने ही गजपति ; एक लाख नव सहस्र साढ़े तीन सौ पैदल ; और पैंसठ सहस्र छ सौ दस अश्वपति ; यह अक्षौहिणी का प्रमाण है.

ऐसी तेईस अक्षौहिणी उस के साथ थीं, और उन में से एक एक राक्षस ऐसा बली था सो मैं कहां तक वर्णन करूं. महाराज! जिस काल जरासंध सब असुर सेना साथ ले धांसा दे चला. उस काल दशों दिशा के दिक्पाल लगे थर थर कांपने, और पृथ्वी न्यारी ही बोझ से लगी छात सी हिलने ; निदान कितने एक दिनों में चला चला जा पहुंचा, और उस ने चारों ओर से मथुरापुरी को घेर लिया ; तब नगर निवासी अति भय खाय श्री कृष्णचंद के पास जा पुकारे, कि महाराज ; जरासंध ने आय चारों ओर से नगर घेरा, अब क्या करें और किधर जांय.

इतनी बात के सुनते ही हरि कुछ सोच बिचार करने लगे ; इस में बलराम जी ने आय प्रभु से कहा, कि महाराज! आप ने भक्तों का दुःख दूर करने के हेतु अवतार लिया है, अब अग्निंतन धारण कर असुररूपी वन को जलाय भूमि का भार उतारिये. यह सुन श्री कृष्णचंद. उन को साथ ले उपछेन के पास गये, और कहा कि महाराज! हमें तो लड़ने की आज्ञा दीजे, और आप सब यदुर्वंशियों को साथ ले गढ़ की रक्षा कीजे.

इतना कह जों मातपिता के निकट आये, तो सब नगरनिवासी घिर आये ; और लगे अति व्याकुल हो कहने, कि हे कृष्ण! हे कृष्ण! अब हन असुरों के हाथ से कैसे बचें ; तब हरि ने मातपिता समेत सब को भयातुर देख समझाके

कहा, कि तुम किसी भांति चिंता मत करो, यह असुर दल जो तुम देखते हो सो पल भर में यहां का यहीं ऐसे बिलाय जायगा, कि जैसे पानी के बुलुले पानी में बिलाय जाते हैं। यों कह सब को समझाय बुझाय, ठाढस बंधाय, उन से बिदा हो अस्त्र भरे रथों में बैठलिये।

निकसे दोऊ यदुराय, पहुंचे सु दल में जाय।

जहां जरासंध खड़ा था, तहां जा निकसे; देखते ही जरासंध भी कृष्णाचंद से अति अभिमान कर कहने लगा, अरे! तू मेरे आगे से भाग जा, मैं तुझे क्या मारूं, तू मेरी समान का नहीं, जो मैं तुझ पर अस्त्र चलाऊं; भला बलराम को मैं देख लेता हूं। श्री कृष्णाचंद बोले अरे मूर्ख अभिमानी! तू यह क्या बकता है; जो सूरमा होते हैं सो बड़ा बोल किसी से नहीं बोलते, सब से दीनता करते हैं; काम पड़े अपना बल दिखाते हैं और जो अपने मुंह अपनी बड़ाई मारते हैं, सो क्या कुछ भले कहाते हैं। कहा है कि गरजता है सो बरसता नहीं, तुच्छ से वृथा बकवाद क्या करता है।

इतनी बात के सुनते ही जरासंध ने ज्यों क्रोध किया, त्यों भी कृष्ण बलदेव चल खड़े हुए. उन के पीछे वह भी अपनी सब सेना ले धाया, और उस ने यों पुकारके कह सुनाया, अरे दुष्टो! मेरे आगे से तुम कहां भाग जाओगे, बहुत दिन जीते बचे. तुम ने अपने मन में क्या समझा है, अब जीते न रहने पाओगे; जहां सब असुरों समेत कंस गया है, तहांई सब यदुवंशियों समेत तुम भी भेजूंगा। महाराज! ऐसा दुष्ट वचन उस असुर के मुख से निकलते ही, कितनी एक दूर आय दोनों भाई फिर खड़े हुए. श्री कृष्ण जी ने तो सब अस्त्र लिये, और बलराम जी ने हल मूसल; जो असुर दल उनके निकट गया, तो दोनों बीर ललकारके ऐसे टूटे जैसे हाथियों के यूथ पर सिंह टूटे, भी लगा लोथा बाजने।

उस काल मारू जो बाजता था, सो तो मेघ सा गाजता था; और चारों ओर से राक्षसों का दल जो घिर आया था, सो दल बादल सा छाया था; और अस्त्रों की झड़ी झड़ी सी लगी थी; इसके बीच भी कृष्ण बलराम युद्ध करते ऐसे शोभायमान लगते थे, जैसे सघन घन में दामिनी सुहावनी लगती है।

इतनी कथा सुनाय श्री शुकदेव जी बोले, कि पृथ्वीनाथ! अब लड़ते लड़ते असुरों की बहुत ही सेना कट गई, तब बलदेव जी ने रथ से उतर जरासंध को

बांध लिया, इस में भी कृष्णचंद जी ने आ बलराम से कहा, कि भाई! इसे
जीता छोड़ दो, मारो मत; क्योंकि यह जीता जायगा तो फिर असुरों को साथ
ले आवेगा, तिन्हें मार हम भूमि का भार उतारेंगे; और जो जीता न छोड़ेंगे, तो
जो राक्षस भाग गये हैं सो साथ न आवेंगे. ऐसे बलदेव जी को समझाय प्रभु ने
जरासंध को छुड़ाय दिया; वह अपने विन लोगों में गया जो रथ से भागके बचे थे.

चहुं दिस चाहि करै पछताय, चिगरी सेना गई विलाय.
भयो दुःख अति, कैसें जीजे, अब घर छांडि तपस्या कीजे.
मंत्री तबै करै समझाय, तुम हौ ज्ञानी क्यों पछिताय.
कबहूं हार, जीत पुनि होय, राज देस छांड़े नहिं कोय.

क्या तुम्हा जो अब की लड़ाई में हारे, फिर अपना दल जोड़ लावेंगे, और सब
यदुवंशियों समेत कृष्ण बलदेव को स्वर्ग पठावेंगे, तुम किसी बात की चिंता
मत करो. महाराज! ऐसे समझाय बुझाय जो असुर रथ से भागके बचे थे, तिन्हें
भी जरासंध को मंत्री ने घर ले पहुंचाया; और वह फिर वहां कटक जोड़ने
लगा. यहां भी कृष्ण बलराम रथभूमि में देखते क्या हैं, कि लोहू की नदी बह
निकली है; तिस में रथ बिना रथी नाव से बहे जातें हैं; ठौर ठौर हाथी मरे
पहाड़ से पड़े दृष्ट आते हैं; उनके घावों से रक्त झरनों की भांति झरता है;
गिद्ध गीदड़ काग लोथों पर बैठ बैठ मांस खाते हैं, और आपस में लड़ते जाते हैं.

इतनी कथा कह श्री शुकदेव जी बोले, कि महाराज! जितने रथ हाथी घोड़े
और राक्षस उस खेत में रहे थे, तिन्हें पवन ने तो समेट इकट्ठा किया, और अग्नि
ने पल भर में सब को जलाय भस्म कर दिया; पांच तत्त्व पंच तत्व में मिल
गये; उन्हें आते तो सब ने देखा, पर जाते किसी ने न देखा कि किधर गये.
ऐसे असुरों को मार, भूमि का भार उतार, श्री कृष्ण बलराम, भक्तहितकारी.
उग्रसेन के पास आय, दंडवत कर, हाथ जोड़ बोले, कि महाराज! आप के
पुण्यप्रताप से असुर दल मार भगाया, अब निर्भय राज कीजे, और प्रजा को सुख
दीजे. इतना वचन इनके मुखसे निकलते ही राजा उग्रसेन ने अति आनंद मान
बड़ी बधाई की, श्री धर्मराज करने लगे. इस में कितने एक दिन पीछे फिर
जरासंध उतनी ही सेना ले चढ़ि आया, श्री भी कृष्ण बलदेव जी ने पुनि त्योंही

मार भगाया. ऐसे तेरहंस तेरहंस मद्दोन्मित्थी ले जरासंध उन्नत बेर चढ़ि आया, श्री प्रभु ने मार मार हटाया.

इतनी कथा कह श्री गुरुदेव मुनि ने राजा परीच्छित से कहा, कि महाराज! इस बीच नारद मुनि जी के जो कुछ जी में आई, तो ये एकाएकी उठकर कालयवन के यहां गये. उन्हें देखते ही वह सभा समेत उठ खड़ा हुआ, श्री उसने दंडवत कर, कर जोड़ पूछा कि महाराज! आप का आना यहां कैसे भया?

सुनिके नारद कहं विचारि, मथुरा में बलभद्र मुरारि.

तो बिन तिन्हें हते नहिं कोह, जरासंध सों फछु नहिं होइ.

तू है अमर, और अति बली, बालक हैं बलदेव और हरी.

यों कह फिर नारद जी बोले, कि जिसे तू मेघबरन, कमलनैन, अति सुंदर बदन, पीतांबर पहरे, पीत पट ओढ़े देखे, तिस का तू पीछा बिन मारे मत छोड़ियो. इतना कह नारद मुनि तो चले गये, श्री कालयवन अपना दल जोड़ने लगा. इस में कितने एक दिन बीच उसने तीन करोड़ महाम्लेच्छ अति भयावने एकट्टे किये, ऐसे कि जिनके मोटे भुज गले, बड़े दांत, मैले भेष, भूरे केश, नैन लाल घूंघची से. तिन्हें साथ ले, डंका दे, मथुरापुरी पर चढ़ि आया, श्री उसे चारों ओर से घेर लिया. उस काल श्री कृष्णचंद जी ने उस का व्यवहार देख अपने जी में विचारा, कि अब यहां रहना भला नहीं, क्योंकि आज यह चढ़ आया है. श्री कल को जरासंध भी चढ़ि आवे तो प्रजा दुःख पावेगी, इससे उत्तम यही है कि यहां न रहिये, सब समेत अनत जाय बसिये. महाराम! हरि ने यों विचार कर, विश्वकर्मा को बुलाय, समझाय बुझायके कहा, कि तू अभी आके समुद्र के बीच एक नगर बनाव, ऐसा जिस में सब यदुवंशी सुख से रहैं, पर वे यह भेद न जानें कि ये हमारे घर नहीं, श्री पल भर में सब को वहां ले पहुंचाव.

इतनी बात के सुनते ही, आ विश्वकर्मा ने समुद्र के बीच सुदर्शन के ऊपर, बारह योजन का नगर जैसा श्री कृष्ण जी ने कहा था तैसाही रात भर में बनाय, उसका नाम द्वारका रख, श्री हरि से कहा; फिर प्रभु ने उसे आज्ञा दी, कि इसी समे तू सब यदुवंशियों को वहां ऐसे पहुंचाय दे, कि कोई यह भेद न जाने जो हम कहां आये श्री कौन से आया.

इतना वचन प्रभु के मुख से जों निकला, तों रातों रातही उपछेन वसुदेव समेत विश्वकर्मा ने सब यदुवंशियों को ले पहुंचाया, और श्री कृष्ण बलराम भी वहां पधारे। सरे बीच समुद्र की लहर का शब्द सुन सब यदुवंशी चौंक पड़े, और भांति अचरज कर आपस में कहने लगे, कि मथुरा में समुद्र कहां से आया, यह भेद कुछ जाना नहीं आता।

इतनी कथा सुनाय श्री शुकदेव जी ने राजा परीक्षित से कहा, कि पृथ्वीनाथ! ऐसे सब यदुवंशियो को द्वारका में बसाय, श्री कृष्णचंद जी ने बलदेव जी से कहा, कि भाई! अब चलके प्रजा की रक्षा कीजे, और कालयवन का वध। इतना कह दोनों भाई वहां से चल ब्रजमंडल में आये। इति

॥ ५२ अध्याय ॥

श्री शुकदेव मुनि बोले, कि महाराज! ब्रजमंडल में आते ही श्री कृष्णचंद ने बलराम जी को तो मथुरा में छोड़ा, और आप रूपसागर, जगतउजागर पीतांबर पहने, पीत पट ओढ़े, सब सिंगार किये, कालयवन के दल में आय, उसके सन्मुख हो निकले। वह उन्हें देखते ही अपने मन में कहने लगा, कि हो नहो यही कृष्ण है, नारद मुनि ने जो चिन्ह बताये थे सो सब इस में पाये जाते हैं; इसी ने कंसादि असुर मारे; जरासंध की सब सेना हनी। ऐसे मन ही मन विचार,

कालयवन यों कहे पुकारि, काचे भागे जात मुरारि
आय पहलो अब मोसों काम, ठाढ़े रहो करो संग्राम।
जरासंध हों नाहीं, कंस, यादवकुल को करों विध्वंस।

हे राजा! यों कह कालयवन अति अभिमान कर, अपनी सब सेना को छोड़ अकेला श्री कृष्णचंद के पीछे धाया: पर उस मूर्ख ने प्रभु का भेद न पाया। आगे आगे तो हरि भागे जाते थे, और एक हाथ के अंतर से पीछे पीछे वह दौड़ा जाता था, निदान भागते भागते जब अनेक दूर निकल गये, तब प्रभु एक पहाड़ की गुफा में बढ़ गये; वहां आ देखें तो एक पुरुष सोया पड़ा है। ये भट अपना पीतांबर उसे उढ़ाय, आप अलग एक ओर छिप रहे; पीछे से कालयवन भी दौड़ता हाफता उस अति अंधेरी कंदरा में जा पहुंचा, और पीतांबर ओढ़े विस

मुख को सोता देख उसने अपने जी में जाना कि यह कृष्णही छलकर सो रहा है। महाराज! ऐसे मन ही मन विचार, क्रोध कर उस सोते हुए को एक लात मार, कालयवन बोला, अरे कपटी! क्या मिस कर, साधु की भांति, निश्चिंतार्थ से सो रहा है, उठ मैं तुझे अब ही मारता हूं। यों कह उसने उसके ऊपर से पीतांबर झटक लिया; वह नींद से चौंक पड़ा; और ज्यों उस ने उस की ओर क्रोध कर देखा, तों वह जल बल भस्म हो गया।

इस बीच फिर जरासंध तेरहवीं की अधौहिणी सेना ले मथुरापुरी पर चढ़ि आया, तब भी कृष्ण बलराम अति घबराय के निकले, और उसके सन्मुख आ दिखाई दे उसके मन का संताप मिटाने को भाग चले; तद मंत्री ने जरासंध से कहा, कि महाराज! आप के प्रताप के आगे ऐसा कौन बली है जो ठहरे; देखो वे दोनों भाई कृष्ण बलराम, छोड़के सब धन धाम, लेके अपना प्राण, तुम्हारे त्रास के मारे नंगे पाम्बों भागे चले जाते हैं। इतनी बात मंत्री से सुन जरासंध भी यों पुकारकर कहता हुआ सेना ले उन के पीछे दौड़ा।

काहे इतके भागे जात, ठाढ़े रहो। करो कछु बात।

परत, उठत, कंपत घौं भारी, आई है ठिग मीच तिहारी।

इतनी कथा कह श्री शुकदेव मुनि बोले, कि पृथ्वीनाथ! जब श्री कृष्ण और बलदेव जी ने भाग के नोकरीनीति दिखाई, तब जरासंध के मन से पिछला सब शोक गया, और अति प्रसन्न हुआ, ऐसा कि जिस का कुछ बरनन नहीं किया जाता। आगे श्री कृष्ण बलराम भागते भागते एक गोतम नाम पर्वत, ग्यारह योजन ऊंचा था, तिस पर चढ़गये, और उस की चोटी पर आय खड़े भये।

देख जरासंध कियो पुकारि, गिरिखर चढ़े बलभद्र मुरारि

अब किम हम सों आय पलाय, या पर्वत कों देहु जलाय।

इतना वचन जरासंध के मुख से निकलते ही, सब असुरों ने उस पहाड़ को आ घेरा, और नगर नगर गांव गांव से काठ कबाड़ लाय लाय उसके चारों ओर चुन दिया; तिस पर गड़गूदड़. घी तेल से भिगो, डालकर आग लगादी। जब वह आग पर्वत का चोटी तक लहकी, तव उन दोनों भाइयों ने वहां से इस भांति द्वारका की बाट ली कि किसी ने उन्हें जाते भी न देखा; और पहाड़ जलकर भस्म होगया। उस आग जरासंध श्री कृष्ण बलराम को उस पर्वत के

संभल का मरा खान, अति मुसलमान, सब कर खराब दे, मथुरापुरी में आया, और वहां का राज ले, नगर में ढंढोरा दे उस ने बछना बाना बंठाया; कितने उनसे वसुदेव के पुराने मंदिर से गो छब ठवाये; और उस ने बाप बछने नये बनवाये।

इतनी कथा सुनाय भी गुरुदेव जी ने राजा से कहा, कि महाराज! इस रीति से अराउंध को धोखा दे सो भी कथा बलराम जी तो दुरखा में आय बसे; और अराउंध भी मथुरा नगरी से चल छब खेना से अति आनन्द कथा निःसंब हो, अपने घर आया। इति

॥ बूढ़े बाघ और पथिक की कहानी ॥

एक बूढ़ा बाघ नहाकर कुश हाथ में लिये सरोवर के तीर पर यह कह रहा था कि हे पथिको दान लेने के कंकण को लो। उस की बात सुनकर डर के मारे उस के पास कोई न आता। कोई लोभी पथिक उसे देख के सोचने लगा कि भाग्य से यह मिलता है पर दुष्ट जीव के हाथ में पड़ना न चाहिये क्योंकि बुरे से अच्छी वस्तु के मिलने से भला नहीं होता जो अमृत में विष लगा हो तो वह मृत्यु के लिये है॥ किन्तु सब जगह धन के उपार्जन में संदेह ही है॥ और ऐसा कहा है। मनुष्य संदेह में गये बिना कल्याण नहीं देखता संदेह में जाकर जो जीता रहे तो सुख देखता है॥ पहिले समझलें तब पुकार के कहने लगा कहां तेरा कंकण है॥ व्याघ्र ने हाथ पसारा के दिखलाया। पथिक ने कहा। तुझ जीवघाती पर विश्वास कैसे हो। व्याघ्र बोला। सुन रे पथिक पहिले ही युवावस्था में मैं बड़ा दुराचारी था अनेक गौ और मनुष्यों के वध से मेरे पुत्र और कलत्र मरगये और मैं बंधहीन हो गया। तब किसी धर्मात्मा ने मुझे उपदेश किया कि आप दान धर्म आदि कीजिये। उस के उपदेश से मैं स्नान किया करता दान देता और वृद्ध भी हूँ दांत नख गल गये क्यों कर विश्वासपात्र नहीं हूँ॥

क्योंकि यज्ञ अध्ययन दान तप सत्य धीरता और अलोभ यह आठ प्रकार का धर्म का मार्ग कहा है॥ उन में पहिले चार अर्थात् यज्ञ अध्ययन दान तप देखलाने के लिये भी किये जाते हैं परन्तु पिछले चार अर्थात् सत्य धीरता क्षमा और अलोभ महात्मा ही लोगों में रहते हैं॥ और मुझ को लोभ का इतना

त्याग है कि जिस से अपने हाथ में का भी सुवर्ण का कंकण किसी को दिया
चाहता हूं तोभी व्याघ्र मनुष्य को खाता है इस लोकप्रवाद का निवारण कठिन
है । क्योंकि । लोग चले के पीछे चलनेवाले एवं उपदेश करनेवाली कुटनी का
धर्म के विषय में प्रमाण नहीं करते जैसा गोघाती ब्राह्मणा का ॥ और मैं ने
धर्म शास्त्रों को पढ़ा है । सुन ॥ मरुस्थली में जैसे तृप्ति तैसे ही सुधा से
पीड़ित को भोजन है दरिद्र को जो दान दिया जाता है सो सफल है ॥ जैसे
अपना प्राण प्रिय है वैसे जीवों को भी है इस लिये साधु लोग अपने समान
जीवों पर दया करते हैं । और दूसरे । पर स्त्रियों को माता के समान पराये
द्रव्यों को ढेले के समान सब जीवों को अपने समान जो देखता है वह पंडित
है ॥ और तू दुर्दशा में है इसलिये मैं तुझे दिया चाहता हूं ॥ और ऐसा शास्त्रों
में कहा है कि दरिद्रों का पोषण करना चाहिये धनी को धन देना न चाहिये
रोगी को औषध हित है निरोगी को औषध से क्या ॥ इसलिये इस सरोवर में
स्नान करके सोने के कंकने को लें । इस के उपरांत इस के बचन की अब
प्रतीति करके लोभ के मारे सरोवर में स्नान के लिये पैठा तब वह पथिक बड़े
कीचड़ में ऐसा फसा कि निकल न सका । उसे कीचड़ में पड़ा देख कर व्याघ्र
ने कहा । आह दो तू बड़े कीचड़ में फसा पड़ा है । इसलिये मैं तुझे निकालता
हूं । यह कहकर धीरे धीरे आकर उस व्याघ्र ने पकड़ा तब वह पथिक सोचने
लगा कि किसी का स्वभाव किसी प्रकार से नहीं बदलता ॥ और कि । खिंज का
मन वश नहीं उस की क्रिया स्थायी के स्थान के समान है कुरूपा स्त्री के भूषण
के समान क्रिया के बिना ज्ञान बोझा है ॥ सो मैं ने भला न किया जो उस
हिंसक जीव पर विश्वास किया सभी के स्वभाव परखे जाते हैं दूसरे गुण नहीं
क्योंकि सब गुणों को नांघ कर स्वभाव सिर पर रहता है अर्यात् मनुष्य के सब
गुणों में स्वभाव हो मुख्य है ॥ फिर सोच कर कहने लगा कि ललाट का लिखा
कोई नहीं मिटा सक्का ॥ यह चिंता करता ही था कि व्याघ्र ने उस को मारा
और खाया ॥

॥ फल इस का यह है कि लालच से हानि होती है ॥

॥ जरद्गव गिद्ध और लंबकर्ण बिड़ाल की कहानी ॥

भागीरथी के तीर गृध्रकूट नाम पर्बत पर एक बड़ा पाकर का पेड़ था उस के खोंढरे में निज कर्म भोग से जरद्गव नाम गिद्ध जिस के नख और नयन गल गये थे रहता था कृपा करके उस के जीवन के लिये उस वृक्ष के रहनेवाले पक्षी अपने आहार में से कुछ कुछ निकार देते थे इस से यह जीता था किसी समय लंबकर्ण नाम बिड़ाल चिड़िये के बच्चों के खाने के लिये यहां आया। तब उस को आते देख कर चिड़िये के बच्चे भय से व्याकुल होकर कोलाहल करने लगे। यह सुनकर जरद्गव ने कहा। यह कौन आता है। लंबकर्ण गिद्ध को देखकर डरकर बोला। हाय मैं मारा गया। क्योंकि तब तक भय से डरना चाहिये जब तक भय नहीं आयी आयी भय को देख कर मनुष्य को उचित करना चाहिये। अब इस के पास से भाग नहीं सक्ता सो जैसी होनी हो वैसी हो पहिले में विश्वास उत्पन्न कर के उस के समीप चलता हूं। यह बिचार कर निकट आ कर कहा। हे महाराज में तुम को प्रणाम करता हूं। गिद्ध ने कहा तू कौन है। उस ने कहा। में बिलार हूं। गिद्ध ने कहा दूर चला जा नहीं तो मैं मारडालूंगा। बिलार ने कहा। पहिले हमारी बात तो सुनें तब जो मैं मारने के योग्य हां तो मारियो ॥ क्योंकि। जाति मात्र से क्या कोई कहां मारा अथया पूजा जाता है व्यवहार को जान कर अध्य अथया पूज्य होना चाहिये ॥ गिद्ध ने कहा। कह किस लिये आया है। उस ने कहा। यहां गंगा के तीर नित्य स्नान करता। ब्रह्मचर्य्य ब्रत कर के रहता हूं और आप धर्मात्मा की प्रशंसा सब विषय. सुपात्र पक्षी सर्वदा मेरे आगे करते हैं। इस लिये आप से जो विद्या और धय में बड़े हैं धर्म सुनने को यहां आया हूं। और आप ऐसे धर्मज्ञ जो सुभ्र अतिथि को मारने को उठे ॥ और गृहस्थधर्म यह है कि जो धन न हो तो प्रीतियुक्त वचन ही से अतिथि को पूजना चाहिये ॥ क्योंकि। तृण भूमि जल और चौथी मधुरबाणी ये सब कभी सत्पुरुषों के घर में उच्छिन्न नहीं होतीं ॥ और दूसरे। गुणहीन भी स्त्रीयों पर साधु लोग दया करते हैं चंद्रमा चांडाल के घर में से चंद्रिका को नहीं खींचता ॥ और दूसरे। जिस घर से अतिथि निराश होकर फिर जाता है यह उस को पाप देकर पुण्य लेकर चला आता है ॥ उत्तम भी जाति के घर में नीच भी आगया तो यथा योग्य उस को मानना चाहिये

क्योंकि अतिशय आदरणीय है ॥ गिद्ध ने कहा बिलार को मांस की रुचि होती है और यहां चिड़िये के बच्चे रहते हैं इसलिये में ऐसा कहता हूं यह सुन कर बिलार ने भूमि छू कर कान को छुआ ॥ में ने धर्म शास्त्र को सुनकर राग का त्याग करके यह कठिन चान्द्रायण व्रत धारण किया है । परस्पर विरुद्ध भी धर्मशास्त्रों का इस बात में ऐकमत्य है कि अहिंसा परम धर्म है । क्योंकि जो मनुष्य सब हिंसा से निवृत्त हैं और जो सब कुछ सहते हैं और सब के आश्रय भूत हैं वे लोग स्वर्गगामी होते हैं ॥ धर्म ही एक मित्र है जो मरने पर भी साथ जाता है और सब तो शरीर के साथ नष्ट हो जाते हैं ॥ अब जिस की मांस को जो खाता है दोनों के अन्तर को देखो एक को क्षण भर सुख दूसरा प्राण से जाता है ॥ मरण यह जो दुख पुरुष होता है उस अनुमान से पराये की भी रक्षा की जा सकती है ॥ और सुनो । आप से बन में उत्पन्न साग से भरता है तो इस खलहुत पेट के लिये बड़ा पाप कौन करे ॥ इस प्रकार से विश्वास करा के यह बिलार वृक्ष के खोड़रे में रहने लगा । इस के उपरांत दिनों के बीते चिड़ियों के बच्चों को पकड़ कर खोड़रे में लाकर प्रति दिन खाता जिन के बच्चे खाये गये उन्हों ने शोक से दुःखित होकर बिलाप करते हुए इधर उधर खोजना आरम्भ किया । यह जान कर वह मार्जार खोड़रे से निकल कर भागा गांछ सों पक्षियों ने इधर उधर खोजते २ उस पेड़ के खोड़रे में बच्चों की हड्डियां पायीं । इस के उपरांत उन्हों ने कहा कि इसी अधम ने हमारे बच्चों को खाया है यह बात सब पक्षियों ने निश्चय कर गिद्ध को मारडाला ॥

फल इस का यह है कि जिस से ज्ञान पहचान न हो उस को
अपने घर में बसाना न चाहिये ।

॥ हाथी और सियारों की कहानी ॥

ब्रह्मारण्य में कर्पूरतिलक नाम हाथी था उस को देख कर सब सियारों ने विचारा कि जो किसी उपाय से यह मरे तो हम लोगों का इस की शरीर से चार महीने का भोजन हो । उन में से एक बूढ़े सियार ने प्रतिज्ञा की कि में बुद्धि के प्रभाव से इस का मरण साधूंगा । इस के अनन्तर वह उस कर्पूरतिलक के पास जाकर साष्टांग प्रणाम करके बोला । हे महाराज दया दृष्टि कीजिये ।

हाथी ने कहा तू कौन है कहां से आया है। उस ने कहा। मैं सियार हूं। सब बनवासी पशुओं ने मिल कर आप के पास भेजा है कि बिना राजा के रहना उचित नहीं। सो यहां बन के राज्य पर अभिषेक के लिये आप को जो स्वामी के सब गुणों से युक्त हैं ठहराया है॥ क्योंकि। जो कुल और नीति के आचारों करके अति शुद्ध है प्रतापवान धार्मिक और नीतिकुशल है यह पृथ्वी पर स्वामी होने के योग्य है॥ और दूसरे देखो। पहिले राजा को प्राप्त करें तब भार्या को तब धन को क्योंकि इस लोक में राजा के न रहते कहां से भार्या और कहां से धन॥ और तीसरे। राजा मेघ के समान जीवों का आधार है क्योंकि मेघ के विकल होने पर भी प्राणी जीता रहता है परन्तु राजा के विकल होने पर नहीं॥ प्रायः दण्ड देने से लोग नियत विषय में वर्त्तमान रहते हैं इस परवश जगत में समीचीन आचरण करनेवाला दुर्लभ है दुर्जन प्रति विकल अथवा रोगी अथवा निर्धन पति को भी कुलनारी दण्ड के भय से अंगीकार करती है सो जिस में लग्न की बेला न चली जाय ऐसा करके तुरन्त महाराज आवें। यह कह उठ कर चला। तब राज्य के लोभ से खिंचा हुआ यह कर्पूरतिलक सियार की वाट से दौड़ता हुआ बड़े कीचड़ में धंस गया। तब उस स्वामी ने कहा हे मित्र सियार अब क्या करना चाहिये बड़े कीचड़ में मैं गिरा हूं मरता हूं। फिर कर देखो। सियार ने हंस कर कहा। हे महाराज मेरी पूछ का अवलंबन करके उठो जो मुझ ऐसे की वात पर तुम ने विश्वास किया सो असहायरहित तुम को भोगे॥ और ऐसा कहा है। जब सत्संग से रहित होगे तब दुर्जनों की संगति में पड़ोगे॥ तब बड़े कीचड़ में धंसे हाथी को सियारों ने खाया॥

फल इस का यह है कि जो बात उपाय से होती है वह
पराक्रम से नहीं होती।

॥ नीले सियार और सिंह आदि पशुओं की कहानी ॥

किसी बन में एक सियार था अपनी इच्छा से नगर के आस पास घूमता हुआ नील के कुंड में गिर पड़ा और उस में से निकल न सका और अपने को मृतक के समान दिखला कर ठहरा रहा प्रातःकाल नीलीभांड के स्वामी ने उसे मरा जान के वहां से उठा कर दूर लेजा कर फेंक दिया वहां से भाग के बन में

मया अपने को नीलवर्ण देख कर सोचा कि मैं अब उत्तमवर्ण हूं अपनी महिमा को न बढ़ाऊं यह विचार कर अरण्य के पशुओं को डरा जान कर बोला अरे पशुओ किस लिये तुम लोग मुझे देख कर इस प्रकार से डर कर भागते हो डरना न चाहिये । आज ब्रह्मा ने मुझे बुला कर कहा कि पशुओं में कोई राजा नहीं है इसलिये तुम को मैं पशुओं की राजगद्दी पर बैठाता हूं और तुम्हारा नाम नीलवर्ण रखता हूं जाकर पृथ्वी पर उन सब की रक्षा करो इस लिये मैं यहां आया हूं सो मेरी छत्रछाया के नीचे तुम सब लोग सदा बसो मैं नीलवर्ण नाम राजा तीनों लोक में पशुओं का रक्षक तुम्हारा हूं यह सुन कर सिंह आदि सब पशु स्वामी प्रभु आज्ञा दीजिये ऐसा कह कर उस को घेर कर ठहरे तब नीलवर्ण महाराज बोले कि सिंह को हम ने मंत्री की पदवी दी और बाघ को पलंगकी रखवाली दी चीतों को तांबूल का अधिकार दिया हाथियों को द्वारपाल बनाया बानरों को छत्रधारी का काम सौंपा और जो अपनी जाति के लोग थे उन के साथ बात चीत न करता और सब सियारों को गर्दनिया देकर निकलवा दिया इस प्रकार से राज काज करता और सिंह आदि पशु मृगा रोझ शायर आदि मार कर उस के आगे ला रखते और वह प्रभु के धर्म के अनुसार सब को बांट देता इस प्रकार से अरण्य में राज करता था । एक दिन सियारों के झुंड को बोलते सुना उन के शब्द को सुन कर वह उस की शरीर में रोयें खड़े हो आये और मारे आनन्द के आंखें आंसू से भर गईं उठ कर आप भी ऊंचे स्वर से हांव हांव करने लगा सिंह आदि पशुओं ने उस का हलुआना सुन कर जाना कि यह सियार है क्या एक तो मारे लज्जा के सिर नीचे किये हुए खड़े रहे फिर आपस में कहने लगे कि अरे इस ठग सियार ने हम लोगों को धोखा दिया ऐसा कह कर बोले कि इस को मारडालो मारडालो यह सुन कर वह भागने को चाहा पर सिंह आदिखों ने उस को पकड़ कर टुकड़े टुकड़े कर मारडाला ॥

फल इस का यह है कि जो और को ठगा चाहता है
सो आप ही ठगा जाता है ।

———————

॥ महाराणी दमयन्ती की कथा ॥

विदर्भ नगर में राजा भीमसेन की कन्या दमयन्ती रहती थीं उन का रूप
और गुण सारी पृथ्वी पर प्रसिद्ध हो गया उन के विवाह के लिये स्वयंवर रचा
गया तहां देश देश के राजा लोग आये उन में निषध देश के राजा वीरसेन के
बेटे जब गुणसम्पन्न अति सुशील धर्मात्मा राजा नल भी थे दमयन्ती ने उन के
रूप और गुण को देखकर जयमाल उन्हीं को पहिनाया और विवाह किया
बारह बरस तक दोनों सुख आनंद से रहे और एक लड़का और एक लड़की
उन को हुई । राजा नल पासा खेलने को बहुत चाहते थे उन का एक भाई
पुष्कर नाम था उन से इन से खेल हुआ करता राजा नल दांव लगाते लगाते
सारा राज हार गये एक धोता को छोड़ उन के पास कुछ न बचा दमयन्ती को
साथ लेकर विदेश को निकले दमयन्ती ने आगे ही से लड़के लड़की को अपने
नैहर भेज दिया था । पुष्कर ने अपने राज में ढोंढ़ी फिरवा दी थी कि जो कोई
राजा नल को अपने घर में रहने देगा वह जान से मारा जायगा । राजा नल
को तीन दिन रात बिना अब पानी के बीत गया चौथे दिन नदी के तीर जा-
कर चुल्लू से पानी पिया और बन में कन्द मून फल खा के रानी समेत दिन
काटने लगे । नल ने दमयन्ती को बहुत समझाया कि तुम बहुत कोमल और
सुकुमार हो ऐसी विपत्ति में कैसे साथ रह सकोगी हम चाहते हैं कि तुम अपने
पिता के घर जाके रहो जो ईश्वर की दया होगी तो फिर हम तुम एकट्ठे हो
जायंगे इस बात को सुनतेही दमयन्ती विलाप कर रोने लगी और बोली कि
हे स्वामी हे प्रिय ऐसा कठोर वचन आप अपने मुखारविन्द से क्यों कहते हैं
क्या पिता के घर में आप के संग से अधिक सुख आनन्द मिलेगा क्या खाना
पहिनना आप के दर्शन से अधिक सुखदायक होगा जो आप मुझे छोड़ें भी तो
मैं आप को कभी त्याग नहीं सकती जो फिर कभी आप ऐसा वचन कहियेगा
तो मैं अपना प्राण तजूंगी । यह कह के अपने बायें को राजा के गले पर रख
कर एक पेड़ के नीचे सो गयी राजा मन में सोचने लगे कि जो स्त्री राजमंदिर
में फूलों की सेज पर डरकर पैर रखती थी वह इस दुर्गम बन में कांटों के ऊपर
क्योंकर चल सकेगी मैं अब कुछ रह सकता पर इस प्राणप्यारी को इस विपत्ति
में कैसे देखूंगा यह मुझे कभी न छोड़ेगी जो मैं इसे यहां छोड़ दूं तो यह किसी

न किसी प्रकार से अपने पिता के घर चली जायगी निदान यह सोच बिचार
कर उस सुशीला गुणवती और पतिव्रता को उस पेड़ के नीचे छोड़ कर आप
एक ओर चल दिये नल के पास कुछ कपड़ा पहिनने को न था एक चिड़िया
पकड़ने के लिये अपनी धोती उस पर फेंकी वह चिड़िया धोती समेत उड़गयी
जब विपत्ति आती है तब सब सामग्री ऐसी ही हो जाती है निदान अब राजा
नल ने चाहा था कि दमयन्ती को यहाँ छोड़ कर किसी और जगह चला आऊं
उस समय दमयन्ती को आधी साड़ी फाड़कर अपने पहिनने को लेली थी और
आधी उस की शरीर पर छोड़ दी थी मनुष्य का मन भगवान ने अद्भुत बनाया
है किसी का बहुत कोमल किसी का बहुत कड़ा । उस समय नल की दशा
नल ही जानते थे कुछ दूर जाकर दमयन्ती को देखने को फिर लौटे फिर कुछ
सोच विचार कर फिर चले । निदान जब महाराज दूर निकल गये और दमयन्ती
की आंख खुली तो उन को अपने पास न देखकर छाती पीटने और हाथ
पटकने लगीं मूर्छित होकर भूमि पर गिरपड़ीं आंसू की धारा बहती जाती थी
और रो रो कर पुकारती थी कि हे प्राणपति मुझ दासी को किस अपराध से
आप ऐसे जंगल में अकेली छोड़कर चले जाते हैं अपने उस बचन को चेत करो
जो बियाह के समय आप ने कहा था कि मैं जीते जी तुम से अलग कभी न
होऊंगा महाराज बेग आके मेरी सुध लीजिये और मेरे मन के खेद को दूर
कीजिये दमयन्ती का विलाप सुन कर सब जीव जंतु चर अचर व्याकुल हो
गये थे दमयन्ती रोती बिसूरती उस घने जंगल में चारो ओर फिरने लगी अचानक
एक अजगर वहां आकर उन को घेरा और चाहा कि काटे उसे देख कर दमयन्ती
चिल्लाने लगीं भाग से वहां एक व्याधा आ गया उस ने इन की पुकार सुनी
और निकट गया तो देखता क्या है कि अजगर उन को काटा चाहता है एक
बाघ ऐसा मारा कि वह अजगर मरगया पर यह व्याधा दमयन्ती को अजगर से
भी अधिक दुखदायी हुआ कि मोह के वश में होकर उस पतिव्रता का सत
खोने को चाहा दमयन्ती चिचिया के और पिता पिता उस को कछ के धर्म की
बहुत ही बातें सुनाने लगीं पर जब देखा कि वह अधम अब किसी प्रकार से
नहीं मानता तो व्याकुल होकर के भी भगवान अंतर्यामी घट घट निवासी से
प्रार्थना करने लगीं कि हे दीनबन्धु दयासागर जो मैं सती हूं तो यह दुष्ट मेरा

व्रत भंग न करे और बहुत समय जलकर राख हो जाय धन्य भगवान और कैसी उस की अपरंपार महिमा है कि व्याधा ने इस बात से क्रोध करके दमयन्ती के मारने को बाण चलाया परंतु वह तीर उसी को लगा और मरगया। इस पीछे दमयन्ती रोती बिलखती जंगल पहाड़ों में ढूंढती फिरती सिंह और हाथियों से बचती हुई सुबाहुनगर में पहुंची वहां के राजा के रानी के पास दासी बन कर रहने लगी। संयोगन उस के पिता के भेजे हुए ब्राह्मण ढूंढते २ वहां पाकर विदर्भ नगर में ले गये। राजा नल उस के विरह में व्याकुल होकर घूमते फिरते अयोध्या में आ निकले और अपना नाम बाहुक रखकर वहां के राजा ऋतुपर्ण के सारथी बने। दमयन्ती के पिता नल के खोजने के लिये नगर नगर गांव गांव ब्राह्मण भेजे उन में से एक ब्राह्मण अयोध्या से यह समाचार लाया कि बाहुक नाम एक सारथी जो राजा ऋतुपर्ण के यहां है दमयन्ती का नाम सुनकर आंख में आंसू भर लाया वह अपने को सारथी छोड़ के और कुछ नहीं कहता यह सुनते ही दमयन्ती ताड़गयी कि हो न हो कि मेरा स्वामी राजा नल यही है यह सोच बिचार अपने पिता से प्रार्थना की कि उन को बोलावें। भीमसेन ने राजा नल को बुलाया पर वे न आये तब दमयन्ती ने अपने पिता से कह कर राजा ऋतुपर्ण के पास यह संदेशा भेजवाया कि अब राजा नल के मिलने की कुछ आशा नहीं है इसलिये अब दमयन्ती का दूसरा स्वयंवर होगा आप कृपा करके यहां आइये और स्वयंवर का दिन ऐसा समीप ठहराया कि बिना राजा नल के हांके कोई घोड़ा उतने काल में अयोध्या से विदर्भ तक न पहुंच सके। राजा नल रथ हांकने को विद्या में बड़े प्रसिद्ध थे। राजा ऋतुपर्ण बहुत घबराये कि इतने काल में विदर्भ कैसे पहुंच सकूंगा यह बात सुनकर नल ने महाराज से निवेदन किया कि महाराज चिंता न करें मैं आप को स्वयंवर के दिन से पहिले ही पहुंचाऊंगा। निदान ऐसा ही हुआ कि ऋतुपर्ण स्वयंवर के दिन से पहिले पहुंचे राजा भीमसेन ने राजा ऋतुपर्ण का बड़ा आदर मान किया परंतु वहां स्वयंवर की कुछ रचना न थी और न कोई दूसरा राजा वहां आया था यह अपने मन बड़ा लज्जित हुआ नल ने घोड़े को घोड़ग्याले में बांधकर भीमसेन के सारथी के पास खटिये पर पड़रहा। दमयन्ती ऋतुपर्ण के पहुंचने का समाचार सुनकर बहुत घबड़ायी और मन में संकल्प किया कि वो नल से

भेंट न हुई तो अपने प्राण का त्याग करूंगी निदान अपने सखी केसनी को ऋतुपर्ण के सारथी को खोजने को ढूंढ़ाने भेजा केसनो ने आकर नल से कहा कि दमयन्ती आप का समाचार पूछती हैं नल बोले कि मैं अयोध्या के राजा का सारथी हूं और नाम मेरा बाहुक है दमयन्ती का स्वयंवर सुन के राजा को हम यहां ल्याये हैं परंतु यह बड़े अचरज की बात है कि राजा नल की स्त्री दमयन्ती ऐसी पतिव्रता होकर दूसरे पति की अभिलाषा करे ठीक है कि जब मनुष्य के दिन बुरे आते हैं तो पुत्र और कलत्र भी अपने नहीं रहते ॥ केसनी बोली है बाहुक तुम राजा नल का भी कुछ पता ठेकाना बता सकते हो देखो तो उन्हों ने बड़ी निर्दयता का काम किया कि उस अबला को जंगल में गाढ़ सिंह भुजगरों के साथ छोड़कर कहां चला गया दमयन्ती ने उन के विरह में अच जल का त्याग कर दिया केवल उन के नाम का जपा करती हैं राजा नल की आंखों से दमयन्ती की यह दया सुनकर आंसू की धारा बह चली बोला कि स्त्री अपने पति से कितनाहूं कष्ट पावे परंतु औरों के सामने पति की निन्दा करना उचित नहीं है जो राजा नल दमयन्ती को बन में न छोड़ आते तो उन का प्राण भी न बचता और जो नल ने कोई निर्दयता का काम भी किया होता तो दमयन्ती को चमा करनी चाहिये क्योंकि दुख पड़ने पर मनुष्य की मति ठिकाने नहीं रहती इतना कह कर नल फिर रोने लगे । केसनी उन की दया देख वहां से जाकर सब समाचार दमयन्ती से कहा सुनते ही दमयन्ती ने जान लिया कि यही मेरा स्वामी राजा नल है । केसनी से कहा कि फिर तू उन के पास जाकर देख कि वे क्या कर रहे हैं और मेरे लड़के लड़कों को भी अपने साथ लेतीजा जब वे सब राजा नल के पास आये तो लड़के लड़की को देख राजा नल की आंख से आंसू की धारा बह चली और दोनों को छाती से लगा के कहने लगे कि ऐसे ही बेटा बेटी हमारे भी हैं बहुत दिन से मैंने उन को नहीं देखा इन को देख के वे मुझे चेत पड़े अब इन को इन की मां के पास पहुंचा दो ये अनाथ आज नल के लड़के हैं कल किसी दूसरे के हो जांयगे खो दो धन्य है कि एक पति छोड़ती और दूसरा करलेती रात बीतने पर मैं देखूंगा कि राजा नल की पतिव्रता रानी दमयन्ती किस प्रकार दूसरा स्वामी करती है । यह सब समाचार सुन केसनी ने दमयन्ती से आके कहा और यह

भी कहा कि यह तो कोई ग्विलवन पुरुष है क्योंकि जितनी सामग्री हमारे यहां
से राजा ऋतुपर्ण के यहां भेजी गयी थी हम ने थात की थात में सब पका कं
चिह्न करडालनी दमयन्ती ने कहा आ जो जो उस ने पकाया है थोड़ा थोड़ा सत्र
मेरे पास ले था कंछनी आयें लेआयी । दमयन्ती ने चीखा तो उन में वही
स्वाद पाया जो राजा नल के हाथ के बनाये भोजन में पाती थीं । अपनी मां
के पास जाकर कहने लगीं कि मेरा स्वामी आया मुझे आज्ञा दीजिये तो
घोड़खाने में जाऊं । उस की मां ने कहा कि तुम उन के पास जाव । दमयन्ती
बेटा बेटी में राजा नल के पास गयी राजा नल को सारथी के भेष में तन छीन
मन मलीन देखकर बहुत घबरायी और आंखों से आंसू की धारा बह चली
राजा से कहने लगीं कि स्वामी मुझ अबला को आप ने अंगन में अकेली क्यों
छोड़ा राजा नल लज्जित हो कर थाने कि तुम को मैं कभी न छोड़ सक्ता था
परंतु जिस निर्बुद्धि के कारण मैं सारा राज खोया उसी से तुम्हारा भी विछोह
हुआ पर तुम्हारे बिरह से जो दुख उठाया वह मेरी गर्दार ही जानती है
पतिव्रता स्त्री अपने स्वामी का अवगुण देखकर भी उस की निन्दा नहीं करती
पर तुम तो कल किसी दूसरे की हो जायगी इन अवगुणों में अब तुम्हें क्या
प्रयोजन है । तब दमयन्ती हाथ जोड़कर थानी कि आप के थानाने के निये
राजा ऋतुपर्ण के पास स्वयंवर का पत्र निखवाया था मेरा बिवार दूसरे व्याह
का नहीं था नहीं तो बहुत से राजा लोग यहां आते मेरी प्रतिज्ञा थी कि आज
आप से भेंट न होगी तो मैं आग में जल मरूंगी । निदान यह सब समाचार
राजा भीमसेन और ऋतुपर्ण के पास पहुंचा इस थात को सुनकर वे बहुत
आनन्दित हुए राजा ऋतुपर्ण ने नल से प्रार्थना की कि महाराज मुझ से बड़ी
भूल हुई कि अनजाने मैंने आप को सारथी के काम पर रक्खा हमारे अपराध
को आप क्षमा कीजिये यह कह कर अयोध्या को चले गये । और भीमसेन ने
राजा नल से कहा कि आप अभी निषध देश में न जावें मेरा राज पाट सोजिये
और इसी जगह रहिये परंतु नल ने सुसराल में रहना अंगीकार न किया और
अपने देश में जाने के लिये हठ की । राजा भीमसेन ने एक रथ सोलह हाथी
पांच सौ घोड़े और छ सौ पियादे साथ देकर निषध देश की ओर बिदा किया
और दमयन्ती को अपने पास ही रक्खा । राजा नल ने निषध देश में पहुंच

कर अपने भाई पुष्कर को बोलाकर यह कहा कि एक बार हमारे तुम्हारे साथ फिर पासा हो जो मैं हारूं तो तुम्हारा दास होकर रहूं और जो तुम हारो तो मेरा सारा हारा तुम्हा राज फेर दो। अब की पारी भगवान की ऐसी दया हुई कि राजा नल जीता और पुष्कर हारा और मारे डर के कांपने लगा तब नल ने समझाया कि इस में तुम्हारा क्या अपराध है यह सब अपने दिनों का फेर है जिस प्रकार पहिले काम करते थे उसी प्रकार करते रहो फिर नल ने दमयन्ती को भी बेटा बेटी समेत विदर्भ नगर से अपने पास बुलवा लिया और बहुत काल तक सुख चैन करते रहे जैसा दिन इन का फिरा भगवान सब का फेरे॥

॥ ऋतु ॥

जब लट्टू फिराया जाता है तब वह अपनी गूंझ की नोक पर घूमता है। यह नोक फिरती है परन्तु भूमि पर अपने ठिकाने को नहीं पलटती। पर जब तक गति बनी रहती है तब तक लट्टू के और सब भाग अपने स्थान को लगातार पलटा करते हैं क्योंकि वे ऐसे वर्तुलघेरे में घूमते हैं जिसका केन्द्र नहीं ठीक गूंझ के ऊपर रहता है। फिरकी समान फिरती हुई पृथ्वी पर भी एक स्थान है जो उसके फिरने के विषय में टीका ठीक लट्टू की गूंझ की नोक के सदृश है और जो वह पृथ्वी फिरने के समय किसी ठोस वस्तु के आधार पर होती तो वह स्थान सत्य करके पृथ्वी की गूंझ की नोक के तुल्य होता। यह स्थान ध्रुव कहलाता है। पृथ्वी के दो ध्रुव सामने सामने हैं और इन ध्रुवों के बीच में एक सीधी रेखा अवश्य करके रहती है जो गति के विषय में ठीक ध्रुवों ही की नाईं स्थित है अर्थात् पृथ्वी के जितने भाग इस रेखा पर पड़ते हैं गो सब ऐंठा करते हैं परन्तु फिरते नहीं जैसे एक डोरा अंगुली और अंगूठे के बीच में तागकर बटें तो ऐंठता है। ऐंठती रेखा जो पृथ्वी के ध्रुवों के बीच फैली हुई है सो उसकी धुरी कहलाती है। फिरती हुई पृथ्वी का प्रत्येक भाग जो उसकी धुरी में नहीं पड़ता सो उसी धुरी की चारों ओर फिरता है जैसे पहिये की पुट्ठी धुरी की चारों ओर घूमती है। तीसरे चित्र में वृत्ताकार जो सकीर है सो जो पृथ्वी का घेरा माना जाय और प प की लें वा बिंदु माने जांय जिन पर ऐंठन होती है तो धुरी पृथ्वी के आर पार प से प तक बिन्दु रेखा की

नाई एक सीधी लकीर होगी । पृथ्वी का प्रत्येक अंश जो इस बिन्दुरेखा पर न हो सो उसकी चारों ओर बड़े वा छोटे वर्तुलपथ में सदा फिरा करेगा ॥

पृथ्वी की पृष्ठ के वे देश जो आमने सामने के धुवों के ठांचो बीच हैं अर्थात् जो दोनों धुवों से समान अन्तर पर हैं सो निरक्षदेश कहलाते हैं । वे आठ सहस्र मील के व्यास के बड़े वर्तुल में और एक मिनिद में शोनस मील के वेग से घूमते हैं । जो स्थान निरक्ष और ध्रुव के बीच आधो आध अन्तर पर हैं सो तिहाई छोटे वर्तुल में एक मिनिद में ग्यारह मील के वेग से भ्रमण करते हैं । तथ्यपि आधी दूर की अपेक्षा एक ध्रुव के कुछ निकट है इस निमित्त वह इस से कुछ न्यून वेग से फिरता है । जो लोहे की छड़क को एक गाड़ी लयदन से चले और प्रसिद्ध अतिशीघ्र गति से अठारह गुण अधिक वेग से ठीक पश्चिम को जाय तो वह पृथ्वी की पृष्ठ पर ठीक उतना शीघ्र एक ओर जायगी जितना शीघ्र कि वह पृष्ठ शून्य में दूसरी ओर फिरेगी । कील पर फिरने को छोड़कर जो पृथ्वी की और कोई गति न होती तो वह गाड़ी यद्यपि एक घंटे में ६०० मील के वेग से पृथ्वी की पृष्ठ पर दौड़ती तथापि वह सचमुच शून्य में जहां की तहां ही रहती । एक नदी के आर पार आमने सामने के तटों से तने हुय रस्से को पकड़कर जो कोई मनुष्य एक चलती हुई वाष्पनौका की छत पर उसके माथे से पतवार की ओर चले तो जैसी उसको दशा होगी तैसी ही ठीक ठीक उस गाड़ी की दशा होती । ऐसा मनुष्य फुरती से एक ओर जायगा और उसी समय जिस नाव पर वह चलेगा सो उसके तले उतनाही शीघ्र सामने दूसरी ओर खिसकती जायगी । जो वह रस्सा पकड़कर नाव पर से पैर उठा ले और लटक जाय तो उसका सब घम बच जायगा क्योंकि तब भी वह नाव को अपने तले से ठीक उसी प्रकार निकल जाते देखेगा जैसा कि उस पर चलते हुय देखता । इसी भांति जो लोहे की छड़क को गाड़ी पृथ्वी की पृष्ठ पर से उठा ली जाती और ऊपर थंभी रहती तो उस पर से कोई जन पृथ्वी को भी तले से सरक जाते देखता । चाहे गाड़ी घंटे भर में छ से मील के वेग से पृथ्वी को पृष्ठ पर पश्चिम को चलती चाहे पृथ्वी की पृष्ठ से उठा ली जाती और एक ओर को अपनी चाल से और दूसरी ओर की पृथ्वी की गति से रहित हो जाती दोनों अवस्था में एक ही लीला होती ॥

जिस धुरी पर पृथ्वी फिरती है यह ऐसी कि चौथे चित्र के पहिले क्षेत्र में
[जिस में छ सूर्य का स्थान माना गया है] सीधी देख पड़ती है तिरछी सीधी
सूर्य की ओर नहीं रखती । जो वह इसी रीति से रखती तो पृथ्वी की एक
अलग अर्थात् निरक्षदेशप्रकाशक चौड़ी रेखा की बाईं अलग में कभी कुछ भी
घाम न आता । जैसे एक चिड़िया को लोहे की सींक में गोदकर सींक की एक
अलग को तो भाग की ओर सींधी रक्खें और दूसरी अलग को फेरकर भाग से
दूर रक्खें और उस चिड़िया को भूंजें तो जो दशा उसकी होगी सोई दशा उस
अवस्था में पृथ्वी की होती । परन्तु जिस धुरी पर पृथ्वी फिरती है यह ऐसी
कि चित्र के दूसरे क्षेत्र में है ऐसी उस लकीर पर लम्बरूप नहीं है जो सूर्य की
ओर जाती है । जो वह इस प्रकार से होती तो पृथ्वी की पृष्ठ पर प्रत्येक स्थान
जो ध्रुव की किसी ओर होता उसका अपना ठीक आधा चक्कर घाम में और
दूसरा आधा छांह में रहता इस रीति से दिन और रात छब ठौर बराबर होते ।
परन्तु रात दिन समान नहीं होते और केवल भिन्न भिन्न स्थानों ही में वे घट
बढ़कर नहीं होते परन्तु बरस के भिन्न भिन्न समय में वे एक ही ठौर घट बढ़
हुआ करते हैं । दिन रात के घट बढ़ का कारण यह है कि पृथ्वी का एक ध्रुव
सामने के ध्रुव की अपेक्षा सूर्य की ओर प्रायः सदा अधिक फिरा रहता है ।
सूर्य की ओर जो ध्रुव फिरा रहता है तिसके बहुतसो पास के स्थान पृथ्वी की
धुरी पर अपने चक्कर के आधे से अधिक घाम में रहते हैं और आधे से थोड़ा
छांह में । जो एक चिड़िया को लोहे की सींक में गोदकर भूंजें और सींक को
इस रीति तिरछी पकड़ें कि उसका एक टांक नीचे भाग की ओर हो और दूसरा
टांक ऊपर की अलग भाग से दूर हो तो जब सींक फेरी जायगी तब चिड़िया
के वे सब भाग जो नीचे के टांक के बहुतसो नेरे होंगे सो भाग के सामने बहुत
रहेंगे और उनको आंच बहुत लगेगी । ठीक ठीक ठीक इसी भांति पृथ्वी सूर्य से
तिरछी रहती है । परन्तु जिस दिशा में सूर्य होता है उस से ठीक एक ही
झुकाव पर पृथ्वी की धुरी नहीं रहती । धुरी का प्रत्येक ध्रुव सूर्य की ओर किसी
समय की अपेक्षा किसी समय में अधिक फिरा रहता है । यह व्यवस्था इस हेतु
को गई है कि पृथ्वी की तिरछी स्थिति की क्षति किसी प्रकार पूरी हो जाय
और पृथ्वी की पृष्ठ का प्रत्येक भाग अंछा चाहिये वैसा सूर्य के तेज में आछरा

ओसरी आया करे । वह बहुत करके एक चिड़िया की स्थिति के समान है जिसे एक शींक में गोदकर भूंजें और शींक ऐसी तिरछी पकड़ें कि कभी तो उसका एक टांक और कभी दूसरा भाग की ओर थोड़ा सा अधिक फिरा रहे जिस में चिड़िया के सब भाग आंच के फैलाव में पड़ें । जब पृथ्वी की धुरी का एक ध्रुव सूर्य की ओर फिर जाता है तब पृथ्वी की पृष्ठ के वे सब भाग भी जो उस ध्रुव की अलंग रहते हैं सूर्य के तेज में अधिक पड़ते हैं और तब उन में गरमी की ऋतु होती है । जब दूसरा सामने का ध्रुव सूर्य की ओर बढ़ता है तब उन में जाड़ा आता है । अपनी धुरी पर पृथ्वी के फिरने से दिन को रात और रात को दिन हुआ करता है । उस धुरी का एक टांक सूर्य के पास वा दूर होजाता है तब ऋतु बदलती है । पृथ्वी की पृष्ठ पर प्रत्येक स्थान चौबीस घंटे में पृथ्वी की धुरी की चारों ओर घूम आता है परन्तु धुरी का प्रत्येक ध्रुव केवल बरस के अन्त में दूसरी बार सूर्य के सामने बहुत निकट हो जाता है । जो सूर्य के स्थान से पृथ्वी के स्थान तक एक सीधी रेखा खींची जाय और इस पर जो एक लम्ब पड़े तो इन दोनों के बीच में जितना अन्तर होगा उसकी तिहाई से कुछ न्यून अन्तर पर पृथ्वी की धुरी उस लम्ब से झुकी समझो इसी लिये प्रत्येक ध्रुव बारी बारी से कुछ सूर्य की ओर आता है । जैसी पांचवें चित्र के पहिले चेन में पृथ्वी की धुरी देख पड़ती है वैसी ही आधी ग्रीष्म ऋतु में रहती है उस काल में वह्नलयह के अत्यन्त निकट जो ध्रुव है सो सूर्य की ओर हो जाता है । परन्तु आधे जाड़े में वह धुरी जैसी दूसरे चेन में देख पड़ती है वैसी रहती है इसी निमित्त वही ध्रुव और वह्नलयह भी सूर्य से दूर हो जाता है । और वह जैसी तीसरे चेन में है वैसी मध्यवर्ती ऋतुओं में रहती है इसी कारण तब दोनों ध्रुव सूर्य के उन्मुख रहते हैं तिस पर भी सूर्य की ओर की दिशा से धुरी झुकी रहती है ॥

पृथ्वी के निरक्षदेशों में रात दिन सदा बराबर होते हैं । वहां सूर्य छ बजे भोर को उदय होता है और छट्ठे बजे सांझ को अस्त होता है इस निमित्त वह सदा बारह घंटे दृष्टि के बाहर और बारह ही घंटे दृष्टिगोचर रहता है ॥

ग्रीष्म काल में गरमी दो बातों से होती है पहिली तो यह कि पृथ्वी के जिस भाग में यह ऋतु होती है उस पर सूर्य अधिक सिंथार्ई और तेज से तपता

है और दूसरी यह कि सूर्य एक एक बेर बहुत काल तक निरन्तर तपता है। जाड़े के सूर्य से गरमी का सूर्य एथ्वी की पृष्ठ को बहुत ही अधिक तपाता है और आठ घंटे के स्थान में षोलह घंटे उसे एक एक बेर तपाता है। इस लिये पृथ्वी की पृष्ठ और जो वायु उस पर रहती है सो वर्ष के अन्य कालों की अपेक्षा उस समय अधिक तप जाती है॥

प्रतिदिन सूर्य आकाश में दुपहरी तक चढ़ता है तब उसके पीछे सांझ तक ढलता है फिर अदृश्य हो जाता है। परन्तु दुपहरी में सूर्य का चढ़ाव जाड़े की अपेक्षा गरमी में ऊंचा होता है इस निमित्त सूर्य को प्रतिदिन चढ़ने और ढलने में अधिक काल लगता है और इसी से दिन बड़ा होता है। पृथ्वी की पृष्ठ के जिस भाग पर हम रहते हैं सत्यता में सूर्य की ओर उसके अधिक फिरने के कारण से सूर्य आकाश में चढ़ते देख पड़ता है। जैसे जैसे वह स्थान सूर्य की ओर चला जाता है तैसे तैसे उसके सामने के आकाश का अधोभाग उसके आगे धसता जाता है और सूर्य के नीचे चला जाता ज्ञान पड़ता है। परन्तु आकाश-सम्बन्धी अधोभाग के सूर्य के तले धसने का देखने में वही फल होता है जैसे कि आकाश में सूर्य के ऊपर चढ़ने का। इसलियइस में ज्यों ज्यों गरमी आती है त्यों त्यों सूर्य दुपहरी को आकाश में चढ़ता जाता है जब तक कि ठीक हमारे मस्तक के ऊपर की दो तिहाई मार्ग से थोड़ा अधिक नहीं हो जाता परन्तु इस से ऊंचा कभी नहीं होता। इसलियइस और उस के बहुत निकट का ध्रुव सूर्य की ओर इतना नहीं फिरे रहते कि उस से अधिक सूर्य उठता देख पड़े॥

॥ शकुन्तला ॥

अंक ४

स्थान तपोवन

(दोनों सखी फूल बीनती आयीं)

अनसूया।   हे सखी प्रियम्बदा हमारी सहेली शकुन्तला का गान्धर्व विवाह सुभा और पति भी उसी के समान मिला इससे हमारे मन को सुख हुआ परन्तु फिर भी चिन्ता न मिटी॥

प्रियम्बदा । सखी और क्या चिन्ता रह गयी ॥

अनसूया । आज वह राजर्षि तपस्वियों का यज्ञ पूरा कराकर अपनी राजधानी हस्तिनापुर को बिदा हुआ है वहां रनवास में पहुंचकर जाने यहां की सुध रहेगी या न रहेगी ॥

प्रियम्बदा । इस की कुछ चिन्ता मत करो ऐसे गुनवान मनुष्य कभी निर्लज्ज नहीं होते हैं अब चिन्ता की बात यह है कि न जानें पिता कन्व इस वृत्तान्त को सुनकर क्या कहेंगे ॥

अनसूया । मेरे मन में तो यह भासती है कि वे इस वृत्तान्त से प्रसन्न होंगे ॥

प्रियम्बदा । क्यों ॥

अनसूया । इस लिये कि उनका संकल्प था कि यह कन्या किसी गुनवान को दें सो देव ने वैसा ही योग मिला दिया फिर वे क्यों अप्रसन्न होंगे ॥

प्रियम्बदा । सत्य है (फूलों की टोकरी को देखकर) हे सखी जितने फूल पूजा के लिये चाहियें उतने तो बीन चुकीं ॥

अनसूया । अब थोड़े से शकुन्तला के गौरिपूजा कराने के लिये और बीन लें ॥

प्रियम्बदा । यछा (दोनों फूल बीनने लगीं)

(नेपथ्य में) मैं आता हूं

अनसूया । (कान लगाकर) हे सखी ऐसा बोल जान पड़ता है मानो कोई अतिथि आश्रम में आया है ॥

प्रियम्बदा । क्या दर है शकुन्तला वहां बनी है ॥

अनसूया । शकुन्तला है तो परन्तु उसका मन ठिकाने नहीं है चलो इतने ही फूल बहुत हैं (चलदीं) (नेपथ्य में) हे अतिथि का निरादर करनेवाली मैं तुझे भाप देता हूं कि जा जिस पुरुष के ध्यान में तू ऐसी मग्न बैठी है कि तैंने मुझ तपस्वी को भी आया न जाना वही तेरा निरादर करेगा और फिर तू उस के सन्मुख होकर अपनी सुधि दिलावेगी तो भी वह तुझे ऐसा भूल जायगा जैसा कोई उन्मत्त मनुष्य चैतन्य होकर उन्मत्तता की कही बातों को भूल जाता है ॥

प्रियम्बदा । हाय हाय बुरी पुर्छ किसी तपस्वी का अपराध बेसुधी में शकुन्तला से बना ॥

अनसूया ।   (आगे देखकर) ठीक है तभी रिखिसरे दुर्बासा बेग बेग लौटे जाते हैं ॥

प्रियम्बदा ।   इन को छोड़ और किसी को ऐसी सामर्थ्य नहीं है कि अपराधी को शाप से भस्म करदे है अनसूया तू पैरों पड़कर जैसे बने तैसे इन को मनाना तब तक मैं उन के लिये अर्घ संजाती हूं ॥

अनसूया ।   मैं जाती हूं ॥

प्रियम्बदा ।   (दौड़कर चली इससे पांव रपट गया) हाय उतावली होकर मैंने फूलों की टोकरी गिरायी अब कहीं ऐसा न हो कि पूजा उल्लंघन हो जाय (फूल बीछे लगी)

(अनसूया फिर आयी)

अनसूया ।   हे सखी इनका स्वभाव बहुत टेढ़ा है और क्रोध इतना है कि किसी भांति मनाये नहीं मानते हैं परंतु तौ भी मैंने कुछ सीधे कर लिये ॥

प्रियम्बदा ।   इनका थोड़ा सीधा होना भी बहुत है तुम यह कहो कि कैसे मने ॥

अनसूया ।   जब किसी भांति न माने तब मैंने पैरों में गिरकर यह बिन्ती की कि हे महा पुरुष तुम को इस ने आगे नहीं देखा था इससे तुम्हारे प्रभाव को नहीं जानती थी अब इस कन्या का अपराध छमा करो ॥

प्रियम्बदा ।   तब क्या कहा ॥

अनसूया ।   तब बोले कि मेरा शाप भूठा नहीं होता है परंतु जब इस का पति अपनी मुदरी को देखेगा तब शाप मिट जायगा यह कहकर अन्तरध्यान होगये ॥

प्रियम्बदा ।   तो कुछ आशा है क्योंकि जब वह राजर्षि चलने को सुधा था तब अपनी अंगूठी जिस में उस का नाम खुदा था शकुन्तला की उंगली में पहना दी थी और उस को तुरन्त पहचान भी लेगा यही शकुन्तला के लिये अच्छा उपाय है ॥

अनसूया ।   आओ अब चलें देवियों है प्रार्थना करें ॥

प्रियम्बदा ।   हे अनसूया देख बांये कर पर कपोल धरे पति के वियोग में प्यारी सखी कैसी चिन्ती बन रहीं है दूसरे की तो क्या चलायी इसे अपनी भी सुध नहीं है ॥

अनसूया। हे प्रियम्वदा यह गूढ़ की बात हम से तुम जानें शकुंतला का मत सुनाओ क्योंकि उसका स्वभाव कोमल बहुत है॥

प्रियम्वदा। ऐसा कौन होगा जो मल्लिका की लहलही लता पर तत्ता पानी छिड़के (दोनों गयीं)

(कन्व का एक चेला आया)

चेला। महात्मा कन्व ऋषि प्रभासतीर्थ को चा गये हैं और मुझे आज्ञा दी है कि देख या रात्रि कितनी रहा है तो मैं रात देखने को बाहर आया हूँ (इधर उधर फिरकर आकाश की ओर देखता हुआ) अहा यह तो प्रभात हो गया चन्द्रमा और सूर्य्य इस संसार की सम्पत्ति विपत्ति की अनित्यता का कैसा अनुमान करातें हैं भायधिपति तो इस समय अस्त होनेपर है और यदुपति अरुण को सारथी किये उदय हुआ चाहता है इन की शोभा उदय अस्तपर बढ़ घट होती है ऐसे ही सज्जन मनुष्य सुख दुःख में धीरज रखतें हैं इन की घटतीं बढ़तीं इस संसार के उतार चढ़ाउ का दृष्टान्त है वहीं कमलादिनी जिस की शोभा की बड़ाई होती थी अब चन्द्रास्त में दृष्टि को आनन्द नहीं देती केवल सुगंधि रह गयी है और ऐसी कुम्हला गयी है जैसे अपने प्यारे के वियोग में अबलाजन व्यथित होती हैं देखो बेर के पत्तोंपर ओस की बूंदों का अरुण कैसी शोभा देता है दाभ की फुटी से मोर निद्रा छोड़ छोड़ बाहर निकसतें हैं यज्ञ स्थानों से भाग भाग कर मृग टीले पर खड़े कैसे ऐंड़ातें हैं वही चन्द्रमा जो गिरिराज सुमेरु के सिर पर पांव धरता और अन्धकार को मिटाता हुआ मध्यआकाश में विष्णुधाम तक चढ़ गया था अब अपना तेज गंवाकर नीचे को आता है ऐसे ही इस संसार में बड़े मनुष्य भ्रति यम से अपनी कामना को प्राप्त होतें हैं फिर तुरन्त उतरना पड़ता है॥

(अनसूया कुछ विचारती हुई आयी)

अनसूया। (आप ही आप) यद्यपि शकुन्तला तपोवन में इतनी बड़ी हुई है और इंद्रियों का सुख नहीं जाना है तो भी लगन ने यह दशा उस की कर दी है आय राजा ने किसी अनंति दुखको साथ की है॥

चेला। (आप ही आप) अब होम का समय हुआ गुरु से चल कर कहना चाहिये (बाहर गया)

अनसूया । रैन बीतगयी में अभी सोते से भी नहीं उठी हूं और जो उठी भी होती तो क्या करती हाथ पैर तो कहने ही में नहीं है अब निरदयी कामदेव का मनोरथ पूरा हुआ कि उसने एक मिथ्याबादी राजा के बस में हमारी सीधी सख्री सखी को डाल कर एक दगा को पहुंचाया है और जो यह फल दुर्वासा के श्राप का नहीं है तो क्या हेतु है कि धर्मात्मा राजा ने ऐसे बचन देकर अब तक संदेसा भी न भेजा अब यह उचित है या नहीं कि उस सुन्दरी को हम राजा के पास भेजें अथवा और भी कोई उपाय है जिससे हमारी प्यारी सखी का बिरह मिटे उस का तो कुछ अपराध नहीं है पिता कन्व तीर्थ कर के भागये परन्तु उन से यह बात कहने को कि शकुन्तला का बिवाह राजा दुष्यन्त से हो गया है और गर्भवती भी है मेरा हियाव नहीं पड़ता है हे देव अब क्या उपाय करें जिससे शकुन्तला की बिया दूर हो ॥

(प्रियम्बदा आयी)

प्रियम्बदा । अनसूया चलो शकुन्तला की बिदा का उपचार करें ॥

अनसूया । (आश्चर्य्य से) सखी तू क्या कहती है ॥

प्रियम्बदा । अभी में शकुन्तला से यह बात पूछने गयी थी कि रात को चैन से सोयी या नहीं ॥

अनसूया । सो तब ॥

प्रियम्बदा । सो वह तो सिर झुकाये बैठी थी इतने में पिता कन्व निकट आकर उससे मिले और यह शुभ बचन बोले कि हे पुत्री बड़े मंगल की बात है कि आज प्रातःकाल जब ब्राह्मणा ने अग्निकुंड में आहुति दी तब यद्यपि यज्ञ के धुयें से उस की दृष्टि धुंधुली होरही थी तोभी आहुति अग्नि के बीच में पड़ी इसलिये अब तुम को में अधिक दुःख में न रक्खूंगा आज तुम्हारी बिदा एक घुटी से उस राजा के रनवास को करदूंगा जिस ने तुम्हारा पाणियग्रहा किया है ॥

अनसूया । हे सख्री जो बातें मुनि के पीछे हुई थीं सो उन से किस ने काहदीं ॥

प्रियम्बदा । जब मुनि यज्ञस्थान के निकट पहुंचे तब आकाशवाणी कहगयी ॥

अनसूया । (चकित होकर) तू किसी अचम्मे की बात कहती है ॥

प्रियम्बदा ।   सखी सुन आकाश्ववाणी ने यह कहा कि हे ब्राह्मणी जैसे होम की अग्नि से चमी गर्भवती होती है तैसे ही तेरी बेटी ने पृथ्वी की रचा के निमित्त राजा दुष्यन्त से एक भव्य तेज का लिया है ॥

अनसूया ।   (आनन्द से प्रियम्बदा को भेटकर) हे सखी यह सुनकर मुझे बड़ा सुख हुआ परन्तु सखी के बिछोह का दुःख भी है इसलिये आज हमारा हर्ष शोक समान है ॥

प्रियम्बदा ।   सखी को सुख होगा इससे हम को भी कुछ शोक न करना चाहिये ॥

अनसूया ।   मैंने इसी दिन के लिये उस नारियल में जो वह देखो आम के वृच्च पर लटकता है नागकेसरि भर रक्खी थी तुम उसे उतार कर कमल के पत्ते में रक्खो तब तक मैं थोड़ा सा गोरोचन और मिट्टी और दूब मंगलकार्य्य के लिये लेआऊं ॥

प्रियम्बदा ।   बहुत अच्छा (प्रियम्बदा ने नागकेसरि ली और अनसूया गयी) (नेपथ्य में) हे गौतमी शारंगरव और शारद्वत मित्रों से कहदो कि शकुन्तला के संग जाना होगा ॥

प्रियम्बदा ।   (कानलगाकर) अनसूया विलंब मत करो पिता कन्व हस्तिनापुर के जानेवालों को आज्ञा देते हैं ॥

(अनसूया सामिग्री लिये आयी)

अनसूया ।   मैं आयी चलो (दोनों गयीं)

प्रियम्बदा ।   (देखकर) वह देखो शकुन्तला सूर्य्य उदय का स्नान करके खड़ी है और बहुत सी ऋषियों की स्त्री टोकरियों में तंदुल लिये आशीष देरही हैं चलो हम भी आशीष दे आवें ॥

(शकुन्तला और गौतमी और तपस्वियों की स्त्रियां आयीं)

१ तपस्विनी ।   हे राजवधू तू पति की प्यारी हो ॥

२ तपस्विनी ।   तू सूरवीर पुत्र की माता हो (आशीर्वाद देकर तपस्विनी गयीं)

दो सखी ।   (शकुन्तला के निकट आकर) कहो सखी स्नान अच्छे हुय ॥

शकुंतला ।   (आदर से) सखियो भली आईं यहां बैठो कुछ बातें करें (दोनों बैठगयीं)

अनसूया। तुम नेक ठैरो तौ में कुछ मंगलनेग करदूं॥

शकुंतला। तुम करोगी सो अच्छा ही करोगी परन्तु फिर तुम से मिलने का अवसर कठिन हो जायगा॥

(यह कहकर आंसू डाल दिये)

दो० सखी। सखी ऐसे मंगल समय जब कि तू सुख भोगने आती है रोना उचित नहीं है (यह कहकर दोनों ने आंसू डालदिये और वस्त्र पहराने लगीं)

प्रियम्वदा। सखी तेरे इस सुंदर अंग को तौ अच्छे वस्त्र आभरण चाहियें थे परन्तु अब ये ही साधारण फूल पत्ते आश्रम में मिल सके हम पहराती हैं॥

(कन्व का चेला अच्छे अच्छे वस्त्र आभूषण लेकर आया)

चेला। रानी को ये वस्त्र आभूषण पहराओ (देखकर सब सखी चकित होगयीं)

गौतमी। हे पुत्र हारीत ये वस्त्र आभूषण कहां से आये॥

चेला। पिता कन्व के तपप्रभाव से॥

गौतमी। क्या यह मन में बिचारते ही प्राप्त हो गये॥

चेला। नहीं महात्मा काश्यप की आज्ञा हुई कि शकुन्तला के निमित्त वृक्षों से फूल ले आओ आयुस होते ही तुरन्त किसी बनदेवी ने कोमल हाथ उठा कर चन्द्रमा के तुल्य श्वेत साड़ी दी किसी ने महावर के लिये लाह्यारस दिया कोई भूषण बनाने लगी॥

प्रियम्वदा। कमल के मकरन्द को मधुक की मक्खी भी सिर झुकाती है॥

गौतमी। (शकुन्तला को देखकर) बनदेवियों से वस्त्राभरण मिलना यह शगुन तुझे सासरे में राजलक्ष्मी का दाता होगा॥

(शकुन्तला लजागयी)

चेला। गुरुजी मालिनी के स्नानों को गये हैं वहीं आकर यह वृतान्त बनदेवियों के सत्कार का उन से कहूंगा (गया)

अनसूया। (आभूषण पहराती हुई) हे सखी हम बनवासिनियों ने ऐसे भूषण आगे कभी न देखे थे इसचे हम ज्यौंके त्यौं पहराना नहीं जानती हैं परन्तु मैं अपनी चित्र बिद्या के बल से शृंगार कराती हूं॥

शकुन्तला। (मुस्कुराकर) हां तेरी चतुराई को मैं जानती हूं॥

(कन्व कुछ बिचार करते हुए आये)

कन्व ।   (आप ही आप) आज शकुन्तला जायगी इसछे उत्कंठा करके मेरा हृदय स्नेह के बस आंसुओं से भरा आता है जब मुझ बनवासी की यह दशा है तो गृहस्थियों की क्या गति बेटी बिदा होने के समय होती होगी (इधर उधर मन बहलाने के लिये टहलने लगे)

प्रियम्बदा ।   सखी शकुन्तला अब तुम्हारा यथोचित शिंगार हुआ इस साड़ी को जो बनदेवियों ने दी है पहरो ॥

(शकुन्तला ने उठ कर साड़ी पहरी)

गौतमी ।   हे पुत्री पिता कन्व मिलने को आये हैं ॥

शकुंतला ।   (उठ कर लज्जा से) पिता में नमस्कार करती हूं ॥

कन्व ।   पुत्री जैसी प्यारी राजा ययाति को शर्मिष्ठा हुई तैसी तू अपने पति को होगी और जैसा चक्रवर्त्ती पुत्र पुरु शर्मिष्ठा के हुआ तैसा ही तेरे होगा ॥

गौतमी ।   ऋषि के बचन सत्य होंगे ॥

कन्व ।   आओ बेटी हुताशन की प्रदक्षिणा करलो (सबने प्रदक्षिणा की) यही अग्नि जो बेदी में प्रज्वलित होकर नैवेद्य को लेती है परन्तु मंत्र पढ़ी दाभ को यद्यपि आस पास बिछी है परन्तु बाधा नहीं पहुंचाती यही अग्नि जो हव्य के गंध से पापों को नाश करती है तेरी रक्षा करेगी (शकुन्तला ने प्रदक्षिणा दी) अब पुत्री तू शुभ घड़ी में बिदा हो (चारों ओर देखकर) संग आनेवाले शिष्य कहां हैं ॥

(सारंगरव और शार्ङ्गत आये)

दो भाई ।   मुनि जी हम ये हैं ॥

कन्व ।   पुत्र सारंगरव अपनी बहन को गैल बताओ ॥

सारथी ।   आओ भगवती इधर आओ (सब चले)

कन्व ।   हे तपोबन के वृक्षों जिस शकुन्तला ने तुम्हारे बिना सींचे कभी जल भी नहीं पिया और जिसे यद्यपि पुष्पपत्र के गहने बनाने का चाउ था परंतु प्यार के मारे तुम्हारे फूल पत्ते कभी न तोड़े और बड़ा आनन्द सदा तुम्हारे मौरने के समय माना इसको तुम पति के घर जाने की आज्ञा दो (कोयल बोली) यह देखो बनदेवियों ने आज्ञा दी (भाग्यवायी शकुन्तला को

यह याचा मंगलकारी हो और उस के सुख के निमित्त मार्ग में पवन फूलों
का पराग बरसावे कमलसंयुक्त निर्मल जल के ताल उस को पर्यटन में सुख
दें और वृक्षों की सघन छाया सूर्य्य के तेज से रक्षा करे ॥

सारधी ।   यह आशीर्वाद किस ने दिया कोकिला ने या तपस्वियों की उछवाविनी
बनदेवियों ने ॥

गौतमी ।   हे पुत्री तपस्वियों की हितकारी बनदेवी तुझे आशीर्वाद देती हैं
तू भी इन को प्रणाम कर (शकुन्तला ने फिरकर नमस्कार किया) ॥

शकुन्तला ।   (प्रियम्वदा से धीले धीले) हे प्रियम्वदा आर्यपुत्र से फिर भेट
होने का तो मुझे बड़ा उत्साह है परंतु इस बन को जिसमें इतनी बड़ी
हुई हूं छोड़ते आगे को पांउ नहीं पड़ते हैं ॥

प्रियम्वदा ।   अकेली तुझी को शोक नहीं है ज्यों ज्यों तेरे बिदाहोने का
समय निकट आता है तेरे बिरह से बन में बिथा सी छायी जाती है देख
हरिणियों ने घासचरना छोड़दिया है मोर नाचना भूल गये हैं वृक्षों के पत्ते
तेरे बिछोह की भांति से पीले हो हो कर ऐसे गिरते हैं मानों आंसू टपके ॥

शकुन्तला ।   पिता आज्ञा दो तो इस माधवीलता से भेट लूं क्योंकि इससे
मेरा बहिन का सा नेह है ॥

कन्व ।   बेटी मिलले में भी तुम्हारे नेह को जानता हूं ॥

शकुन्तला ।   (लता से भेटकर) हे बनज्योत्सनी यद्यपि तू आम का आश्रय
ले रही है तो भी भुजा पसार के मुझ से मिलले अब मैं तुझ से दूर जा
पड़ूंगी परंतु मन तुझी में रहेगा पिता इस लता को मेरी ही समान गिनियो ॥

कन्व ।   बेटी मेरे मन में बड़ी चिन्ता रहती थी कि तुझे अच्छा पति मिले
सो अपने सुकृतों से तिने योग्य बर पाया अब मैं तेरी प्यारी लता का भी
बिवाह इस आम से जो उस के निकट मोर रहा है करदूंगा तू विलंब मत
करे बिदा हो ॥

शकुन्तला ।   (दोनों सखियों के पास जाकर) हे सखियो प्यारी माधवी को
मैं तुम्हें सौंपती हूं ॥

दो सखी ।   सखी हमें किसपो सौंपे जाती है ॥

(दोनों ने आंसू डालदिये)

कन्व। अनसूया इस समय रोना न चाहिये शकुन्तला को धीरज बंधाओ॥

(सब आगे को चलें)

शकुन्तला। हे पिता अब यह हरिणी जो गर्भ के बोझ से चलने में अलसाती है और आश्रम के निकट चरती है अने तब इस की कुशल कहला भेजना भूल मत जाना॥

कन्व। न भूलूंगा॥

शकुन्तला। (कुछ चल कर और फिरकर) यह कौन है जो मेरे अंचल को नहीं छोड़ता है॥

(फिर पीछे फिरकर देखा)

कन्व। यह वही मगछौना है जिसको तूने पुत्र सम पाला है यह वही है जिसका मुंह जब कभी दाभ से चिरजाता था तू इंगोट का तेल लगाती थी और जिस को तूने समा के चांवल खिला खिला कर इतना बड़ा किया है अब यह अपनी पालनेवाली के चरण क्योंकर छोड़े॥

शकुन्तला। अरे छौना तू मेरे लिये क्यों रोता है तेरी मा तो तुझे जन्ते ही छोड़ मरी थी मैंने पाल कर तुझे इतना बड़ा किया है तेछे ही मेरे पीछे पिता कन्व तेरा पालन करेंगे अब तू लौट जा (आंसू डालती चली)

कन्व। बेटी यह समय रोने का नहीं है हम सब फिर मिलेंगे आंसूओं से तेरी दृष्टि रुक रही है इससे ऐसा न हो कि ऊंचे नीचे में पाउं पड़े अब तू अपने धीरज से आंसूओं को रोक॥

सारथी। हे महात्मा सुनते हैं कि प्यारे मनुष्यों को पहुंचाने वहीं तक जाना चाहिये जहां तक जलाशय न मिले अब यह सरोवर का तट आगया आप हमको आज्ञा देकर आश्रम को सिधारो॥

कन्व। तो आओ छिनमात्र इस बट को छाया में ठेरलें (सब छाया में गये) राजा दुष्यन्त को क्या संदेशा भेजना योग्य है (बिचार करने लगा)

अनसूया। (शकुन्तला से धीले धीले) हे सखी आज इस आश्रम में सब का चित्त तुझी में लगा है और छब तेरे बिछोह में उदास हैं देख चकई कमल के पत्तों में बैठी बहुतेरा बोलती है परन्तु चकवा उत्तर नहीं देता चोंच से चुगा छोड़ तेरी ही और निहार रहा है॥

कन्व ।   पुत्र सारंगरव जब तू राजा के सन्मुख पहुंचे तब शकुन्तला को आगे करके मेरी ओर से यह कहियो कि हम तपस्वियों को केवल तप के धनी जानो और अपने ष्रेष्ठ कुल को बिचार कर इस लड़की पर भी सब रानियों की भांति वही स्नेह रक्खो जो तुम्हारे हृदय में आप से आप इस को और उत्पन्न हुआ है इससे अधिक हम क्या मांगे और विशेष प्यार तो भाग्य के आधीन है ॥

सारथी ।   आप का संदेशा मैंने भली भांति गांठ बांध लिया ॥

कन्व ।   (शकुन्तला की ओर बड़े नेहसे) हे पुत्री अब तुझे भी कुछ सीख दूंगा क्योंकि यद्यपि हम बनवासी हैं तो भी लोक के व्यवहारों को भली भांति जानते हैं ॥

सारथी ।   विद्वान पुरुषों से क्या छुपा है ॥

कन्व ।   बेटी सुन जब तू रनवास में बास पावे तब पति का आदर और गुरुजनों की सुश्रूषा करियो सोतों में सपत्नी भाव से मत रहियो सहेली की भांति टहल करियो कदाचित पति तिरस्कार भी करे तो भी उसकी आज्ञा से बाहर मत बूजियो नौकर चाकरों को एकसा समभियो और अपस्वार्थी मत बूजियो जो कुलवधू इस धर्म में चलती हैं वे अच्छी गृहस्थिनी कहलाती हैं और जो इससे विमुख होती हैं सो कुल कलंकिनी होती हैं जब पति सन्मुख आवे तो उठकर आदर कीजो और जो कुछ वचन वह कहे सो नम्रता से सुनलीजो उस के चरणों में दृष्टि रखियो और बैठने को आसन दीजो पति की सेवा आप कीजो उससे पीछे सोइयो और पहले जागियो यह सब कुलवधुओं के मुख्य धर्म बड़ों ने कहे हैं कहो गौतमी यह शिक्षा कैसी है ॥

गौतमी ।   कुलवधुओं के लिये यह उपदेश बहुत श्रेष्ठ है पुत्री इस को भूल मत जाना ॥

कन्व ।   बेटी आ मुझ से और अपनी सखियों से एक बेर फिर मिलने ॥

शकुंतला ।   क्या प्रियम्बदा और अनसूया यहीं से आश्रम को लौट जायंगी ॥

कन्व ।   बेटी इन को लौट जाने की आज्ञा दे क्योंकि अभी जब तक क्वारी हैं इन को नगर में जाना योग्य नहीं है गौतमी तेरे संग जायगी ॥

शकुंतला। (कण्व घे भेटकर) हाय में पिता की गोद से न्यारी होकर मलयगिरि घे उखाड़े चंदन के पौधे की भांति विठुनी भूमि में कैसे जीऊंगी॥

कन्व। पुत्री ऐसी विकल मत हो जब तू घरकी धनी होगी और राजा पति मिलेगा तब वैभव के कामों में यद्यपि कभी कभी व्याकुल हो जायगो परन्तु इस दुःख का कुछ बहुत स्मरण न रहेगा और फिर जब तेरे तेजस्वी पुत्र का जन्म होगा तब इस विछोह को संपूर्ण भूल जायगी (शकुन्तला छवि के पैरों में गिर पड़ी) मेरे आशीर्वाद से तेरी मनोकामना पूरी होगी॥

शकुंतला। (दोनों सखियों के पास आकर) भाभी सखियो दोनों एकहरी संग भुजा पसार के भेटलो॥

अनसूया। (दोनों मिलीं) ही सखी कदाचित राजा तुरन्त तुझको न पहचान ले तो यह मुन्दरी जिसपर उस का नाम खुदा है दिखादीबो॥

शकुंतला। (घबराकर) सखी तेरे इस बचन ने तो मेरा हृदय कंपादिया॥

प्रियम्बदा। प्यारी डरमत नेह में झूठी शंका बहुधा उठती हैं॥

सारथी। अब दिन बहुत चढ़गया है चलो बिदा हो॥

शकुंतला। (फिर आश्रम की ओर देखकर) हे पिता इस आश्रम को कब फिर देखूंगी॥

कन्व। बेटी जब कुछ काल पति के साथ तुझे बीत लेगा और तेरे महाबली पुत्र हो लेगा तब उस पुत्र को राज्य सौंपकर अपने पति सहित इस आश्रम में तू फिर आवेगी॥

गौतमी। चलने का समय बीताजाता है अब पिता को लौट जाने दे मुनीखी आप जाओ॥

कन्व। हे बेटी मेरे नित्यकर्म में बिघ्न मत डाले (स्वास लेकर) मेरा शोक न घटेगा क्योंकि तेरे सुकुमार हाथों के बोये धान कुटी के सामने नित्य दृष्टि के सोंही रहेंगे अब सिधारो मार्ग मंगलकारि हो (गौतमी और दोनों मिषो सहित शकुंतला गयी)

दो सखी। (बियोग से शकुंतला की ओर देखकर) अब तो सखी दृष्टों की ओट हुयी॥

कन्व । (स्वास लेकर) बेटियो अब तुम्हारी छुट्टी गयी तुम इस शोच को त्याग कर हमारे साथ आओ ॥

दो सखी । पिता शकुंतला बिना तपोबन सूना लगता है ॥

(सब लौटे)

कन्व । सत्य है तुम को ऐसाही दिखायी देता होगा (बिचार करते हुय चले) शकुंतला को बिदा करके आज मैं सुचित्त हुआ बेटी किसी दिन पराये ही घर का धन होती है आज मेरा चित्त ऐसा प्रसन हुआ है मानो किसी की धरोहर देदी ॥

॥ रामायन बा० ॥

दो० । शतानंदपद बंदि प्रभु बैठे गुर पद्ध आइ ।

चलहु तात मुनि कह्देउ तब पठवा जनक बुलाइ ॥

चौ० । सीयस्वयंवर देखिय आई । इस काज धौं देखि बड़ाई ॥

लपन कहा असभाजन सोई । नाथ कृपा तव जापर होई ॥

हरषे मुनि सब मुनिबरबानी । दीन्ह अशीस सबहिं सुख मानी ॥

पुनि मुनिबृन्द समेत कृपाला । देखन चले धनुषमखसाला ॥

रंगभूमि आये दुौ भाई । अस सुधि सब पुरवासिन पाई ॥

चले सकल गृहकाज बिसारी । बालक युवा जरठ नर नारी ॥

देखी अनक भीरि भइ भारी । सुचि सेवक सब लिये हंकारी ॥

तुरत सकल लोगन पह जासू । आसन उचित देहु सब काहू ॥

दो० । कहि म्दु बचन बिनीत तिन बैठारे नर नारि ।

उत्तम मध्यम नीच लघु निज निज थल अनुहारि ॥

चौ० । राजकुंवर तेहि अवसर आये । मनहु मनोहरता छबि छाये ॥

गुनसागर नागर बर बीरा । सुंदर स्यामल गौर सरीरा ॥

राजसमाज बिराजत रहे । उड़ुगन मह अनु युग विधु पूरे ॥

जिन के रही भावना जैसी । प्रभुमूरति देखी तिन तैसी ॥

देखहिं भूप महा रनधीरा । मनहु बीररस धरे सरीरा ॥

डरे कुटिल नृप प्रभुहिं निहारी । मनहुँ भयानक मूरति भारी ॥
रहे असुर छल ओ नृपवेषा । तिन प्रभु प्रगट काल सम देखा ॥
पुरबासिन देखे दोौ भाई । नरभूषन लोचनसुखदाई ॥

दो०। नारि बिलोकहिं हरषि हिय निज निज रुचि अनुरूप ।
जनु सोहत सिंगारधरि मूरति परम अनूप ॥

चौ०। बिदुषन प्रभु विराटमय दीसा । बहु मुख कर पग लोचन सीसा ॥
जनकजाति अवलोकहिं कैसे । सज्जन सगे प्रिय लागहिं जैसे ॥
सहित विदेह विलोकहिं रानी । सिसु सम प्रीति न जाति बखानी ॥
योगिन परम तत्त्वमय भासा । सांत सुद्ध मन सहज प्रकासा ॥
हरि भक्तन देखेउ दोौ भ्राता । इष्टदेव इव सब सुखदाता ॥
रामहिं चितव भाव जेहि सीया । सो सनेह सुख नहिं बचनीया ॥
उर अनुभवति न कहि सक सोऊ । कवन प्रकार कहै कवि कोऊ ॥
एहि विधि रहा आसि जस भाऊ । तेहं तस देखेउ कोसलराऊ ॥

दो०। राजत राजसमाज महँ कोसलराजकिसोर ।
सुंदर स्यामल गौर तनु बिस्वबिलोचनचोर ॥

चौ०। सहज मनोहर मूरति दोऊ । कोटि काम उपमा लघु सोऊ ॥
सरदचंदनिंदक मुख नीके । नीरजनयन भावते जी के ॥
चितवनि चारु मारमदहरनी । भावति हृदय जाय नहिं बरनी ॥
कल कपोल श्रुति कुंडल लोला । चिबुक अधर सुंदर मृदु बोला ॥
कुमुदबंधु कर निंदक हाँसा । भृकुटी बिकट मनोहर नासा ॥
भाल बिसाल तिलक झलकाहीं । कच बिलोकि अलिअवलि लजाहीं ॥
पीत झीतनी छिरन सुहाई । कुसुमकली बिच बीच बनाई ॥
रेखा रुचिर कंबु कल ग्रीवां । जनु त्रिभुवनसुखमा की सीवां ॥

दो०। कुंजरमनिकंठाकलित उर तुलसी की माल ।
वृषभकंध केहरि ठवनि बलनिधि बाहु बिसाल ॥

चौ०। कटि तूनीर पीत पट बांधे । कर सर धनुष बाम बर कांधे ॥
पीत यज्ञ उपबीत सुहाई । नखसिख मंजु महा छबि छाई ॥

देखि लोग सब भये सुखारे । एकटक लोचन टरहिं न टारे ॥

हरषे जनक देखि द्वौ भाई । मुनिपदकमल गहे तब जाई ॥

करि बिनती निज कथा सुनाई । रंगभवनि सब मुनिहि दिखाई ॥

अर्घ अर्घ आसनि कुंवर बर दोऊ । तहँ तहँ चकित चितव सब कोऊ ॥

निज निज रुचि रामहिं सब देखा । कोउ न जान कछु मर्म बिसेषा ॥

भलि रचना नृप सन मुनि कहेऊ । राजा मुदित महा सुख लहेऊ ॥

दो॰ । सब मंचन तें मंच एक सुंदर बिसद बिसाल ।
मुनि समेत द्वौ बंधु तहँ बैठारे महिपाल ॥

चौ॰ । प्रभुहि देखि सब नृप हिय हारे । जनु राकेसउदय भये तारे ॥

हरषि प्रतीति तिन्ह के मन माहीं । राम चाप तोरब सक नाहीं ॥

बिनु भंजेउ भवधनुप बिसाला । मेलिहि सीय रामउर माला ॥

अस बिचारि गवनहु घर भाई । जय प्रताप बल तेज गंवाई ॥

बिहसे अपर भूप सुनि बानी । जे अबिबेक अंध अभिमानी ॥

तोरेहु धनुप ब्याह अवगाहा । बिनु तोरे को कुंवरि बिवाहा ॥

एक बार कालहु किन दोरई । सिय नित समर जितब हम सोरई ॥

यह सुनि अपर भूप मुसुकाने । धर्मसील हरिभक्त सयाने ॥

दो॰ । सीय बियाहब राम गर्व दूर करि नृपन कर ।
जीति को सक संग्राम दसरथ के रनबांकुरे ॥

चौ॰ । बुधा मरहु जानि गाल बजाई । मनमोदक नहिं भूख बुताई ॥

सिख हमारि सुनु परम पुनीता । जगदंबा जानहु जिय सीता ॥

जगतपिता रघुपतिहिं बिचारी । भरि लोचन छबि लेहु निहारी ॥

सुंदर सुखद सकल गुनराशी । ये द्वौ बंधु संभु उर बासी ॥

सुधा समुद्र समीप बिहाई । मगजल निरखि मरहु कत धाई ॥

करहु जाइ जा कहँ जोइ भावा । हम तौ आजु जन्मफल पावा ॥

अस कहि भले भूप अनुरागे । रूप अनूप बिलोकन लागे ॥

देखहिं सुर नभ चढ़े बिमाना । बरषहिं सुमन करहिं कल गाना ॥

दो॰ । जानि सुभ्रध्रुर सीय तब पठवा जनक बुलाइ ।
चतुर देखि सुंदरि सकल सादर चलीं लवाइ ॥

चौ॰। सियसोभा नहिं आइ बखानी । जगदंबिका रूपगुनखानी ॥
उपमा सकल मोहि लघु लागी । प्राकृत नारि अंगअनुरागी ॥
सीय बरनि तेहि उपमा देई । को कवि कहै अजस को लेई ॥
जौं पटतरिय तीय सम सीया । जग अस युवति कहां कमनीया ॥
गिरा मुखर तनु अर्द्ध भवानी । रति अति दुखित अतनु पति जानी ॥
बिष बारुनी बंधु प्रिय जेही । कहिय रमा सम किमि बैदेही ॥
जौं छबि सुधा पयोनिधि होई । परम रूपमय कच्छप सोई ॥
सोभा रजु मंदर संगारू । मथै पानिपंकज निज माझू ॥

दो॰। जदपि बिधि उपजी लछि जब सुंदरता सुखमूल ।
तदपि सकोच समेत कवि कहहिं सीय सम तूल ॥

चौ॰। चलीं संग लै सखीं सयानी । गावत गीत मनोहर बानी ॥
सोह नवल तनु सुंदर सारी । जगतजननि अतुलित छबि भारी ॥
भूषन सकल सुदेस सुहाये । अंग अंग रचि सखिन्ह बनाये ॥
रंगभूमि अब सिय पगु धारी । देखि रूप मोहे नर नारी ॥
हरषि सुरन्ह दुंदुभीं बजाईं । बरषि प्रसून अप्सरा गाईं ॥
पानिसरोज सोह जयमाला । अवलोक चिते सकल महिपाला ॥
सीय चकित चित रामहि चाहा । भये मोहबस सब नरनाहा ॥
मुनि समीप बैठे दोउ भाई । लगे ललकि लोचन निधि पाई ॥

दो॰। गुरुजनलाज समाज बड़ि देखि सिय सकुचानि ।
लगी बिलोकन सखिन्ह तन रघुबीरहि उर आनि ॥

चौ॰। रामरूप अरु सियछबि देखी । नर नारिन परिहरी निमेषी ॥
सोचहिं सकल कहत सकुचाहीं । बिधि सन बिनय करहिं मन माहीं ॥
हरु बिधि बेगि जनक जड़ताई । मति हमारि अस देहु सुहाई ॥
बिनु बिचार पन तजि नरनाहू । सीय राम कर करैं बिवाहू ॥
जग भल कहहिं भाव सब काहू । हठ कीन्हें अंतहु उर दाहू ॥
यह लालसा मगन सब लोगू । बर सांवरो जानकी जोगू ॥
तब बंदी जन जगब बुलाये । बिरुदावलि कहत चलि आये ॥
कह नृप आइ कहहु प्रन मोरा । चले भाट सिय हरष न थोरा ॥

दो० । बोले बंदी बचन बर सुनहु सकल महिपाल ।
पन बिदेह कर कहहिं हम भुजा उठाइ बिसाल ॥

चौ० । नृप भुजबल बिधु सिवधनु राजू । गरुअ कठोर बिदित सब काजू ॥
रावन बान महा भट भारे । देखि सरासन गवँहिं सिधारे ॥
सोइ पुरारि कोदंड कठोरा । राजसमाज आजु जेइं तोरा ॥
त्रिभुवनजय समेत बैदेही । बिनहिं बिचार बरै हठि तेही ॥
सुनि पन सकल भूप अभिलाषे । भट मानी अतिसय मन माखे ॥
परिकर बांधि उठे अकुलाई । चले इष्टदेवन सिर नाई ॥
तमकि ताकि तकि सिवधनु धरहीं । उठइ न कोटि भांति बल करहीं ॥
जिन के कछु बिचार मन माहीं । चाप समीप महीप न जाहीं ॥

दो० । तमकि धरहिं धनु मूढ़ नृप उठइ न चलइँ लजाइ ।
मनहुँ पाइ भट बाहु बल अधिक अधिक गरुआइ ॥

चौ० । भूप सहस दस एकहि बारा । लगे उठावन टरइ न टारा ॥
डगइ न संभु सरासन कैसें । कामी बचन सती मन जैसें ॥
सब नृप भये जोग उपहांसी । जैसें बिनु बिराग सन्यासी ॥
कीरति बिजय बीरता भारी । चले चापकर बरबस हारी ॥
बीछत भये हारि हिय राजा । बैठे निज निज आसन समाजा ॥
नृपन बिलोकि जनक अकुलाने । बोले बचन रोष जनु साने ॥
दीप दीप के भूपति नाना । आये सुनि हम जो पन ठाना ॥
देव दनुज धरि मनुज सरीरा । बिपुल बीर आये रनधीरा ॥

दो० । कुंअरि मनोहरि बिजय बड़ि कीरति अति कमनीय ।
पावनहार बिरंचि जनु रचेउ न धनुवमनीय ॥

चौ० । कहहु काहि यह लाभ न भावा । काहु न संकरचाप चढावा ॥
रहेउ चढाउब तोरब भारै । तिल भरि भूमि न सकेहु छुड़ाई ॥
जाब जानि कोउ मारै भट मानी । बीर बिहीन मही मैं जानी ॥
तजहु आस निज निज यह आजू । लिखा न बिधि बैदेहि बिवाजू ॥
सुकृत जाइ जौं पन परिहरऊं । कुंअरि कुंवारि रहेउ का करऊं ॥

जौं जनितें बिनु भट भुंइ भारें । तौ धन करि होत्थें न हंछारें ॥
जनकबचन सुनि सब नर नारी । देखि जानकिहिं भये दुखारी ॥
सांवे नयन कुटिल भई भौंहैं । रदपट फरकत नयन रिसांहैं ॥

दो० । कहि न सकत रघुबीरडर सगे बचन जनु बान ।
नाथ रामपदकमल सिर बोले गिरा प्रमान ॥

चौ० । रघुबंसिन महं जहं कोउ होई । तेहि समाज अस कहइ न कोई ॥
कही जनक अति अनुचित बानी । बिद्यमान रघुकुलमनि जानी ॥
सुनहु भानुकुलपंकजभानू । कहौं सुभाव न कछु अभिमानू ॥
जौं राउर अनुसासन पावौं । कंदुक इव ब्रह्मांड उठावौं ॥
काचे घट जिमि डारौं फोरी । सकौं मेरु मूलक इव तोरी ॥
तव प्रतापमहिमा भगवाना । को बापुरो पिनाक पुराना ॥
नाथ जानि अस आयसु होऊ । कौतुक करौं बिलोकिय सोऊ ॥
कमलनाल जिमि चांप चढ़ावौं । सत जोजन प्रमान लँ धावौं ॥

दो० । तोरौं छत्रकदंड जिमि तव प्रतापबल नाथ ।
जौं न करौं प्रभुपदसपथ पुनि न धरौं धनु हाथ ॥

चौ० । लखन सकोप बचन जब बोले । डगमगानि महि दिग्गज डोले ॥
सकल लोक सब भूप डेराने । सियहिय हरष जनक सकुचाने ॥
गुर रघुपति सब मुनि मन माहीं । मुदित भये पुनि पुनि पुलकाहीं ॥
सैनहि रघुपति लखन निवारे । प्रेम समेत निकट बैठारे ॥
बिस्वामित्र समय सुभ जानी । बोले अति सनेह मृदु बानी ॥
उठहु राम भंजहु भवचापू । मेटहु तात जनक परितापू ॥
सुनि गुरुबचन चरन सिर नावा । हरष बिषाद न कछु उर आवा ॥
ठाढ़ भये उठि सहज सुभाये । ठवनि जुवा मगराज लजाये ॥

दो० । उदित उदयगिरिमंच पर रघुबर बालपतंग ।
बिकसे संत सरोजबन हरषे लोचन भृंग ॥

चौ० । नृपन केरि आसा निसि नासी । बचन नखत अवली न प्रकासी ॥
मानी महिप कुमुद सकुचाने । कपटी भूप उलूक लुकाने ॥

भये बिलोकि कोक्ष मुनि देवा । बरषहिं सुमन जनावहिं सेवा ॥
गुरुपद बंदि सहित अनुरागा । राम मुनिन सन आयसु मांगा ॥
सहद्रर्षि चले सकल जगस्वामी । मत्त मंजु कुंजर बर गामी ॥
चलत राम छब पुरनरनारी । पुलक पूरितनु भये सुखारी ॥
बंदि पितर सुर सुकृत संभारे । जो कछु पुन्यप्रभाव हमारे ॥
तो शिवधनुप मनाल कि नार्है । तोरहिं राम गनेस गुसार्है ॥

दो० ।   रामहिं प्रेम समेत लखि सखिन समीप बुलाइ ।
        सीता मातु सनेहबस बचन कहे बिलखाइ ॥

सो० । सखि सब कौतुक देखनहारे । जोउ कहावत हितू हमारे ॥
कोउ न बुझाइ कहइ नृप पाहीं । ये बालक अति हठ भल नाहीं ॥
रावन बान छुआ नहिं चापा । हारे सकल भूप करि दापा ॥
सो धनु राजकुंवरकर देखौं । बाल मराल कि मंदर लेखौं ॥
भूप सयानप सकल सिरानी । सखि बिधिगति कछु जाति न जानी ॥
बोली चतुर सखी मृदु बानी । तेजवन्त लघु गनिय न रानी ॥
कहं कुंभज कहं सिंधु अपारा । सोखेउ सुजस सकल संसारा ॥
रविमंडल देखत लघु लागा । उदय तासु त्रिभुवनतम भागा ॥

दो० ।   मंत्र परम लघु जासु बस बिधि हरि हर सुर सर्ब ।
        महा मत्त गजराज कहं बस कर अंकुस खर्ब ॥

सो० । काम कुसुम धनुसायक लीन्हे । सकल भुवन अपने बस कीन्हे ॥
देवि तजिय संसय भ्रम ज्ञानी । भंजब धनुष राम सुनु रानी ॥
सखीबचन सुनि भइ परतीती । मिटा विषाद बढ़ी अति प्रीती ॥
तब रामहिं बिलोकि बिदेही । सभय हृदय बिनवति जेहि तेही ॥
मनहीं मन मनाव अकुलानी । होउ प्रसन्न महेस भवानी ॥
करहु सुफल आपनि सेवकाई । करि हित हरहु चापगरुआई ॥
मननायक अरु दायक देवा । आजु लगे कीन्ही तव सेवा ॥
बार बार बिनती सुनि मोरी । करहु चापगुरुता अति थोरी ॥

दो० ।   देखि देखि रघुबीर तन सुर मनाव धरि धीर ।
        भरे बिलोचन प्रेमजल पुलकावली सरीर ॥

दो0। नीके निरखि नयन भरि सोभा । पितुपन सुमिरि बहुरि मन छोभा ॥

अहह तात दारुन हठ ठानी । समुझत नहिं कछु लाभ न हानी ॥

सचिव सभय सिख देइ न कोई । बुध समाज बड़ अनुचित होई ॥

कहँ धनु कुलिसहु चाहि कठोरा । कहँ स्यामल मृदु गात किसोरा ॥

बिधि केहि भांति धरौं उर धीरा । सिरिसुसुमन क्रिमि बेधिधि दोरा ॥

सकल सभा को मति भइ भोरी । अब मोहि संभुचाप गति तोरे ॥

निज जड़ता लोगन पर डारी । होउ दरब रघुपतिहि निहारी ॥

अति परिताप सीय मन माहीं । लव निमेष युग सम चलि जाहीं ॥

दो0।   प्रभुहि चितइ पुनि चितव महि राजत लोचन लोल ।

खेलत मनसिज मीन जुग जनु बिधुमंडल डोल ॥

सो0। गिरा अलिनि मुख पंकज रोकी । प्रगट न लाज निसा अवलोकी ॥

लोचनजल रघु लोचन कोना । जैसें परम कृपन कर सोना ॥

सकुची व्याकुलता बढ़ि जानी । धरि धीरजु प्रतीति उर आनी ॥

तन मन बचन मोर मन सांचा । रघुपतिपदसरोज मन रांचा ॥

तौ भगवान सकल उरबासी । करिहहिं मुहि रघुपति की दासी ॥

जेहि के जेहि पर सत्य सनेहू । सो तेहि मिलत न कछु संदेहू ॥

प्रभुतन चितइ प्रेमतन ठानी । कृपानिधान राम सब जानी ॥

सियहि बिलोकि तकेउ धनु कैसें । चितव गरुड़ लघु व्यालहि जैसें ॥

दो0।   सयन लखेउ रघुबंसमनि ताकेउ हरकोदंड ।

पुलकि गात बोलें बचन चरन चापि ब्रह्मगंड ॥

दो0। दिसकुंजरतु कमठ अहि कोला । धरहु धरनि धरि धीर न डोला ॥

राम चहहिं संकरधनु तोरा । होहु सजग सुनि आयसु मोरा ॥

चाप समीप राम जब आये । नर नारिन सुर सुकृत मनाये ॥

सब कर संसय अरु अग्यानू । मंद महीपन कर अभिमानू ॥

भृगुपति केरि गरब गरुआई । सुरमुनिबरन केरि कदराई ॥

सिय कर सोच जनकपछितावा । रानिन कर दारुन दुखदावा ॥

संभुचाप बड़ बोझिल पाई । चढ़े आइ सब संग बनाई ॥

रामबाहुबल सिंधु अपारा । चहत पार मगहिं कोउ कनधारा ॥

दो० । राम विलोके लोग सब चित्र लिखे छे देवि ।
चितवै सीय कृपायतन जानी बिकल बिसेषि ॥

चौ० । देखी बिपुल बिकल वैदेही । निमिषि बिहात कल्प सम तेही
तृषित बारि बिनु जो तनु त्यागा । मुये करै का सुधा तड़ागा
का बरषा जब कृषी सुखाने । समय चूक पुनि का पछिताने
अस जिय जानि जानकी देखी । प्रभु पुलके लखि प्रीति बिसेषी
गुरहिं प्रनाम मनहिं मन कीन्हा । अति लाघव उठाइ धनु लीन्हा
दमकेउ दामिनि जिमि घन माहीं । पुनि धनु नभमंडल सम भयऊ
लेत चढ़ायत खैंचत गाढ़े । काहु न लखा देख सब ठाढ़े
तेहि छन मध्य राम धनु तोरा । भरेउ भुवन धुनि घोर कठोरा

छं० । भरि भुवन घोर कठोरखव रवितजि तजि मारग चले ।
चिक्कुरहिं दिग्गज डोल महि अहि कोल कूरम कलमसे ॥
सुर असुर मुनि कर कान दीन्हे सकल बिकल बिचारहीं ।
कोदंड भंजेउ राम सुलछी जयति बचन उचारहीं ॥

दो० । संकर चाप जहाज सागर रघुबर बाहु बल ।
बूड़े सकल समाज चढ़े जे प्रथमहिं मोहबस ॥

चौ० । प्रभु दोउ खंड चाप महि डारे । देखि लोग सब भये सुखारे
कौतिकरूप पयोनिधि पावन । प्रेमबारि अवगाह सुहावन
राम रूप राकेस निहारी । बढ़ी कोच पुलकावलि भारी
बाजे नभ गहगहे निसाना । देवबधू नाचहिं करि गाना
ब्रह्मादिक सुर सिद्ध मुनीसा । प्रभुहि प्रसंसहिं देहिं असीसा
बरषहिं सुमन रंग बहु माला । गावहिं किंनर गीत रसाला
रही भुवन भरि जय जय बानी । धनुषभंगधुनि जात न जानी
मुदित कहहिं अरु तहँ नर नारी । भंजेउ राम संभुधनु भारी

दो० । बंदी मागध सूतगन बिरद बदहिं मतिधीर ।
करहिं निछावरि लोग सब हय गय लिख धन मनि चीर ॥